STAN MUSIAL

STAN MUSIAL

A BIOGRAPHY

Joseph Stanton

BASEBALL'S ALL-TIME GREATEST HITTERS

GREENWOOD PRESS
WESTPORT, CONNECTICUT • LONDON

Library of Congress Cataloging-in-Publication Data

Stanton, Joseph, 1949–

    Stan Musial : a biography / Joseph Stanton.

      p.   cm. — (Baseball's all-time greatest hitters)

    Includes bibliographical references and index.

    ISBN 978–0–313–33609–6 (alk. paper)

    1. Musial, Stan, 1920–   2. Baseball players—United States—Biography.

3. St. Louis Cardinals (Baseball team)—History.   I. Title.

  GV865.M8S73   2007

  796.357092–dc22

  [B]   2007022818

British Library Cataloguing in Publication Data is available.

Library of Congress Catalog Card Number: 2007022818
ISBN-13: 978–0–313–33609–6

First published in 2007

Greenwood Press, 88 Post Road West, Westport, CT 06881
An imprint of Greenwood Publishing Group, Inc.
www.greenwood.com

Printed in the United States of America

The paper used in this book complies with the
Permanent Paper Standard issued by the National
Information Standards Organization (Z39.48–1984).

10 9 8 7 6 5 4 3 2 1

FOR MY PARENTS,
WHO WERE GREAT ADMIRERS OF STAN MUSIAL.

CONTENTS

SERIES FOREWORD

The volumes in Greenwood's "Baseball's All-Time Greatest Hitters" series present the life stories of the players who, through their abilities to hit for average, for power, or for both, most helped their teams at the plate. Much thought was given to the players selected for inclusion in this series. In some cases, the selection of certain players was a given. **Ty Cobb**, **Rogers Hornsby**, and **Joe Jackson** hold the three highest career averages in baseball history: .367, .358, and .356, respectively. **Babe Ruth**, who single-handedly brought the sport out of its "dead ball" era and transformed baseball into a home-run hitters game, hit 714 home runs (a record that stood until 1974) while also hitting .342 over his career. **Lou Gehrig**, now known primarily as the man whose consecutive-games record Cal Ripken Jr. broke in 1995, hit .340 and knocked in more than 100 runs eleven seasons in a row, totaling 1,995 before his career was cut short by ALS. **Ted Williams**, the last man in either league to hit .400 or better in a season (.406 in 1941), is widely regarded as possibly the best hitter ever, a man whose fanatical dedication raised hitting to the level of both science and art.

Two players set career records that, for many, define the art of hitting. **Hank Aaron** set career records for home runs (755) and RBIs (2,297). He also maintained a .305 career average over twenty-three seasons, a remarkable feat for someone primarily known as a home-run hitter. **Pete Rose** had ten seasons with 200 or more hits and won three batting titles on his way to establishing his famous record of 4,256 career hits. Some critics have claimed that both players' records rest more on longevity than excellence. To that I would say there is something to be said about longevity and, in both cases, the player's excellence was the reason why he had the opportunity to keep playing, to keep tallying hits for his team. A base hit is the mark of a successful plate appearance; a home run is the apex of an at-bat. Accordingly, we could hardly have a series titled "Baseball's All-Time Greatest Hitters" without including the two men who set the career records in these categories.

Joe DiMaggio holds another famous mark: fifty-six consecutive games in which he obtained a base hit. Many have called this baseball's most unbreakable record. (The player who most closely approached that mark was Pete Rose, who hit safely in forty-four consecutive games in 1978.) In his thirteen seasons, DiMaggio hit .325 with 361 home runs and 1,537 RBIs. This means he *averaged* 28 home runs and 118 RBIs per season. MVPs have been awarded to sluggers in various years with lesser stats than what DiMaggio achieved in an "average" season.

Because **Stan Musial** played his entire career with the Cardinals in St. Louis—once considered the western frontier of the baseball world in the days before baseball came to California—he did not receive the press of a DiMaggio. But Musial compiled a career average of .331, with 3,630 hits (ranking fourth all time) and 1,951 RBIs (fifth all time). His hitting prowess was so respected around the league that Brooklyn Dodgers fans once dubbed him "The Man," a nickname he still carries today.

Willie Mays was a player who made his fame in New York City and then helped usher baseball into the modern era when he moved with the Giants to San Francisco. Mays did everything well and with flair. His over-the-shoulder catch in the 1954 World Series was perhaps his most famous moment, but his hitting was how Mays most tormented his opponents. Over twenty-two seasons the "Say Hey Kid" hit .302 and belted 660 home runs.

Only four players have reached the 600-home-run milestone: Mays, Aaron, Ruth, and **Barry Bonds**, who achieved that feat in 2002. Bonds, the only active player included in this series, broke the single-season home-run record when he smashed 73 for the San Francisco Giants in 2001. In the 2002 National League Championship Series, St. Louis Cardinals pitchers were so leery of pitching to him that they walked him ten times in twenty-one plate appearances. In the World Series, the Anaheim Angels walked him thirteen times in thirty appearances. He finished the Series with a .471 batting average, an on-base percentage of .700, and a slugging percentage of 1.294.

As with most rankings, this series omits some great names. Jimmie Foxx, Tris Speaker, and Tony Gwynn would have battled for a hypothetical thirteenth volume. And it should be noted that this series focuses on players and their performance within Major League Baseball; otherwise, sluggers such as Josh

Gibson from the Negro Leagues and Japan's Sadaharu Oh would have merited consideration.

There are names such as Cap Anson, Ed Delahanty, and Billy Hamilton who appear high up on the list of career batting average. However, a number of these players played during the late 1800s, when the rules of baseball were drastically different. For example, pitchers were not allowed to throw overhand until 1883, and foul balls weren't counted as strikes until 1901 (1903 in the American League). Such players as Anson and company undeniably were the stars of their day, but baseball has evolved greatly since then, into a game in which hitters must now cope with night games, relief pitchers, and split-fingered fastballs.

Ultimately, a list of the "greatest" anything is somewhat subjective, but Greenwood offers these players as twelve of the finest examples of hitters throughout history. Each volume focuses primarily on the playing career of the subject: his early years in school, his years in semi-pro and/or minor league baseball, his entrance into the majors, and his ascension to the status of a legendary hitter. But even with the greatest of players, baseball is only part of the story, so the player's life before and after baseball is given significant consideration. And because no one can exist in a vacuum, the authors often take care to recreate the cultural and historical contexts of the time—an approach that is especially relevant to the multidisciplinary ways in which sports are studied today.

Batter up.

ROB KIRKPATRICK
GREENWOOD PUBLISHING
FALL 2003

Chronology

1920 Stanislaus Francis Musial is born on November 21. His father calls him by the Polish nickname Stashu, which is often shortened to Stash by his friends. The name Stanley Frank will come into use when he starts school.

1937 He signs a contract with the St. Louis Cardinals on September 29, a little less than two months before his seventeenth birthday.

1938 He begins his professional career as a pitcher for the Cardinals' Class D team at Williamson, West Virginia.

1940 Briefly optioned to a Class B ball club, he finds, to his disappointment, that he has been assigned to remain at the Class D level, this time in Daytona Beach. Helped by the kindly mentorship of manager Dickie Kerr, Musial improves as a pitcher but also plays frequently in the outfield because of the small number of players on the roster. On August 11 he falls hard on his shoulder while making an acrobatic catch in the outfield. The injury proves to be serious, effectively ending his prospects as a pitcher.

1941 Ollie Vanek, skipper for the Class C team in Springfield, Missouri, after some hesitation, agrees to accept the sore-armed young pitcher. Musial's outstanding hitting begins to attract attention. Vanek helps Stan master the art of fielding the outfield. In late July, Musial is leading the league in hitting at Springfield with a .379 average when he is called up to the Class AA team in Rochester, New York, where he also leads the league with a .326 average. Brought up to the majors to help the Cardinals in a tight pennant race with the Dodgers, musial hits .426 in the closing days of the 1941 season as the Redbirds fall short of the pennant, Stan's rise from marginal status in Class C ball all the way to the majors in one season is a remarkable feat. In 1941, he leads each of his three leagues in hitting when he was playing in them but does not get enough at bats in any league to be eligible for consideration for a hitting championship.

1942   The Cardinals, fielding one of the best teams in the history of the franchise, win 106 games during the regular season. Musial plays in his first World Series. The Cardinals defeat the Yankees in five games.

1943   With an average of .357, Musial leads the league in hitting for the first time. In fact, he leads the National League in most categories and is selected for the MVP award for the first time. The Cardinals again face the Yankees in the World Series, losing in five games this time.

1944   The Cardinals win the National League pennant for the third year in a row. In a surprise development the other St. Louis team, the Browns beat out the Yankees to win the American League pennant. The All-St. Louis World Series is won by the Cardinals four games to two.

1945   He enlists in the Navy and is stationed at Pearl Harbor in Hawai'i. He plays in an eight-team league on O'ahu along with a number of other Major League ball players.

1946   Released from service because his father is seriously ill, Musial rejoins the Cardinals in time for the 1946 season. The Cardinals again win the pennant and defeat the Boston Red Sox in an exciting seven-game World Series. Musial hits .365 during the regular season to win his second batting championship.

1947   Bothered by appendicitis and tonsillitis, Musial has a difficult year physically but still manages to hit .312.

1948   This is Musial's best statistical year. If not for injuries late in the season, he might have had a shot at hitting over .400. He ends with an average of .376 and leads the Major Leagues in most hitting categories. In the home-run department his thirty-nine falls one short of the lead. Musial's overall hitting performance in 1948 is considered one of the most dominating in the history of baseball. Among the highlights are four different games in which he has five hits.

1949   He enters into a partnership in a restaurant business with Julius "Biggie" Garagnani. Stan decides to go for more home runs early in the season and his batting average remains lower than usual. When he stops pressing for homers, the hits come fast and furious again. Despite his early-season slump, Musial still manages to hit .338.

1950 On April 28, Musial slips in soft dirt running the bases at Forbes Field and injures the ligaments in his left knee. Paradoxically, Musial goes on a hitting rampage during the weeks immediately following the injury. He theorizes that his is because an injury forces him to concentrate on simply meeting the ball. He hits .346 to win his third batting championship.

1951 He gets the most votes in the balloting for the All-Star roster of the National League. Musial gets three hits in four times at bat in the All-Star contest, including a home run off Eddie Lopat, who had bragged before the game that he had figured out a foolproof way to get Musial out. Stan hits .355 for the regular season to win his fourth batting title.

1952 On February 14, with reporters on hand to witness the event, Cardinals' owner Fred Saigh offers Musial a contract with the salary amount left blank and asks Stan to name his figure. A surprised Musial, thinking that demanding a raise would reduce the amount available for the rest of the team, indicates he would sign for the same salary he had received in 1951. On September 9, he gets his 2000th hit off Philadelphia's Curt Simmons. His .336 average earns him his fifth batting championship and his third in a row.

1954 On May 2, in St. Louis in a doubleheader against the New York Giants, one of the best teams of that year, Musial goes four for four with three home runs. He hits two more home runs in the second game, thereby accomplishing the rare feat of hitting five homers in one day.

1955 He hits a walk-off home run to win the All-Star Game for the National League at Milwaukee's County Stadium. It is the fourth of his six career All-Star Game home runs.

1956 Cardinals' GM Frank Lane makes plans to trade Musial to the Phillies for pitcher Robin Roberts. When Cardinals' owner August Busch hears about the deal, he vetoes it. Musial is elected "Player of the Decade" by the vote of sports writers responding to a *Sporting News* survey. In this vote he beats out Ted Williams, Joe DiMaggio, and Bob Feller.

1957 He badly injures his left shoulder and arm during a game in Philadelphia on August 23, but manages to come back quickly. He wins his seventh and final batting crown with a .351 average.

1958 With a double off Moe Drabowsky in Wrigley Field on May 13, Musial becomes the eighth hitter in the history of Major League Baseball to get 3,000 hits. The milestone seemed all the more rare because the last previous player to join the 3,000-hit club had been Paul Waner who had reached that plateau way back in 1941. The Cardinals participate in a post-season exhibition series in Japan. *Sports Illustrated* names Musial "Sportsman of the Year."

1959   Musial is advised by the Cardinals management to take it easy during the winter to conserve his energy for the season. Unfortunately, he follows this advise and is never able to rise above an early season slump, in part because he is often kept out of the lineup and is never able to find his timing at the plate. He hits .255, the lowest average of his career.

1960   Although his business interests mean that he could easily afford to quit playing, as some urge him to do after his disappointing 1959 season— Musial refuses to quit on a low note and determinedly undergoes an exercise regimen to prepare for the season. When he is not given the opportunity to play, he finds himself reconsidering the possibility of retirement, but, when all the Cardinals' other left-field options falter, Musial gets a chance to play and concludes the season hitting well.

1961   On June 23, in a game in Busch Stadium against the Giants he hits two homers and drives in seven runs to help the Cardinals to a 10-5 victory. Musial plays this game with numerous maladies—including an abscessed tooth, a bad cold, and a pulled leg muscle. His performance on this occasion is another example of his ability to play with a high level of concentration when hurt.

1962   He becomes one of the biggest stories in sports in 1962 by hitting .330 and competing for the batting crown at age forty-one. Among the many batting marks Musial sets in 1962 is his breaking of Honus Wagner's record for most hits in the National League. One of his best days of the Summer comes against the Mets, when he homers in four consecutive at bats, beginning with a game-winning blast on July 7 and then continuing with his first three at bats on July 8.

1963   At the annual Cardinal team picnic, Musial announces he will be retiring after the 1963 season. The Cardinals get hot, winning nineteen of twenty games at one point, raising the possibility that Stan the Man might play in one more World Series, but they lose key games at the end of the season and finish in second place. On September 9, Musial plays in the last of his 3,026 games, smashing his 3,630th hit to knock in his 1,951st RBI.

1964   He becomes Cardinals' vice-president and contributes to management de-cisions for the Redbirds as they win the National League pennant and then defeat the New York Yankees in the World Series. Musial dismisses reporters' suggestions that he should have played one more year. He points out that, if he had stayed with the team, they might not have traded for Lou Brock and, therefore, would not have won the pennant or the series. He is appointed by Lyndon Johnson to head a national physical fitness initiative.

1966   He becomes the General Manager of the Cardinals.

1967 With Musial as GM and Red Schoendienst as manager, the Cardinals win the pennant in dominant fashion and then go on to defeat the Boston Red Sox in the World Series in seven games. He resigns as GM.

1968 An enormous bronze statue of Musial by Carl Mose is unveiled at Busch Stadium on August 4.

1969 He is inducted into the Hall of Fame in Cooperstown on July 29.

2006 Musial, a few weeks shy of his eighty-sixth birthday, throws out the first ball for game five of the 2006 World Series. The Cardinals defeat Detroit to secure their tenth World Series crown.

INTRODUCTION

Stan Musial won seven National League batting crowns, was picked as National League MVP three times, and was twenty-four times an All-Star. When he retired after more than two decades with his one and only major league team, the St. Louis Cardinals, he found himself in possession of twenty-nine National League records, seventeen major league records, and nine All-Star Game records. He retired sixth all-time in number of games played, fifth in RBIs, fourth in hits, and second in total bases. He led the league in hits six times, doubles eight times, triples five times, and slugging percentage six times. He had hit over .300 in seventeen different seasons in the majors and ended with a career average of .331. Though his statistics dipped in a few of his later years, he made an amazing "elderly" comeback in his second-to-last season, batting .330 in 1962 and almost winning another batting crown at the age of forty-one. By the time he hung up his spikes for good, he had racked up a total of 3,630 hits—in remarkably consistent fashion, hitting 1,815 at home and 1,815 on the road. Another sign of his balanced achievement is that he scored 1,949 runs and drove in 1,951. He was a pitcher's (and a fielder's) worst nightmare and a spray hitter with power. His prowess as a player was famously allied with his affability as a person. As his final season drew to a close, his last visits to National League cities were causes for enthusiastic tributes and farewell festivities. Few American athletes have been as unanimously beloved as Stan the Man was as his long and amazing career drew to a close.

Although widely acclaimed during his career and continuously revered in the city of St. Louis, Musial has too often been overlooked and underappreciated, in the years since his retirement, by commentators on baseball, many of whom are located in Northeastern cities such as New York and Boston and whose memories have, therefore, tended to fixate on the great players of their own cities. While these New Yorkish and Bostonian tendencies are the natural way of fandom and are hardly surprising, a lack of chroniclers has tended to leave Musial out of stories in which he was one of the main men, in which he was, indeed, often The Man.

Also working against the remembrance of Stan's greatness is the oft-expressed notion that Stan's low-key, friendly manner and uncontroversial life meant that he was a colorless figure who was newsworthy only because of his astonishing knack for hitting screaming line drives to every part of the field. Musial was thought too nice a guy to be colorful the way a bad boy like Leo Durocher could be colorful. Sometimes, however, nice guys do finish best and from my perspective as a historical writer striving to understand America's most ancient national game there are few sports personalities more fascinating that Stan Musial. Because he seems to embody the sporting ideal of the great athlete as great guy, Musial has become a transcendent figure. There are a multitude of the Leo-Durocher-type wise guys in the history of baseball—that sort of colorful has been a dime a dozen—but there has only been one Stan the Man, the one great player who was equally renowned for being a great guy—the quintessential sports hero, perhaps best visualized, many thought, by an illustration depicting his attentiveness to signing autographs for kids; he was a superstar defined by his genuinely affectionate interactions with fans and sterling personal integrity as well as by his considerable prowess on the field.

By way of further introduction, I would like to briefly mention some of the many facets of the man Ford Frick was to call "baseball's perfect knight." These little glimpses can be regarded as a highlight reel for the book that follows. There were many Stan Musials during his long life: the thin little boy in Donora whose wiry strength and agility developed under the influence of his vigorous working-class parents; the slender teenage basketball and baseball whiz nurtured by various neighborhood mentors; the marginal pitching prospect seemingly lost in the shuffle of the Cardinals' vast and formidably competitive minor-league system; the batter with the corkscrew stance who looked so unpromising that many reporters, coaches, and fellow players predicted he would never amount to much as a hitter; the durable athlete who had a strange way of responding to injury, sometimes reacting to disability by concentrating with such extraordinary determination that he produced some of his best hitting performances while hurt; the superstar hitter so desirous of gaining every possible base that he would explode out of the batter's box, getting the fastest possible start toward first base and then sprinting with every ounce of speed he could muster, striving to get to second, to third, or all the way home. And then there was the forty plus, supposedly over-the-hill athlete who resurrected his vigor and restored himself to topnotch statistical performance by means of vigorous off-season physical regimen. Musial, throughout his playing days, was always the greedy batsman with a hunger for hits so insatiable that, if he had one hit, he had to have two; if he had two hits, he was grimly determined to have three; and, if he had three hits he was frantically anxious to get to the plate to go after the fourth. Famous for his modesty of demeanor, Musial was also fiercely proud of his achievements in baseball and unrelenting in his efforts to turn in the best possible at bats even in those seasons in which his Cardinals were mired in mediocrity. As a baseball executive, the exceptional Stan the Man batted 1.000, helping the Cardinals to a World Series championship in 1967, his one and only season as general manager. As an active member of the Hall of Fame, Stan remained a fixture at HOF induction ceremonies and other events down through the long history of his post-playing life. Outside of baseball there was Musial, the highly successful businessman, establishing a model that many other professional athletes would seek to emulate. Atypical for an athlete-turned-businessman, Stan seemed to possess a Midas touch, probably the result of his sound instincts and attention to detail. He even became a prominent federal bureaucrat when Lyndon Johnson appointed him honcho of a national physical fitness initiative. At home in St. Louis, he was a loyal husband who remained married for life to his high school sweetheart. He was an attentive father and grandfather, and a public figure who overcame shyness to become a popular public speaker. Worthy of particular notice in that regard was his reliance on a pocket-sized musical instrument as a reliable prop to add liveliness to his public appearances. Stan's wielding of the harmonica as a public performer is a good example of his knack for making the best of any difficulty. His shyness, rather than being a limitation, was channeled into a career as Musial the public performer—a player of jokes, magic tricks, and his infamous harmonica. Writing about Stan Musial, the greatest Cardinal of them all, has been a fine opportunity for me to reconnect with the Cardinal fervor of my youth—which has continued, after a fashion, into my exile far from St. Louis. A previous book of mine, *Cardinal Points: Poems on St. Louis Cardinals Baseball* gave me an opportunity to chronicle 100 years of Cardinals baseball. Writing this book on Stan the Man has enabled me to take a close look at one of the central figures of a golden age of baseball, an age in which the Cardinals and their fans were close to the heart of what makes baseball the most national of pastimes. Marooned on my Pacific island, I have been aided in numerous ways by the National Baseball Hall of Fame in Cooperstown as well as by the works of numerous baseball researchers and journalists.

CHILDHOOD IN DONORA

Stan grew up in Donora, Pennsylvania, located just south of Pittsburgh, amidst the mines and mills of the heavily industrialized Mongahela Valley. Stan's love for a game associated with green, Elysian fields of play was nurtured in a gray, polluted, industrial suburb dominated by blast furnaces and zinc works. The grass, where it managed to survive at all, was never greener on this side of the fence.[1]

Donora was populated largely by immigrants, primarily from Russian, Slovak, and Germanic regions. Lukasz Musial, Stan's father, was an immigrant born on a farm in Poland. His mother, Mary Lancos, who was of mostly Czech descent, was born in New York City. Lukasz and Mary met as workers at the American Steel and Wire Company and were married less than a year later. Four daughters— Ida, Helen, Victoria, and Rose—were born to them before the birth of their first boy on November 21, 1920. They named this son Stanislaus but within the family he was known as Stashu. Two years later another boy, Ed, was born to the Musial family.[2] When Stan was about eight years old the family moved from a residence on 6th Street to Grandma Lancos' house on Marelda Avenue. Nine people crowded into a small five-room house. Although there was hardly enough money to buy food for this extended family group, Mary made due by buying potatoes, flour, and sugar in bulk; baking ten loaves of bread at a time in an open-air oven; making cabbage go a long way; concocting such tasty and inexpensive delicacies as pierogi, halucki, and kolatche; and having the kids pick berries for jelly. Most of the chores around the house fell to the female children, as was the tradition in Eastern European households, so Stan and Ed had plenty of time to play.[3]

Baseball became what the two Musial boys played most often. Reflecting back, Stan could not recall the beginning of this preoccupation. "I can't remember when I didn't play. Seems like I was always playing ball."[4]

Stan's mother was strong of body and of personality. As a child Mary Lancos had to help her large family, including her eight siblings, survive the rigors of impoverishment in New York City. At eight years of age she was already laboring as a housekeeper in the big city. While a teenager, she often rowed her father to work back and forth across the Monogahela River.[5] About six feet tall, and strong, she is rumored to have had undeveloped athletic ability. Observers have suggested that Mary Musial had a more direct and substantial influence on her son than did her husband.[6]

Mary recalled that she occasionally played catch with the boys in the yard, because her husband worked such long hours that he was seldom able to do that.[7] James Giglio has discussed another reason for Lukasz's absence from the father-playing-catch-with-sons scenario. Lukasz had a considerable drinking problem. This was not surprising for a man who had to struggle so hard with the heavy labor of his physically demanding job and the multiplying stresses of continuing poverty; but the frequent absence of the father, and the further financial demands that his drinking entailed, exacerbated difficulties for his family and, in particular, seems to have worried his proud and sensitive eldest son.[8]

Stan's father did, however, make at least one very important contribution to the creation of "Stan the Man." A key aspect to the development of Stan's athleticism was his father's insistence that his son train regularly in gymnastics. Stan once mentioned that his real favorite sport as a young child was tumbling. He remembered, "Each week my father took me to the Polish Falcons. The club wasn't far from the house. He took me there and we did tumbling together." Stan often pointed out that one of the benefits of this training was that it taught him how to fall, and he was often to make use of sliding and tumbling tactics in his fielding and base running. It seems likely, moreover, that early exposure to physical training, emotionally enhanced by the intimate participation of his father, enabled and encouraged Stan in the development of the physical discipline, concentration, and coordination that were to help him become an extraordinary athlete. Although there has been much mention of how skinny Stan was in his younger years, the slenderness of his physique only superficially concealed the powerful back and shoulder muscles that gymnastics and related calisthenics enabled him to develop and maintain.[9] Though Lukasz's opposition to Stan's desire to become a professional baseball player usually casts the elder Musial in the role of an obstacle in the path of his son's emergence, it seems clear he helped

Stan's athletic ambitions get the right sort of start by means of his insistence on gymnastics with its attendant training regimen and goal-oriented attitude toward physical development.

A star in both basketball and baseball, the young Musial was encouraged by various mentors. One of the first and most important was Joe Barbao, a neighbor of the Musials, who was a former minor league ball player. When Stan and Ed Musial began playing catch under his watchful eye, Barbao was still managing, pitching, and playing outfield for a semipro team called the Donora Zincs. Barbao's job required him to work loading and reloading intensely hot zinc ovens. Because of the demanding nature of the work, he was expected to work only a "short shift" of three hours each morning, which left him with plenty of time to practice baseball in the afternoons. Barbao often spent time with the Musial brothers, showing them how to play the game. Musial recalled that Barbao talked baseball with him late into the evening, right up until the 9 P.M. mill whistle signaled the curfew hour for the kids of Donora.[10]

Stan began as a formidable pitcher, but he could always hit. Musial pointed out that hardthrowing coordinated left-handed kids frequently become pitchers, in part because the only other important infield position available to them is first base. Although Stan played for various youth teams, he made his biggest splash as a kid pitching against adults. A fifteen-year-old Musial was serving as water boy for the Donora Zincs, when Joe Barbao, lacking a replacement for his starting pitcher who was being badly mauled by the Monessen team, brought Stan in as a relief pitcher in the third inning. At 5'4" and less than 140 lbs, the boyish Musial must have been quite a surprising sight on the mound as he pitched a strong six innings with his hard fastball and wicked curve, getting his adult opponents to strike out thirteen times.[11]

The park where the Zincs played helped Musial develop an important talent. Because trolley tracks made the left-field fence significantly shorter than the right-field fence, Stan worked on driving balls with power to the opposite field, which was to become a key signature of his hitting style. Musial continued to pitch well for the Zincs, but when he lost the first game of the season in 1936, the *Donora Herald* expressed concern for the young hurler, "Musial is too small for steady playing now. He has a world of stuff and a brainy head, but overwork can harm a young player very easily."[12] But Musial was anxious to play more rather than less, and in 1937 he also played for Donora's American Legion team.

Another key mentor emerged when Musial joined the Donora High School team, coached by Michael (Ki) Duda. Duda, whose primary sport had previously been football, was a fiercely competitive, yet deeply compassionate man, who had once considered joining the priesthood. He hated losing and was demanding of

3

his players. He took a special interest in Stan for whom he became a father figure and a valued advisor.[13]

Stan's chief encourager in the basketball direction was James K. Russell, who had been recommended for the Donora position by his coach at Notre Dame, the redoubtable Knute Rockne, whose inspirational coaching style Russell sought to emulate in both football and basketball.[14] The Donora Dragons advanced into the state postseason basketball tournament, with Musial playing a key role as one of the team's most consistent scorers. Just before that tournament, Stan suffered from pneumonia-like symptoms and was nursed back to health in Coach Russell's home. Stan was to continue playing for independent basketball teams sponsored by area merchants, such as Buick dealer Frank Pizzica, who was to become another of Musial's closest friends and advisors.[15]

The story of Musial's signing with the Cardinals has been told and retold, beginning with the version captured in J. Roy Stockton's 1942 article for *The Saturday Evening Post*.[16] As more fully explained in the book Bob Broeg wrote in collaboration with Musial, the potential of Stan's play impressed Andrew French and Ollie Vanek, who were the business manager and field manager respectively for the Monessen Class D farm team of the St. Louis Cardinals. These two representatives of Branch Rickey's empire made repeated visits to the Musial home, endeavoring to persuade Lukasz to sign a contract that would start his son on a career in professional baseball. Stan's father wanted him to pursue the possibility of a basketball scholarship and a college education. Stan's teachers and coaches—in particular Ki Duda and James Russell—were also urging him toward college, and there does seem to have been prospects along those lines.[17]

The argument in the Musial household came to a dramatic conclusion, Stan's passionate desire to play professional baseball swayed his mother to his cause, but his father remained firm in his commitment to the idea of Stan going to college. French got up, preparing to leave. He remarked that this might be Stan's last chance to sign up with a professional team. Only sixteen years old at the time, Stan felt his world was coming to an end and burst into "tears of disappointment, anger and frustration." Mary Musial dried Stan's tears then stood up, angry and determined. Though a tall, imposing, and strong-willed woman—she would usually defer to her husband in most matters, as was "the old-world custom." But she felt her husband was wrong and did not want her son to miss out on what seemed to be his last chance to have the life he so obviously wanted. "Lukasz," she asked her husband, "Why did you come to America?" When he answered, "Because it's a free country, that's why," she seized on the point and declared, "That's right, Lukasz. . . . and in America a boy is free NOT to go to college, too." Lukasz yielded, grumbling, "All right, Stashu, . . . if you want baseball enough to pass up college, then I'll sign."[18] This vivid and touching account of Musial's signing, as presented in his autobiography—is the most frequently retold story regarding Stan's relationship with his parents.[19]

Despite having signed the contract with the Cardinals, Musial remained eligible to play high school basketball for one more year because, in accordance with the practice in those days, the Cardinals did not file the contract with Major League Baseball until June of the following year. Stan's outstanding year on the basketball court resulted in pressure from his teachers and some of his coaches to take advantage of the possibilities of a college scholarship.

Russell strongly advocated college, as did Charles Wunderlich, another of the Donora coaches, who took his advocacy a step further by bringing Stan to meet H. C. Carlson, the coach at the University of Pittsburgh who was, apparently, willing to offer Stan a scholarship.

On the other side of the question, Ki Duda told Stan that he would not be able to dedicate himself to college studies while dreaming baseball dreams,[20] but the person Stan gave most credit for helping him make his decision in favor of baseball, was a member of the Donora High School staff who would seem to be a highly unlikely advocate for choosing a career in pro sports over a college education. Although Miss Helen Kloz, the Donora High School librarian, was customarily a strong proponent of college, Miss Kloz echoed Duda's sentiments, pointing out to Stan that baseball was what he wanted most to do and that he might end up having regrets if he did not try to make it in the professional game while he was still young and able to give it his best effort.[21]

Stan frequently expressed the view, in later years, that he wished he had gone to college. In many speeches and interviews he was to urge young people to complete a college education, if given that opportunity. He often confessed to feeling he had missed out on an all-important means to self-improvement.

Although basketball did not, finally, lead Stan to college, it did lead him to Lillian. One of Musial's basketball teammates, Dick Ercius, introduced Stan to an attractive young lady named Lillian Labash. Lil was later to joke that she fell in love with Stan's legs, while watching him on the basketball court.[22]

In the interim before Musial officially became a Cardinal, other teams expressed an interest in him, and Stan, not having heard from the Cardinals since the signing, and apparently having a somewhat unfavorable view of that organization due, perhaps, to negative publicity the Redbirds were getting because of Commissioner Kenesaw Mountain Landis' campaign against the extensiveness of Branch Rickey's farm system or to lingering dissatisfaction over the low salary the Cardinal's were offering him. Whatever the reason for it, Stan was rumored to have had contact with the Yankees and underwent a tryout with his hometown team, the Pittsburgh Pirates, where he made a good impression on Pie Traynor, who had been one of his childhood heroes. Stan's interest in the Pirates had perhaps been piqued when a Donora sports writer, John Bunardzya, drove Stan to see a game between the Pirates and the Giants at Forbes Field, a park whose beauty made a big impression on young Stan, who had never been inside a major-league stadium before. Though he had grown up close to Pittsburgh, his family's lack of money and his lack of free time due to his active baseball-season schedule, in which he played for multiple teams, had meant that he had never had the opportunity to see a game in person.[23]

The outing provided interesting evidence that Stan possessed the confidence to make it in baseball. In the midst of the game Stan turned to Bunardzya and commented, "I think I can hit big league pitching." In recounting the story years later Musial pointed out that he had said nothing about being confident about pitching to big leaguers. Perhaps he already sensed that it was as a hitter rather than as a pitcher that he would make his mark.[24]

NOTES

1. Stan Musial and Bob Broeg, *Stan Musial: "The Man's" Own Story as told to Bob Broeg* (New York: Doubleday, 1964), 6.

2. Jerry Lansche, *Stan "The Man" Musial: Born to Be a Ballplayer* (Dallas, TX: Taylor, 1994), 5–6.

3. Musial and Broeg, *Stan Musial*, 6–8.

4. John Grabowski, *Stan Musial* (New York: Chelsea House, 1993), 17.

5. Musial and Broeg, *Stan Musial*, 5.

6. James Giglio, *Musial: From Stash to Stan the Man* (Columbia: University of Missouri Press, 2001), 5; Margaret Carlin, "Musial's Mother Cried When He Quit Baseball." *The Pittsburgh Press*, September 15, 1963.

7. Ray Robinson, *Stan Musial: Baseball's Durable "Man"* (New York: Putnam, 1963), 11.

8. Giglio, *Musial*, 9–10.

9. Musial and Broeg, *Stan Musial*, 11.

10. Ibid., 10–11.

11. Ibid., 12–13.

12. Ibid., 13.

13. Giglio, *Musial*, 21.

14. Musial and Broeg, *Stan Musial*, 18–19.

15. Giglio, *Musial*, 18–20.

16. J. Roy Stockton, "Rookie of the Year," *Saturday Evening Post*, September 12, 1942, 29 and 36.

17. Musial and Broeg, *Stan Musial*, 17–20.

18. Ibid., 19–20.

19. Giglio, *Musial*, 25–26. Giglio has expressed doubts about the Pop-wanted-me-to-go-to-college-rather-than-play-pro-baseball theme central to the story of Musial's signing as presented in the autobiography. Giglio contends that Lukasz would have wanted Stan to go immediately into industrial work and would have been opposed to his eldest son undertaking either a career in baseball or a stint in college. Giglio makes an interesting but unconvincing case for this view based on speculations of some Donora residents and Gigio's unsupported assumption that, "Most Eastern European immigrant fathers wanted their sons employed in the factories as soon as possible to supplement the family income." Giglio's vague evidence does not seem to justify rejecting Musial's oft-repeated testimony on this matter. It is worth noting that Stan's mother's version of the story of his signing, told to a reporter in 1963, is basically the same story told by Stan. She explains how she had to have a talk with her husband to persuade him that Stan should be allowed to play baseball rather than go to college, if that was what he wanted (Carlin, "Musial's Mother Cried When He Quit Baseball"). Giglio's view that Stan was lying about this matter, would require that Mary Musial was also lying in 1963.

20. Lansche, *Stan "The Man" Musial*, 9.

21. Musial and Broeg, *Stan Musial*, 21–22.

22. Ibid., 20–21.

23. Giglio, *Musial*, 27–29.

24. Musial and Broeg, *Stan Musial*, 23–24.

Rookie Stan Musial poses soberly in 1942. His expression shows his determination to make a success of his opportunity with the St. Louis Cardinals. *National Baseball Hall of Fame Library, Cooperstown, NY.*

BEATING AROUND THE BUSH

After Musial signed with the Cardinals, he privately told Andrew French that he did not want to start his minor league career with any club that was anywhere near Donora. Although not lacking in confidence in many respects, Musial understood how great the odds were against him in the highly competitive profession in which he wanted so badly to succeed. He did not want to risk being too close to home where any failure would be immediately known to family and friends. But Stan found that putting home behind him was not an easy thing to handle emotionally. He suffered severe homesickness during the 240-mile bus ride to Williamson, West Virginia, to join the Class D team to which he had been assigned, and claims he might have turned around and headed home immediately had he not been met at the bus station by a friendly reception from Lefty Hamilton, a former player who was the general manager of the community-owned Williamson club. Stan's homesickness was compounded by the prospect of the dismal, little, hard-drinking town of about 9,000 souls. He had not expected Williamson to be glamorous but was surprised to find himself in a town even smaller than Donora where they "run out of main street within three blocks."[1]

Musial's first professional manager was Nat Hickey, a tough competitor who had been a star basketball player in the early days of the Boston Celtics. Hickey was irascible on the surface, frequently berating the team for its general failings, but, fortunately for Stan, he maintained a tolerant stance toward the individual failings of his fledgling players. Stan was in sore need of such tolerance, as he suffered from a lack of control and endured considerable embarrassment as he was charged with balk after balk because the deceptive pickoff move he had developed in Donora proved to be disastrously unacceptable in professional baseball. He had taken considerable pride in the deftness of his pickoff technique throughout his younger years, so to have that special bit of prowess declared fraudulent was more than a little distressing for the young pitcher. A few days later Stan had a better outing and won 10–3, but it was already clear that the young pitcher had much to learn.[2]

Stan's first summer in professional baseball was hardly a lucrative venture, but his frugal habits—such as living in a $5-per-week rooming house and making $5 meal tickets stretch as far as possible at the least expensive local restaurant, surviving primarily on cheese sandwiches, hot dogs, and hamburgers[3]—enabled him to actually save a little money to send home out of his $65-per-month salary. During days in which he had free time, Stan discovered the pleasures of playing pool. He wielded the cue stick so often that he later professed he "felt like Minnesota Fats."[4] Stan's ERA for his first minor league season was 4.66. Though his record for the season—six wins and six losses—was not an entirely bad outcome when one considers that he was playing for a mediocre team, it was clear that he had far to go.[5] Wildness was a problem for the young left-hander from the start. In his 110 innings he walked 80 batters.[6] Wid Matthews, a scout for Branch Rickey, put in an optimistic report on Stan's prospects: "Arm good. Good fast-ball, good curve. Poise. Good hitter. A real prospect." Stan later wondered how Mathews had scoped out his hitting potential. Musial had hit only .258 in his own games as well as in occasional pinch-hitting opportunities, but his sixteen hits did include three doubles and a home run.[7] No doubt Williamson's lack of good hitters made Stan's handful of big swings stand out more than they might have otherwise.

Overall, Stan was not discouraged by his low-impact encore in professional ball. The instructional nature of the Cardinals' minor league system had helped him improve and given him confidence that he was making progress. He felt he had "learned a lot . . . about signs, about backing up bases, about breaking to first base on all ground balls hit to the right side of the infield, and about relay throws and cutoffs."[8]

Back in Donora, Stan turned his attention to his senior year of high school. As a professional athlete he was no longer eligible for high school sports, but he was allowed to play on a semipro basketball team coached by Frank Pizzica, a Monongahela City automobile dealer who was to become one of Musial's closest friends and advisers. In one basketball game, the players on an opposing team, unhappy over being soundly defeated by Musial and company, turned rough and slammed Stan against the seats. The Pizzicas marched their team off the court at that point, declaring the game less important than Stan's "baseball future" as "Cardinal property."[9]

Although determined to graduate from high school, Musial's heart was more into athletics than academics as he looked toward the end of his high school experience. In addition to his basketball activities, Stan put in some playing time with Joe Barbao's Zincs and helped Ki Duda coach the Donora high school baseball team. Itching to get back to professional baseball, Stan left Donora as soon as he was sure he had passed his courses. He was already back at Williamson on graduation day. Lil stood in for him at the ceremony and picked up his diploma.[10]

More confident and comfortable in his second season with the West Virginia club, Musial's results were promising in certain respects, but, although he won nine games and lost only two, he gave up eighty-four walks in thirteen games, surrendering more than eight free passes for every nine innings pitched.[11] His ERA of 4.30 was an improvement over the previous year and his eighty-five strikeouts made up somewhat for all those walks, but his manager Harrison Wickel's report to the home office was not optimistic:

> This boy is quite a problem. He is by far the wildest pitcher I have ever seen. . . . He has fair stuff and at times he has a good fast ball and pretty good curve. He will strike out as many as he will walk, but I certainly can't depend on him. . . . I recommend his release because I don't believe he will ever be able to find the plate. I don't think he has enough stuff to get by. I've noticed that when he does get the ball over he is hit rather freely, and I am led to believe that his wildness is his effectiveness. The only place he can pitch is Class D, where the player strikes at almost anything a pitcher tosses up there. I am at a loss to say definitely what to do with him. He has the best habits and is a fine boy.[12]

Although Stan performed better in the second half of the season, in the days after Wickel's pessimistic estimate had gone in, his status as a pitching prospect for the Cardinals was far from secure.

His hitting, however, was showing promise. His average in seventy-one at bats was .352. Because Class D teams carried only fourteen players and Williamson had suffered some injuries, Stan had often been asked to play in the outfield.[13]

Back in Donora, Stan spent much of his off-season working in the Labash grocery store. He and Lil had decided to marry, and, indeed, their first child would be born the following August. Stan has always claimed that they were secretly married on November 21, his nineteenth birthday[14], but it appears that they held off, probably for financial reasons, and did not legally wed until May of 1940 after Lil had joined Stan in his next minor league town, which was Daytona Beach, Florida.[15]

Despite the difficulties of getting by on Stan's small salary, the Musials enjoyed their time in Daytona, an attractive oceanfront community very different from dreary and gritty Williamson.[16] Dickie Kerr, Stan's new manager in Daytona, and Kerr's wife Pep helped Stan and Lil handle what was a decidedly complicated moment in their young lives. The Kerrs took the Musials into their home after Lil's arrival, thus mitigating a multitude of pragmatic and financial obstacles facing the young couple. When Lil gave birth, they named their boy Richard, in honor of Stan's kindly manager.

Stan admired Dickie Kerr for his past achievements as well as his current generosity. Kerr, as a rookie pitcher for the infamous 1919 Chicago White Sox, managed to win two games in the World Series despite the efforts of a group of his "Black Sox" teammates to throw the games. In following seasons, however, Kerr's honesty and excellence went unrewarded. Although he won twenty-one games for the White Sox in 1920 and nineteen in 1921, the team's miserly owner, Charles Comiskey, still refused to give him a raise to a decent wage. When Kerr held out for a pay increase, he was suspended by Comiskey. After playing on semipro and independent teams for three years, he found his skills had deteriorated, and he was never able to regain major-league success. Kerr had, however, never lost faith in baseball and, at the time Musial encountered him, he was happy with his career as a minor league manager.[17]

Musial felt that instruction from Kerr was responsible for greatly improving his success and professionalism as a pitcher. Indeed, his 18–5 record with a 2.62 ERA made him the leagues most successful left-handed pitcher.[18] Stan felt he learned more from Kerr in a few days than he had learned in two seasons at Williamson. Small in stature and not physically gifted, Kerr's success as a pitcher had been hard won and had much to do with his disciplined grasp of the basics of the craft. With Kerr's guidance Musial improved his concentration and command of his pitches, but he confessed that Kerr could only do so much: " . . . I still walked as many as I struck out. Dick Kerr couldn't throw the ball for me."[19] Perhaps more important than the specific skills Kerr developed in Musial was the boost in confidence he gave Stan through his faith in the young man's potential. Kerr had been to the top, and he helped Stan envision himself achieving a similar ascendancy.

Though reports to the Cardinals home office reflected the improvements in Stan's pitching, more and more the emphasis began to shift to the young man's hitting. Wid Matthews reported: "Good fastball, curve fair. Nice poise, big boy.

He can hit and may be too good a hitter to keep out of the game." Similarly, Ollie Vanek, who had recruited Musial for the organization three years earlier, looked past the credible pitching to note the potent bat: "Good form and curve, fast ball a bit doubtful. Also a good hitter. May make an outfielder."[20]

Musial's prospects as a pitcher were considerably reduced on August 11 of his Daytona season when he fell on his arm while making a tumbling catch in the outfield, and lost strength in his throwing arm. The expertise in tumbling that Stan's father had insisted his eldest son develope had enabled the budding outfielder to make spectacular catches in which he would dive for the catch and skillfully absorb the force of the fall by tumbling cleanly and coming up ready to fire the ball into the infield. Stan was to effectively perform this move throughout his career, but in this instance when he was playing centerfield behind Jack Creel, Daytona's best pitcher, Musial dived for a low line drive just as his spikes caught in the turf, causing him to fall hard on the point of his shoulder. The swelling was dramatic and immediate, but X-rays the next day showed no signs of bone damage. The injury was regarded as nothing more than a bad bruise and was treated only with heat, but it became apparent in Musial's last few starts of the season that he had lost much of his zip.

Setting aside the injury, whose future impacts were not yet understood, Stan's summer in Daytona had seen some high points. His record of 18–5 made him one of the best pitchers in the Florida State League. He struck out 176 batters in 223 innings, and, though his wildness led to an unfortunate 145 walks, he was, at least, making some improvement in his strikes-to-walks percentage, as compared with previous seasons. He proved himself a tough competitor, giving up just 179 hits. His hitting was coming along, too, with a .311 average, 126 hits in 405 trips to the plates. His totals included only one home run, but he had ten triples and seventeen doubles.[21]

Kerr's end-of-season comments to a reporter indicated that he felt Musial, if he could gain better control of his pitches, could have a genuine future as a major league pitcher, but Stan's remarks to the same reporter were more ambivalent: "I don't know whether I'm a pitcher or an outfielder," I told him, "I'll let the Cardinals decide that.... When I'm getting hit hard or when I'm hitting hard myself, I want to be an outfielder."[22]

As devastating as Musial's injury was to his prospects as a pitcher, it could be argued that, had he not become damaged goods on the hill, the real Hall-of-Fame-hitter Musial might never have had a chance to stand up. Kerr, one of baseball's most remarkable overachievers on the pitching mound, had helped Stan toward minor-league semi-stardom as a hurler. The relentlessly hardworking and ambitious Musial was poised for a passionate, yet probably only moderately successful, career as a Bush League pitcher. The bum shoulder arrived at a time when Musial's prowess at the bat was becoming obvious. There were no guarantees that this diamond in the rough would be discovered considering the confused status of his prospects as he entered the 1941 season, but, if it had not been for the fateful collision of Stan's shoulder with hard-baked earth the previous August, it seems quite possible he could have become a short-career, moderately successful, pitcher instead of Stan the Man. A retrospective comment by Musial suggests that he understood that his injury might have helped him make a necessary transition in a timely way, "I never would have made the major leagues as a pitcher. My injury merely hastened a switch that was inevitable."[23]

Musial has always said that he gave no thought to quitting professional baseball, despite the grave turn in his fortunes as a pitcher. He claims in the Broeg book that he would have played, "In an E league if they told me to," because "I like baseball too much to ever give it up."[24] But some have speculated that he may have come close to quitting—with a wife and baby to support and no clear prospects for a speedy rise in pro baseball.[25]

NOTES

1. Stan Musial and Bob Broeg, *Stan Musial: "The Man's" Own Story as Told to Bob Broeg* (New York: Doubleday, 1964), 25–27.

2. Ibid., 27.

3. Ray Robinson, *Stan Musial: Baseball's Durable "Man"* (New York: Putnam, 1963), 30–31.

4. Musial and Broeg, *Stan Musial*, 27–28.

5. Jerry Lansche, *Stan "The Man" Musial: Born to Be a Ballplayer* (Dallas, TX: Taylor, 1994), 12.

6. Robinson, *Stan Musial*, 30.

7. Musial and Broeg, *Stan Musial*, 28.

8. Ibid.

9. Ibid., 29.

10. Ibid.

11. Lansche, *Stan "The Man" Musial*, 13.

12. Musial and Broeg, *Stan Musial*, 30–31.

13. Ibid.

14. Lansche, *Stan "The Man" Musial*, 13.

15. James Giglio, *Musial: From Stash to Stan the Man* (Columbia: University of Missouri Press, 2001), 36–37.

16. Musial and Broeg, *Stan Musial*, 31–32.

17. Gigilo, *Musial*, 37.

18. Musial and Broeg, *Stan Musial*, 32.

19. Ibid., 32–33.

20. Lansche, *Stan "The Man" Musial*, 14.
21. Ibid., 15.
22. Musial and Broeg, *Stan Musial*, 35–36.
23. Ibid., 41.
24. Ibid., 36.
25. Giglio, *Musial*, 38–39.

The fleet rookie sensation that sports writers were calling "The Donora Greyhound" exhibits the delight the game of baseball gave him. Though he never tried to steal very many bases, Stan was widely admired for his base running skills, often managing to turn a single into a double or a double into a triple. *National Baseball Hall of Fame Library, Cooperstown, NY.*

NOBODY CAN BE THAT GOOD

1941 was a year of baseball miracles—Joe DiMaggio's fifty-six-game-hitting streak, Ted Williams' .406 batting average, and the remarkably intense pennant races between the Yankees and the Red Sox in the American League and between the Dodgers and the Cardinals in the National League. One of the most surprising events of that year involved the rise of a damaged goods, sore-armed, almost washed-out pitcher from the lower minor leagues to the brink of what would become superstardom on one of the best teams in the history of Major League Baseball.

Because, as we have seen, his prospects as a pitcher were considerably reduced when he fell on his shoulder while making a tumbling catch in the outfield in 1940 and lost strength in his throwing arm, Stan could hardly have realized he was on the verge of greatness as he assessed his prospects in the fall of 1940 and the spring of 1941. There was no way he could have had any sense of how rapidly things were going to turn in his favor; but, in the aftermath of his conversion to a full-time outfielder, his rapid ascension during the 1941 season carried him from the depths of the Cardinal's system to its top farm team at Rochester, and then on to the majors where he hit .426 in the closing days of the 1941 season and helped the Cardinals almost catch the Dodgers. Because Stan's star status held steady from the time of his achieving the Big Leagues until the end of his career, it is hard to remember how precarious his situation was before the tumblers of good fortune clicked into place to enable him to make the most of his talents.

In the early days of the Cardinals' 1941 Class Double-A spring training camp, during which experienced players were evaluated and assigned, Stan found that his arm was strangely weak. It was not sore, but he could not generate the velocity he knew he would have to have to survive as a hurler. Burt Shotten— former major league outfielder and future manager of championship Brooklyn Dodger teams, who was the manager of one of the Cardinals' minor league teams at that time—observed Musial closely and frequently. The critique he delivered in a kindly manner to the worried young man was hardly good news, but it initiated a transition that made possible Musial's amazing emergence in the months ahead: "Son, there's something wrong with your arm. At least, I know you're not throwing hard enough to pitch here. I think you can make it as a hitter. I'm going to send you to another camp with the recommendation that you be tried as an outfielder."[1] Stan was more relieved than disappointed by Shotten's decision. There was a real chance that he might have been released outright. The machine that was the Cardinals' farm system had little patience with players who were not making progress in the lower minor leagues. Unsurprisingly, Musial was anxious about his delicate status. The pitcher Jack Creel who was his roommate at this time, recalled that Stan was uncharacteristically unfriendly toward him for several days after Creel struck him out in a practice session.[2]

It became abundantly clear to Stan that hitting would absolutely have to be his ticket to the next level when he suffered through an unexpected return to the mound. Clay Hopper, who was his manager for a few spring outings, needed a left-handed pitcher to use in relief to shore up a minor-league squad that was in the midst of a pounding by the major-league Cardinals. Stan protested that he was now an outfielder, but Hopper had taken note of Stan's statistically promising performances in past years and was determined to see what the young lefty could do. Stan got out of his first inning without incident, only to be drubbed in the next inning by mammoth home runs by Terry Moore and Johnny Mize. After that Stan pitched several scoreless innings, which lead to Hopper's trying him again a few days later against the Phillies. In that game Stan's ineffectiveness was fully demonstrated as he was hit hard and gave up seven runs in one inning.[3]

No one could doubt, at that point, that Stan's future would be decided by his bat. But, for him to continue with any prospects for success, one of the minor league managers assembled to survey the talent would have to want Stan on his team. Branch Rickey could certainly assign any player to whatever team he deemed appropriate, but Rickey liked to let the decisions emerge from the free interplay of conversation in meetings of the thirty-some managers he had in his system, all of whom were angling for the best possible talent for their individual clubs. Rickey felt these argumentative sessions enabled him to discern who the hottest prospects really were. The managers wanted to succeed at whatever level they were at so they could move up the ladder. The disputes over who would get what players had consequences for the discussants that ensured Rickey was getting honest evaluations.

There was considerable danger that a marginal player could get lost in the shuffle, but Stan was fortunate that one of the managers had reason to take a special interest in his career. Ollie Vanek, manager of the Springfield, Missouri, team had been an early advocate and participant in Musial's signing. When Stan brought up the matter of their past history, Vanek readily recollected "The kid whose father needed so much persuasion to let [him] play." Vanek agreed to let Stan work out with his team for the rest of the spring, but Rickey still had to decide what to do with him for the summer. When Rickey raised the question of Musial in the meeting to determine assignments, there were, at first, no takers. No one wanted him in Class A or Class B. If no one wanted him in Class C, he would return to the extremely risky marginality of a fourth season of Class D ball; but, at last, Ollie Vanek volunteered to take a chance and select Musial for his Class C squad.[4]

Vanek's hopes for Stan resided in his confidence in Stan's athleticism—his quickness, coordination, previous (and perhaps recoverable) arm strength, and "good stroke at the plate." Vanek considered using Stan at first base, a position he would often occupy later, but Vanek had another hitting prospect, Buck Bush, whose slowness made him incapable of playing anywhere other than first. Vanek, himself an outfielder who spent the early summer months playing in the field alongside Musial, educated Stan in outfield essentials and enabled him to make progress toward becoming the great defensive outfielder he was eventually to become. Vanek was especially helpful with regard to judging how to handle line drives, which Stan was, at first, too eager to charge. Vanek calmed the anxious young man down, helping him also with ground balls, showing him how to keep them in front of him despite the bumpy ground of White City Park, an uneven and rocky terrain that caused balls to hop every which way.[5]

Stan made rapid progress at the plate in Springfield and his efforts were noticed. At one game, with Branch Rickey in the stands, Musial figured in all the runs scored by his team by means of a single, a triple, and a home run. He began to show more power more often. In one game against Topeka he contributed three home runs, none of which his wife saw, because she happened to have been changing baby Dickie's diapers each time Stan homered. Things were going so well for Stan that Ollie Vanek predicted that Musial would be in the majors "in a couple years." Neither Musial nor Vanek had any notion that Stan would go up to The Bigs for good before the end of that very summer.[6]

Stan was popular with fans in Springfield due to his slashing line drives at bat, his bold and canny moves on the base paths, and his diving somersault catches in the outfield. Much remarked upon was his quiet, unassuming, yet often joking manner. "Give me a bat with a hit in it," became his standard remark to the bat boy. This affable running gag arose from Stan's shortage of bats and his ongoing effort to ascertain what weight and shape would consistently work best for him. His constant smile became as much his trademark as his already distinctive batting stance. Some Springfield fans, interviewed forty years later, recalled that, despite Stan's exceptional performance at the plate, there was some speculation concerning whether his unusual stance at the plate would work against his chances of making it in the major leagues, a view that many observers shared when they first had a chance to see Stan twist into his characteristic position in the batters' boxes of the big leagues.[7]

Musial was more than happy with how things had been going in Springfield. In his eighty-seven games up to that point he had been hitting .397 with twenty-six homers and ninety-four RBIs. Though he knew he was doing well, the call up to join the Cardinal franchise in Rochester, New York, came as a shock. Content at the prospect of finishing the season in good repute in Class C ball, he suddenly found himself vaulting to Double-A. Stan claims to have been "flabbergasted" by his change in fortunes. Injuries to key players at Rochester created an immediate need, and Musial's great year in Springfield made him an attractive candidate for one of the openings.

The Rochester Red Wings—in fourth place at the time with a 53–47 record—put Musial in right field as soon as he joined them. Another newly recruited outfielder—Erv Dusak, just in from the Mobile, Alabama, team—was put into left field. Dusak outshone Musial on that first night, whacking three hits and making a spectacular catch, while Stan managed only an infield hit. But Stan had made up for that in his first home game in front of the Rochester fans—his four hits included a double and a home run.[8]

That first homestand in upstate New York was a big moment for Musial for another reason. Babe Ruth was there for a special promotion and was asked to put on a batting practice exhibition. The forty-seven-year-old Babe had been out of the game for six years. He was rusty and it took him a while to get his swing going, but he finally connected and lofted one far out of the stadium. Stan was thrilled to be on the bench with this great hero, a player even Stan's father admired, though he was disappointed to witness the potbellied former superstar quickly down a pint of whiskey he had concealed in his pocket. Anxious to impress Babe, Stan was trying too hard and came up with just one single during the ensuing contest.

Stan put on a better performance for another important visitor a few nights later, in Newark, when he got four hits with Branch Rickey sitting in the stands. That Newark series was big for Stan; he had eleven hits in the three games.[9]

Two of those hits in Newark made a particularly strong impression on Tony Kaufman, the Rochester manager, who subsequently sent high praise of Musial to Branch Rickey, which helped persuade the Cardinals' boss that Stan was ready for the majors. Kaufman, who was coaching third, noticed how hard the Newark third baseman, Hank Majeski, was charging whenever a bunt was in the offing. Kaufman told Stan to prepare to bunt; but—in the event Majeski charged the plate—Stan was supposed to push the ball past him. Sure enough Majeski charged when Stan squared around to bunt, and Stan, swinging away instead, slapped the ball into left field for a double. Adding insult to injury, Stan performed the same trick when the game went into extra innings tied at 4–4. Again faking a bunt, Stan whistled a line drive inches from the ear of the startled Majeski, who never dreamt Musial would try the same stunt twice. Stan's second double drove in a run and the Cardinals went on to win. Kaufman's written report in praise of Stan's ice-water-in-the-veins performance helped the young Musial's cause in a big way. Looking back, years later, on his Rochester fake-bunt gambit, Musial noted that despite how easy and effective he found this maneuver to be, he was never to resort to it again in his long career. Stan speculated that this was because his reputation in the majors as a spray hitter kept third base men from "taking liberties." Another factor was that, in his prime as a line-drive-making machine, his managers seldom wanted him to settle for a sacrifice bunt.[10]

With Musial contributing mightily, the Rochester Red Wings made a late run, winning sixteen of twenty to close out the season, and secured a playoff berth. Stan whacked nine hits during the three-game stretch that boosted Rochester into contention for the title. During the playoffs Musial continued to hit well, but the Red Wings were eliminated in the first round.

As the season wound to a close it was announced that the contracts of four of the Rochester players—Musial, George "Whitey" Kurowski, Erv Dusak, and Hank Gornicki—had been picked up by the Cardinals. Delighted with the prospect of having a shot at making the Cards' roster the following spring, Stan was happily content with what he thought was the end of his 1941 season. He caught a train home to Pennsylvania immediately after Rochester was knocked out of the running. The following day, a Sunday, Musial was sleeping at Lil's family's home, when a wire arrived telling Stan to report to St. Louis. An excited, chaotic day of Lil and her mother washing and ironing all of Stan's accumulated dirty clothes was followed by a late night hurried drive in the Labash car to get Stan delivered to the train station in Pittsburgh; however, the last train to St. Louis had already left by the time he got to the station. Stan's trip to the big time would have to wait till the next day.[11]

Stan's sensational play at Rochester, which followed on the heels of his great performance in Springfield, worked out, by happenstance, to have been perfectly timed to vault him to the next level. The injury-plagued 1941 Cardinals, who were in the thick of a pennant race with the Dodgers, had just lost Enos Slaughter to an injury and were in desperate need of a reliable left-handed bat in the outfield.[12] Stan came through for them in spectacular fashion, batting .426 for his first twelve major league games and collecting a crucial twenty hits that were an announcement that a new force to be reckoned with had arrived.[13]

A little background on the situation of the Cardinals is in order at this point to clarify the importance Stan's contributions were to have for that team over the course of the next twenty years. The Cardinals of 1941 were poised for achievements they would not quite attain that year. Branch Rickey's teams, began to emerge with the surprising World Series upset by the Hornsby Cardinals of one of the most dominant teams in the history of baseball, the Ruth-Gehrig Yankees of 1926. The Card's continued to prosper in the 1930s, reaching an antic high point with the Gas House Gang of Pepper Martin, Dizzy Dean, Frankie Frisch, Joe Medwick, and company. The Cardinals meant more to America and American culture than is generally acknowledged—representing, as they did, the little guy, the underprivileged, far-from-New-York-City ordinary folks, who should not have had the ghost of a chance against the several Gotham-funded Behemoth's that dominated Major League Baseball for much of its history. Rickey's cleverness turned St. Louis poverty inside out, finding ways to carefully, frugally, even stingily construct a redoubtable empire of teams he owned or had subtle dealings with. Musial and the excellence of the 1940s Cardinals emerged out of the boiling cauldron of Rickey's creativity, but, after Rickey was gone and the team's potent mix settled down to a simmer, the 1950s were to see Cardinals teams finish out of the money year after year.[14] But in 1941 Musial was the ideal creation of the Rickey machine. Musial perfectly represented the "Cardinal type"—a term Bob Broeg says baseball men of the 1930s and 1940s used to denote "any young, eager, fast athlete who played hungrily and a bit recklessly."[15]

Considering the many injuries to key players the 1941 Cardinals had suffered, their managing to stay close to the powerful Dodger team was a miracle of sorts. In addition to the loss of Slaughter to a fractured collarbone, they had to go without centerfielder Terry Moore for a month after he was beaned by a brush-off pitch; Walker Cooper, their catcher, was out with a broken shoulder; Walker's brother, starting pitcher Mort Cooper, had to have arm surgery; infielder Jimmy Brown's nose had been broken; and first baseman Johnny Mize had a jammed thumb, which meant he could only be used sparingly and was not slugging homers because of problems with gripping the bat.[16]

It just happened that, of the available uniforms, the one that equipment manager Butch Yatkeman judged to be the right size for Stan bore the number 6. Musial would never wear another number in the major leagues, and it became closely identified with him. It was to become the first number ever to be retired by the Cardinals after Stan hung up his jersey for the last time.

With Slaughter out of the line-up, manager Billy Southworth needed left-handed hitting and put Musial into the line-up right away. Because Stan was not a fully known quantity Southworth started out platooning him, using him in the second game of a double hitter against the Boston Braves, managed in those days by a not-yet-famous Casey Stengel. In that contest right-handed, knuckleballer Jim Tobin would provide Stan's first exposure to major league pitching. It was the first time Musial had been faced with a knuckleball, and in his first time at the plate he popped up weakly to the third baseman. Always a fast learner, Musial responded to the challenge by readying a shortened swing and holding back on his stride so that he was in position to "just stroke" the fluttering ball. In his second trip to the plate he lined a double off the wall in right center field to get his first hit in the Bigs. It was a nice touch that his first hit was a double because the frequent hitting of two baggers was to become a Musial trademark. Stan had another hit against the Braves the following day.

In a crucial series against the Chicago Cubs, Musial's budding greatness was announced in a big way. Against Chicago right-hander Paul Ericson he had his first perfect day in the majors as he had three hits in three official chances; one of those hits was a double. As a result of that 3–1 win the Cardinals found themselves closing in on the Dodgers with only nine games left on the schedule. The double-header the next day before a huge crowd was to be an extraordinary outing for the young man only a few days into his major league debut. In the first game, he doubled, singled, and stole second, doubled again, and then finally singled and advanced to second on an infield out.[17]

That last play led to one of the most famous early instances of Musial's capacity for heads-up play. Stan was still on second when Croaker Triplett dribbled a slow roller in front of home plate, and the catcher Clyde McCullough grabbed it and fired the ball to Babe Dahlgren at first base. When the umpire called Triplett safe, both the catcher and the first baseman registered angry protests. Meanwhile, Musial was rounding third and noticing that neither McCollough nor Dahlgren were paying any attention to him. Without hesitation Musial streaked home to score the winning run ahead of the belated throw. After marveling at this heads-up play, Southworth remarked that Musial "was born to play baseball."[18]

Stan also fielded magnificently in that first game. He made two great catches and threw a runner out at the plate, a good sign that his arm strength was returning. In the second game, Stan contributed two more hits and two more acrobatic catches. In response to Musial's sensational play in that double-header, Jimmy Wilson, the manager of the Cubs famously complained, "Nobody can be that good!"[19]

Accepted as a valuable member of the team, Musial was chatting with Terry Moore and Johnny Mize on the train, telling them how happy he was to have come so far from that spring training day when he gave up the two big homeruns to the two of them. Moore and Mize burst into laughter at the realization that the skinny lefthanded pitcher they had clobbered back in April was now their esteemed outfielder. They were, in later years, never reluctant to remind Stan of their first acquaintance with the would-be pitcher that Musial once was.[20]

It was an important occasion for Stan when the Cardinals pulled into Pittsburgh to play in Forbes Field during the last week of the season. With the stands well stocked with his friends and relations come up from Donora, Stan was frustrated that he and his teammates were shutdown in the first game of the double-header that began the Pittsburgh series by the superb pitching of left-hander Ken Heintzelman. Stan made up for it in the second game, getting three hits, including his first major league homerun. It was a special thrill for him to circle the bases of the beautiful "hometown" stadium that had seemed to him so wonderful as a child; hearing its events chronicled on the radio, it had seemed to be an out-of-reach dream kingdom. Having family and friends on hand to witness this special moment made it all the more wonderful. That first dinger was caught by a Donora man who was happy to trade it to Stan for an autographed ball.

General Mills made Stan's first homer a remembrance of radio glory for Stan in another pleasurable way when they awarded him a case of Wheaties. Although he realized it was a silly advertising gimmick, Musial got a big kick out of being the guy who gets the Wheaties after spending his childhood hearing that familiar breakfast-cereal distinction called out by sportscasters to honor the deeds of various Big League heroes. He was now one of those guys![21]

After the triumphant second game of the double-header Stan shyly brought his father into the clubhouse to meet his manager and coaches. Witnessing his father's pleasure and pride somewhat resolved for Stan some of his lingering worries. His father's original opposition to the practicality of Stan's baseball goals had its echo in Stan's internal awareness that success could elude him in this challenging field of endeavor. Bringing Lukasz into the midst of this moment of achievement served to put at least some of the fears to rest. Stan still had much to prove in the years ahead, but it was a big relief to him to be able to show his "Pop" dramatic evidence that the baseball decision had not been a mistake.

Two games later came a richly ambivalent moment for Stan Musial and the Cardinal tradition he was to come to symbolize. The Donora community united to celebrate a Stan Musial Day at Forbes Field. Musial's excited pride over this unexpected development was mingled with a tinge of embarrassment and a few particles of self-inflicted pressure. Stan loved the honor but worried about what he saw as its premature nature, worrying because he felt he "really hadn't done anything yet." Still, it was quite a thrill for him to find that Monongela Valley had turned out in force. A school holiday had even been granted in Donora so kids would not have to play hookey. It was also a satisfying moment of shared pride for Stan and his parents amidst their family and friends. So touched was Stan that he "didn't know whether to laugh or cry," but he rose to the occasion and got two hits. Unfortunately, the rest of the Cardinals did not fare as well and the team lost to the Pirates 3–1, resulting in their official elimination from the pennant race. Full of the joy of his Day, Musial also felt the grim anguish of his teammates who had played so well against the odds despite their injury-depleted roster, only to find themselves falling just short of their goal.[22]

There was some speculation after the season concerning what might have happened if the Cardinals had brought the remarkable Musial up to the majors earlier in the season. Johnny Mize, one of Branch Rickey's bitterest critics, claimed that Rickey wanted only a close pennant race to pack in the stadium and maximize profits and that the Mahatma preferred not winning the pennant, or after that the World Series, because it enabled him to keep players' salaries down. Bringing up hot prospects like Musial only for the last few days of a pennant race resulted, Mize felt, in a frenzied losing finish rather than what might have been a comfortable Cardinal triumph.[23] Mize's angry point of view fails to take into account, however, how sudden and unexpected Musial's emergence was, even in view of his impressive numbers at Springfield and Rochester. In fact, of the Cardinals' several late season call-ups, it was Dusak—a big, hard-hitting, fast-running, slick-fielding, hard-throwing, and can't-miss-outfield prospect—from whom the most was expected. Unfortunately for Erv, he could not hit a major-league curve ball and never caught on with the Cards or anybody else. If Rickey had thought to bring up someone sooner in the summer, it most likely would have been the brawny Dusak, rather than the slender, less-proven Musial, a failed pitcher scrambling against the odds to transition to the outfield. One outcome of Mize's disgruntled point of view is that Cardinals' management, weary of all his complaining, decided to sell him. The loss of Mize was one of a number of unfortunate by-products of the low-budget strategies of Rickey and Breadon.[24]

Musial's sudden emergence was among the most compelling stories of the 1941 season. Kyle Crichton, looking back on 1941 from 1947, described the situation:

> The Brooklyn Dodgers were winning their first pennant under Leo Durocher, and the Cards were breathing on their napes at every step. Every game during those last days was a national crisis and Musial was thrown as a sacrifice into this den of tigers. In 12 spectacular games he batted .426 and almost saved the pennant for the . . . eager St. Louis rooters.[25]

Stan's remarkable 1941 saw him have the highest batting average in three different leagues, but he did not put in enough appearances in any one league to qualify him for the title.[26] Back in Donora after his surprising ascension, Stan's gift for friendship kept him grounded. At a Donora Zinc Works Athletic Association banquet held to honor Stan it was his old, beloved mentor Joe Barbao who presented him a wristwatch and a trophy. In attendance at that gathering was the most famous of Pirate Hall of Famers, Honus Wagner, who was to become another of Stan's good friends. It just so happened that many of the hitting records Musial was eventually to set involved the breaking of Honus' longstanding marks.[27]

If the Cardinals had not been so depleted the miraculous emergence of Musial would probably have been delayed at least until 1942, and, given the ebb and flow of minor league promotions and Musial's tendency to not hit well in spring training, it is possible that the realization of his dream might have been further hindered. Certainly Stan's lack of offensive production in Florida in the spring of 1942 presented a problem, but his phenomenal performances in 1941 assured him a place on the Cardinals major league roster. Although the pressure he put on himself to live up to everyone's expectations in the training season of 1942 must have contributed to his slump, Stan's spring troubles in that year were of the same ilk as those he would have in future springs. As a veteran he was to theorize that the nature of the Florida ballparks with their "high blue skies, waving palm trees in the background and no proper backdrop" worked against his need to see the ball well to hit up to his standard, but, as a young rookie with no guarantees for the future, his poor Grapefruit League numbers in 1942 were an upsetting development.[28]

Despite the disappointing spring, most everyone was expecting great things from Stan. Casey Stengel went on record as saying that Musial would be a force to be reckoned with for the next twenty years, a prediction that would be borne out dramatically twenty years later by Stan's remarkable 1962 performance in his penultimate season. Doubts about where and how much Stan would play in 1942 were resolved by the time the Cardinals reached St. Louis. Manager Billy Southworth, whom Stan credited with being exactly the sort of supportive manager a young player needs, expressed confidence in his budding star. "Don't worry, Stan," Southworth assured him. "You're my left fielder. You can do it." In pre-season exhibition games against the Browns Musial immediately began to hit well, in part, Stan felt, because "those double-decked big league stands . . . provided a better batting background."[29]

Reassurance was also at hand when Branch Rickey tore up Stan's $400-a-month contract and raised it to $700-a-month. In terms of today's baseball contracts those dollar amounts seem laughably tiny, but for Stan and Lil it was an important shift in their fortunes. Lil was able to move out of her parents' house in Donora and join Stan in an inexpensive apartment they found in St. Louis.[30]

Musial was getting his start on an extraordinary team. Despite their break-even play in the first few weeks of the season, the 1942 Cardinals would go on to be regarded as one of the best teams in franchise history. Musial has often said they were the best team he ever played on.

With exceptional defense, a strong and deep pitching staff, hitting for average and for power, and remarkable speed on the base baths—they were a culmination of sorts for Branch Rickey's long-cultivated farm system. No one player had spectacular numbers—Slaughter and Musial had the highest averages at .318 and .315 respectively—but averages, hustle, and speed were available at every position. Even catcher Walker Cooper could run.[31] A New York cartoonist had characterized them as St. Louis Swifties, meaning that they were like Mississippi River Boat gambling swindlers because of their knack for stealing games from the Dodgers, but the nickname stuck because the fleet Redbirds were so adept at taking extra bases at the least opportunity.[32] Centerfielder Terry Moore was widely regarded as among the best at the position in the history of the game, and Slaughter and Musial often pulled off amazing plays to the left and right of him. The infield was anchored by "The Octopus," Marty Marion, one of baseball's first tall short stops, whose incredible range and soft hands enabled him to handle much of his side of the infield. Whitey Kurowski at third base remarkably excelled despite a disability. His deformed right arm had more gristle than bone below the elbow because of an awkwardly healed childhood injury. His shortened limb became the key to his teaching himself to be a vicious pull hitter, who fiercely crowded the plate, and everyone marveled at his play at third, especially the way he could rocket that ball across the infield with his muscular little wing.[33]

The Cardinals had extraordinary pitching available to them in 1942—including Mort Cooper (brother of catcher Walker Cooper), Harry Brecheen, Murray Dickson, Howard Krist, Max Lanier, George Munger, and a promising rookie named Johnny Beazley. Their hitting, however, was slow to get started. Musial was getting his whacks, but much of the rest of the team seemed not quite awake. What got the Cardinals going in a big way, as it so often did during those years, was a series against the Dodgers. Leo Durocher's aggressive tactics and taunting shouts always seemed to stimulate the Cardinals to play their best despite the formidable team the defending National League Champion Dodgers put on the field.[34] The year's first incursion of Dodger blue into Sportsman's park stimulated the Redbirds to sweep Brooklyn in the three-game series. But then the Dodgers returned the favor in Brooklyn, winning four out of a five game series in mid-June. An Associated Press article gave up on the Cardinals' chances at that point: "The ambitions of the Cardinals to make it a two-club race for the National League pennant were all but totally wrecked today."[35]

Musial's hitting, however, had been developing nicely. In the one game the Cardinals beat the Dodgers in that June series, Stan had a triple and a homer. His batting average stood at .315 at the time of the selection of the All-Star team and many felt Musial was unjustly overlooked, but, looking back, Stan felt his nonselection made sense, as there were already five other Cardinals picked for the team and he was, at that point, still an incompletely proven rookie.[36] The Cardinals found themselves trailing the Dodgers by eight and half games at the break for the All-Star game.[37]

The sale of one of the Cardinals' highest salaried pitcher, Lon Warneke, to Chicago for the waiver price was viewed by some fans as a sign that owner Sam Breadon was ready to concede the season and cut his losses, but the Cardinal staff was still well armed as star newcomer Johnny Beazley demonstrated by pitching a shutout victory against the Giants the day after the sale of the "Arkansas Hummingbird." Besides, as Broeg has pointed out, Warneke had begun to give up too many home runs. The loss of Warneke proved essential to the Cardinals resurgent season because it cleared a slot for Beazley's emergence.[38]

On August 5 the Cardinals found themselves ten games behind the Dodgers. The Redbirds were to overcome that deficit by winning forty-three games and losing only eight over the remainder of the season. Mort Cooper's great pitching over that stretch was key to the Cardinals' rise. Cooper's month-long struggle to win his fourteenth game had sparked the superstitious thought that he was being held back to thirteen wins because his uniform number was 13. After he borrowed Gus Mancuso's number 14 jersey and won victory number fourteen, he decided to borrow a uniform for every game. He won his fifteenth wearing his brother's 15. It must have been quite a sight to see him pitch his next game squeezed into little Ken O'Dea's number 16 jersey, but he won that one, too, claiming constriction helped him concentrate. Keeping, more or less, to this policy, Mort pitched his way to twenty-two wins and the year's MVP award.[39]

The Cardinals' cause was also aided by a peculiar theme song. Since the days of the Gas House Gang and Pepper Martin's "Missouri Mudcats," there had tended to be eccentric musical liveliness in the Cardinals' clubhouse. Often in 1942 impromptu performances graced victory celebrations for the Cards with trainer Doc Weaver leading the way on mandolin. Musial contributed on slide whistle and by beating time on lockers with coat hangers. In later years this musical jokiness was to be reborn in Musial's tendency to play the harmonica on the spur of any odd moment. The Cards' "inspirational" theme song for 1942 emerged due to a liking Harry Walker had for a novelty record by Spike Jones, a spoof country western ballad called "Pass the Bisquits, Mirandy," which wryly narrated the ridiculous tale of a murderous mountaineer and his wife's deadly pastry. With their stand-up-comic trainer manning his little record player, "Mirandy" blared out after every victory during the team's amazing stretch drive, with many of the players joining in for a raucous accentuation of the chorus.[40]

As the pennant race concluded, the Cardinals needed only a split of a double-header against the Cubs to clinch. The Dodgers kept up the pressure by winning their final game against the Phillies, but the Cardinals put an exclamation point on their great run to the championship by winning both their games. Musial would always recall "the joy" of squeezing the final out for the National League championship, pulling in and hugging to his chest a long fly ball by Clyde McCullough. Stan could take pride in having been a key player in what more than one commentator has called "the greatest stretch drive in baseball history." Though the Dodgers had had a marvelous season, winning 104 games, they could not keep up with the Cardinals, whose remarkable 106 wins were the highest total by a National League champion since the Pirates of 1909.[41]

The 1942 Cardinals, mentioned by Musial and others as among the best teams ever to play the game, was not overwhelming in any one offensive category, but their overall team speed and balanced attack made them difficult to beat.[42] Add to this their outstanding pitching from Mort Cooper (22–7 with a 1.78 ERA), Johnny Beazley (21–6 with a 2.13 ERA), Max Lanier (13–8 with a 2.98 ERA), Howie Krist (13–3 with a 2.51 ERA), and then there were the early season victories of Lon Warnecke before he was passed along to the Cubs.[43] The pitchers were aided by the wide range and sure hands of the St. Louis outfielders. In particular, Terry Moore was thought by many to be the best defensive centerfielder in baseball, despite the claims some made for the elegance afield of Joe DiMaggio.[44] Musial proved among the swiftest of the Cards and a fine fielder. As his arm strength returned, he was to surprise and cut down quite a few base runners who had hoped to take advantage of his reputedly weakened limb.

Though Musial's .315 average was not as high as would come to be his norm, he had more than lived up to the high expectations held for him because of his performance at the end of 1941. Contributing seventy-two RBIs, eighty-seven runs, thirty-two doubles, ten triples, and ten home runs—Stan proved he was a star to stay and not just the late-season flash in the pan that some skeptics characterized him as, when he was in his early season slump. The beauty of Stan's lever swing, his odd corkscrew batting stance, his speed from home to first, and his opportunistic base running generally—all these aspects of Stan's talent, hustle, picturesqueness, and evident desire had made him a crowd favorite.[45] J. Roy Stockton's calling Musial "the rookie of the year," in an article for the *Saturday Evening Post*, met with wide agreement, though their was no official award of that sort in 1942.[46]

The Yankees were heavy favorites to trample the Cardinals in the World Series. The Yanks had not lost to a National League opponent since their loss to the 1926 Cardinals, and they had dominated the American League in 1942, winning by ten games. Yankee hitting, pitching, and defense were all considered nonpareil. But the loose and lively Cardinals who had gotten used to having fun winning game after game during their improbable stretch drive came into the Series with no lack of confidence and with no particular feelings of awe before the Yankees against whom they had played well during spring training. The team's high spirits were aided by the cheerleading antics of their trainer, Doc Weaver, who did things like rigging up a light to flash green when the Cards were batting and red when the Yanks were at the plate, and devising a "double-whammy" witchcraft gesture to aim at Yankee players, which was whimsically echoed by most of the players on the Cardinals bench.

The Yankees asserted themselves in the first game of the series in Sportsman's Park, scoring seven unanswered runs by the time they had finished batting in the ninth inning, but the Redbirds came on strong in their half of the ninth, gaining back four of the runs. Musial was disappointed that he made the first and last outs in that inning, but he was cheered by the late rally, which demonstrated that the Cards were not going to lie down for the mighty Yankees. Stan's last at bat was one of those rare occasions in his career when he decided to go for a home run. Always a good low-ball hitter, Stan had visions of lifting one of the low pitches Spud Chandler was firing at him onto the grandstand roof, but he ended up grounding out sharply to end the game.

He redeemed himself the next day driving in Slaughter with a single to give the Cardinals a 4–3 lead going into the ninth inning, which rookie pitcher Johnny Beazley held onto, helped by a great throw by Slaughter to nail Yankee pinch-runner as he attempted to advance from first to third on a hit to right field. Slaughter's spectacular play was a dramatic sign of the Cardinals' determination to prevail.[47]

As the Series moved to Yankee Stadium, some of the Cardinals' wives, including Lil Musial, decided to save money by remaining in St. Louis to await the concluding games, which, as it turned out would never be played, when the Cardinals shocked the baseball world by defeating the Yankees the next three games in "The House That Ruth Built." Musial found that stadium an exciting but difficult place to play. Here he was a young man barely into his twenties, who had been playing Class C ball for much of the previous season, facing the enormous three-tiered ballpark, filled to the brim with a World Series record of 69,123 fans. At times he had trouble seeing the ball coming at him in left field due to an October haze, worsened by drifting smoke from thousands of cigarettes and complicated by late-afternoon shadows, but he held his own, aided occasionally by the extraordinary talents of centerfielder Terry Moore, who, in one case, made an amazing diving catch after Musial had fallen down in pursuit of the ball.[48]

Outstanding pitching by Cooper, Beazley, and surprise starter Ernie White, and inspirational play by many Cardinals, capped off by Whitey Kurowski's dramatic home run to win the final game, earned the Cardinals a remarkable five-game victory over the Yankees. The Cardinals had gained as many victories against the Yankees in one series as eight National League teams had collectively won since 1927. Musial's low average of .222 was to be typical of his hitting problems in championship games, bothered as he always was by the way white-shirted fans in packed centerfield stands wreaked havoc with the ability to see pitches as they left the pitcher's hand, an ability that was always key to his being the outstanding hitter he usually was. But Stan had played very well overall, under tremendous pressure, and he was immensely proud and grateful for his first full season as a major leaguer.[49]

Who would have guessed that the young man of twenty-one years tearfully saying goodbye to his friends at Pennsylvania Station in New York City on an October day in 1942 was an extraordinarily happy fellow whose most impossible dream had just come true? Stan Musial of the World Champion St. Louis Cardinals had arrived at the top of the baseball world and was emerging as one of the greatest hitters to ever play the game, but, even years later, after his list of achievements had grown long, he would still speak of his good fortune with astonishment. It is important to be clear on this point. Musial was never lacking in self-confidence, and never lacking in appreciation for his own talents. His fierce determination to succeed was based in a rock-solid sense of his own worth and potential. Still, as a child of The Depression, Stan understood how easily a person could be without recourse, and the total collapse of his prospects as a pitcher had made quite clear that things could go wrong and a dead end could be reached. So imposing was Musial to become that it is hard to bring into focus how fragile his first arrival at success must have seemed to him in one part of his mind. Stan never ceased to think of himself as "lucky"—a word he often used in interviews.

NOTES

1. Stan Musial and Bob Broeg, *Stan Musial: "The Man's" Own Story as Told to Bob Broeg*, (New York: Doubleday, 1964), 37–38.

2. James Giglio, *Musial: From Stash to Stan the Man* (Columbia, MO: University of Missouri Press, 2001), 39.

3. Musial and Broeg, *Stan Musial*, 38.

4. Ibid., 39–40.

5. Giglio, *Musial*, 43; Musial and Broeg, *Stan Musial*, 40; Neal Russo, "Vanek's Decision 25 Years Ago Made Stan Musial a Cardinal." *St. Louis Post-Dispatch*, January 1, 1962.

6. Musial and Broeg, *Stan Musial*, 41–42.

7. Giglio, *Musial*, 48–49; Jerry Lansche, *Stan "The Man" Musial: Born to Be a Ballplayer* (Dallas, TX: Taylor, 1994), 31.

8. Musial and Broeg, *Stan Musial*, 42.

9. Ibid., 43.

10. Ray Robinson, *Stan Musial: Baseball's Durable "Man"* (New York: Putnam, 1963), 40–41; Giglio, *Musial*, 54; Musial and Broeg, *Stan Musial*, 43–44.

11. Musial and Broeg, *Stan Musial*, 45.

12. Peter Golenbock, *The Spirit of St. Louis: A History of the St. Louis Cardinals and Browns* (New York: HarperCollins), 237.

13. Musial and Broeg, *Stan Musial*, 52.

14. Rickey harvested the crops of his farms for more than victories. Many players and journalists regarded Rickey's dealings as economically self-serving and sometimes not in the best interests of the Cardinals. Rickey often sold promising minor league players for cash and routinely sold or traded his veteran stars as soon as he felt they were slightly past their prime but still ranked highly enough to yield big payoffs. See Golenbock, *The Spirit of St. Louis*, 247–250.

15. Musial and Broeg, *Stan Musial*, 47.

16. Ibid.

17. Ibid., 48–49.

18. Lansche, *Stan "The Man" Musial*, 26.

19. Musial and Broeg, *Stan Musial*, 49–50.

20. Lansche, *Stan "The Man" Musial*, 26–27.

21. Musial and Broeg, *Stan Musial*, 50–51.

22. Giglio, *Musial*, 58–59; Musial and Broeg, *Stan Musial*, 51–52.

23. Peter Golenbock, *The Spirit of St. Louis: A History of the St. Louis Cardinals and Browns* (New York: HarperCollins), 214 and 239; Lansche, *Stan "The Man" Musial*, 27–28.

24. John Snyder, *Cardinals Journal* (Cincinnati, OH: Emmis Books, 2006), 320.

25. Kyle Crichton, "Ace in the Hole." *Collier's*, September 13, 1947, 14–15, 56.

26. Golenbock, *The Spirit of St. Louis*, 233; Lansche, *Stan "The Man" Musial*, 27.

27. Giglio, *Musial*, 59; Musial and Broeg, *Stan Musial*, 52.

28. Musial and Broeg, *Stan Musial*, 53.

29. Giglio, *Musial*, 67–68; Musial and Broeg, *Stan Musial*, 54.

30. Musial and Broeg, *Stan Musial*, 54–55.

31. Mel Freese, *The Glory Years of the St. Louis Cardinals, Volume 1, The World Championship Seasons* (St. Louis, MO: Palmerston & Reed, 1999), 102.

32. Bob Broeg and Jerry Vickery, *The St. Louis Cardinals Encyclopedia* (Chicago, IL: Contemporary Books), 39.

33. John Snyder, *Cardinals Journal* (Cincinnati, OH: Emmis Books, 2006), 323; Joseph Stanton, *Cardinal Points: Poems on St. Louis Cardinals Baseball* (Jefferson, NC: McFarland, 2002), 36.

34. Musial and Broeg, *Stan Musial*, 55.

35. Quoted in Lansche, *Stan "The Man" Musial*, 32.

36. Musial and Broeg, *Stan Musial*, 57.

37. Lansche, *Stan "The Man" Musial*, 31–32.

38. Broeg and Vickery, *The St. Louis Cardinals Encyclopedia*, 40.

39. Snyder, *Cardinals Journal*, 325; Stanton, *Cardinal Points*, 27.

40. Musial and Broeg, *Stan Musial*, 60; Stanton, *Cardinal Points*, 28.

41. Giglio, *Musial*, 76–77; Musial and Broeg, *Stan Musial*, 65.

42. Ray Robinson and Christopher Jennison, *Greats of the Game* (New York: Abrams, 2005), 189–191; Giglio, *Musial*, 65–66.

43. Lansche, *Stan "The Man" Musial*, 39–40.

44. Freese, *The Glory Years of the St. Louis Cardinals*, 105–106.

45. Lansche, *Stan "The Man" Musial*, 40.

46. J. Roy Stockton, "Rookie of the Year." *Saturday Evening Post*, September 12, 1942, 29, 36.

47. Musial and Broeg, *Stan Musial*, 66–71.

48. Giglio, *Musial*, 78–80.

49. Musial and Broeg, *Stan Musial*, 66–73.

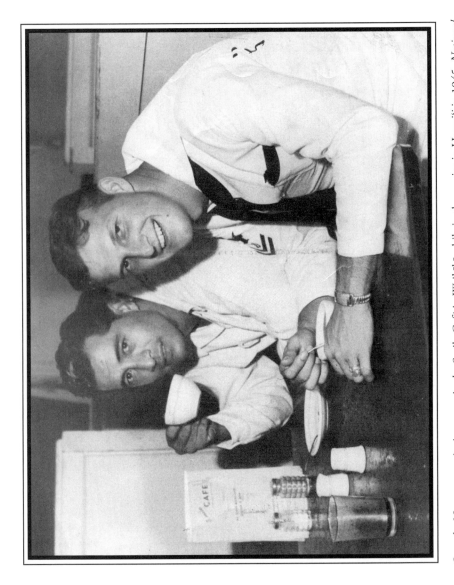

Stan the Navy man enjoying a cup in the Smile Café in Waikiki while in the service in Hawai'i in 1945. *National Baseball Hall of Fame Library, Cooperstown, NY.*

STAN BECOMES THE MAN

Although worried about the eruption of the Second World War and what it might mean for his country, his family, and himself—Musial had much to be optimistic about with regard to his baseball future once Roosevelt encouraged Major League Baseball to continue to operate despite the crisis.

The Cardinals lost a number of key players to the military draft, but were in better shape than many teams because of the depth of their farm system and the fortunate retention of such key players as Whitey Kurowski, Marty Marion, and Johnny Hopp, each of whom had ongoing medical conditions that qualified them for deferments. Musial—as the father of a young child and the supporter of elderly parents—was protected from immediate induction. It happened, too, that the Donora area had a large supply of draft eligible young men, which put Musial further down the list than he might have been otherwise. Further solidifying Musial's protection from immediate induction was his off-season job in zinc mining, which was considered an essential industry.

At first it looked like Musial might be seeing more zinc than baseball in 1943 as he staged his first holdout. Tightfisted owner Sam Breadon had already lightened his salary burdens by giving Branch Rickey his walking papers and taking over as his own general manager and his balance sheet was also helped because several of his military-bound players had resided at the higher end of the pay scale, but Breadon was afraid that wartime conditions would keep attendance low. Despite Stan's emerging stardom, Breadon offered him only a $1,000 raise that would put him at $5,500. Advised by one of his Donora mentors, auto dealer Frank Pizzica, Stan composed a letter to Breadon that made the strategic mistake of arguing that he deserved a raise to $10,000 because he would have to work "even harder" in 1943 due to the loss of fellow outfielders Terry Moore and Enos Slaughter to military service. Breadon wrote back dismissing this claim and asserting sternly that Stan would have no more to do in the year ahead, pointing out that Stan should be "the kind of ball player that gave all [he] had in every game." Breadon, in turn, overstated his case by arguing that Stan was greedy and unrealistic in wanting to get paid more than other great Cardinals outfielders—such as Hafey, Medwick, Moore, and Slaughter—had earned in their second year. Musial responded that comparing current salaries to Depression-era salaries was hardly appropriate. Breadon then breezily urged Stan to come to St. Louis and talk it over, mentioning in a genially menacing way that the Cardinals would pay for Stan's return ticket to Donora should he decide not to play in 1943. Wisely, Stan decided to stay in Donora, and Breadon, no doubt more worried about losing his budding star than he wanted to appear, sent Eddie Dyer, at that time Breadon's farm system director, with a counteroffer. Pizzica was out of town, and Stan, who was eager to start playing, signed a contract for $6,250. Musial's first holdout was over. Despite all the expressions of anxiety by owners about what war-related austerities would do to the baseball business, Breadon and most of the other owners turned profits during the war years.[1]

When Danny Litwhiler joined the Cardinals in 1943, he was amazed at what low salaries the Cardinals stars were making. Branch Rickey had wielded the reserve clause and his dazzling combination of charm and intimidation to create a culture in which rock-bottom salaries were the norm for championship talents, and Breadon, though lacking the charm, had continued to hold the line. Litwhiler particularly noted the surprising underpayment of Musial. "It seems crazy. His wife told my wife that they thought I was rich, because I had a car. Stan couldn't afford to buy a car. Rickey was no longer there, but it didn't matter. Breadon had learned how to do it."[2]

Wartime restrictions dictated that all teams hold their spring training sessions closer to home. The Cardinals set up camp in Cairo, Illinois. Players were advised to bring heavy clothes and long underwear and to be prepared to deal with rain and snow. Despite arriving a week late to the camp Musial was soon ready for action. He had played basketball and exercised throughout the winter so he was close to peak condition when he arrived in Cairo.

At the start of the season hitters were frustrated by the use of balls that contained a rubber substitute called balata. Unlike the prewar balls that featured rubber surrounding a top-quality cork center, the new balls contained a low-grade, ground cork encased in balata, a not entirely rubbery substance concocted from the sap of tropical trees. Regular rubber was restricted because of wartime urgencies. As a result of this deadened ball, most games were low scoring. Joe

Gordon's home run for the Yankees eleven games into the season was the first hit in the major leagues in 1943.[3] On May 9, a livelier baseball came into use and a barrage of homers ensued. Musial, ever the canny hitter, had managed to hit well during the balata drought. His average the day before the return of live balls stood at .323 and he had managed to bang five doubles and three triples by following the Wee Willie Keeler strategy of hitting them "where they ain't."[4] Musial's speed and his ability to spray his drives to all fields gave him some advantages over more predictable hitters whose averages plunged when the balata ball took the sting out of their swing.

The Dodgers kept close to the Cardinals until July when the intense rivalry erupted with Leo Durocher encouraging Dodger pitcher Les Webber to aim for Musial's head—inducing the Card's primary tough guy, Walker Cooper, to step on the foot of Augie Galan at first base, which in turn inspired Mickey Owen to jump on Cooper's back. The ensuing melee involved most players on both teams. As so often happened when Durocher encouraged hostilities, the enraged Cardinals played their best ball and swept the Dodgers that four-game series and the pennant race was virtually over. The Cardinals went on to run away from the National League, coming in first by eighteen games.

Stan made his first All-Star Game appearance in 1943. He had one hit, a double, in four at bats and drove in a run with a sacrifice fly, but the American League won 5-3. Musial's All-Star double was off a left-handed pitcher, as were many of his big hits in 1943. Manager Billy Southworth no longer platooned Musial, realizing that he was dangerous against every sort of pitching. That season saw Stan win his first MVP award and his first batting championship with a .357 average. Among his 220 hits were forty-eight doubles, twenty triples, and thirteen home runs.

Stan gave some of the credit for his hitting for a higher average in 1943 than in 1942 to the decision to play him in right rather than left field. The switch was the result of the Cardinals' acquisition of left-fielder Danny Litwhiler from Philadelphia. Stan told Litwhiler that the throws he had to make from left field often had to be across his body, which aggravated his sore arm. The right field throw was easier on his arm and enabled him to heal from his minor-league injury. Less pain in the arm, Stan felt, contributed to his having an easier time swinging freely and comfortably every time he came to bat.[5]

The 1943 World Series gave the Yankees a chance to exact revenge for their embarrassing five-game loss to the Cardinals in the 1942 Series. Completely turning the tables, the Yanks lost only the second game. That second game was especially memorable for the Cardinals because of what it meant to the Cooper brothers, whose father had died the day before. The Coopers decided to go ahead and play in tribute to their father and Mort got the clutch 4-3 victory with Walker catching the last out of the game, a foul ball pop-up that he managed to snag. Although Musial was to say in the many postseason talks he was to give to groups of servicemen that the Yankees "deserved to win" because they "played better ball" and "had the better pitching"—every game but one was close and could have gone either way. Even the worst game for the Cards, the 6-2 loss in the third game, would have also been close if not for Cardinal errors and a clutch three-run triple by the Yanks.[6] Marty Marion felt that the Cardinals were distracted and not at their best in the 1943 World Series. "I don't know what happened, but we didn't have the intensity, the desire to win like we had in 42. It was a war year. I don't think our minds were on it, to tell the truth, and that's a poor excuse, because they beat us. And they played under the same circumstances. But we didn't seem to have the same feeling."[7]

The loser's share of for the 1943 World Series was $4,321.99. Not bad for a week's work, especially when one considers that it equaled approximately two-thirds of the salary Stan earned for the entire season.

After putting in a stint in the zinc works, Musial went on a six-week tour to entertain the troops in Alaska and the Aleutian Islands. Stan joined Dixie Walker, Hank Borowy, Danny Litwiler, and Frank Frisch for these meet-and-greet sessions in the cold North. They showed newsreel footage of the World Series, autographed baseballs, and answered questions. The many Cardinal fans and sympathizers Stan encountered amongst the troops all demanded to know why the Cards had lost to the Yanks.[8] Stan's good-sportsmanly praise for the Yankee performance was one of the first high-profile instances of the gracious demeanor that was to earn him a reputation for gentlemanly behavior that has long enhanced his legend. Stan has come to embody for many the concept that, contrary to Durocher's famous dictum, nice guys can finish first.

Stan had no concerns about his contract for 1944. Stan's impressive stats for 1943, including his .357 average, made Breadon want to lock him into a multiyear deal. Although Stan was quite proud of his raise in pay to be followed by raises in the two following years—Breadon calculated that the scaled payments of $10,000 for 1944, $12,500 for 1945, and $13,500 for 1946 were going to be bargain rates if Musial continued to be the superstar he appeared to have become. Breadon hoped to stave off, at least for a while, any claims Musial and his supporters might have made to bring his wages up to the level of big-ticket stars such as Ted Williams.

The depth of the Cardinals' farm system served them well in 1944. They were able to field a strong team despite the losses of many players to the military draft. Many of their competitors did not fare as well, and the Red Birds dominated the National League, winning 105 despite a losing record in September after the pennant race had been decided. Had it not been for their losing fifteen of twenty games in September, the Cardinals might have had a shot at setting a record for most games won in a season. One of the causes of the Card's September slump was the loss of Musial for ten days due to an injured knee sustained in a collision in the outfield with Deb Garms. Anxious to help his team get back to winning, Musial returned to play too soon and lost some points from his batting average as he struggled at the plate. Even with that falling off Musial's hit .347 for the season coming in second behind Brooklyn's Dixie Walker's .357.

The 1944 World Series was a rare affair; it was an all St. Louis series because the Browns had managed to win the championship by one game on the very last day of the season. It was an unusual moment for baseball fandom in St. Louis. The Browns had been overshadowed by the Cardinals since the rise of the Redbirds under Branch Rickey in the 1920s, and the failure of the Browns to live up to their potential despite the heroics of their great star George Sisler. The Browns unexpected, last-minute beating out of the mighty Yankees for the pennant in 1944 with a team jerry-rigged from castoffs and remnants was an exciting redemption of sorts for an organization that had seemed to have lost all hope for greatness. Lil Musial, observing the tremendous fanfare that surrounded the Browns' clinching of the championship, remarked, "This is a *Brownie* town."[9]

The heavily favored Cardinals did not have an easy time with the Browns. The Cardinals lost the first game 2-1, despite Mort Cooper's strong two-hit pitching; unfortunately one of the hits was the game-winning, two-run homer by George McQuinn. The Cards might have lost the second game, too, had it not been for a pinch single by Ken O'Dea and a fine fielding play at a crucial moment by relief pitcher Blix Donnelly. The 3-2 win in the second game was a lifesaver because the Browns went on to win the third game 6-2. In the next contest Musial contributed three hits, including a homer, and Harry Brecheen came through with a clutch pitching performance in the Cardinals' 5-1 win. Now the Series was tied with a pair of victories for each team. The Cardinals won the next two games to take the championship.[10]

The double allegiance of the fans, many of whom had been enthusiastic supporters of both teams all year, created a unique situation in which the cheering was nonstop no matter which team was winning. As Danny Litwhiler explains, "When a Brown would get up and do something, there would be a terrific roar, and when the Cards did something, it would be the same thing, so you really wouldn't know what happened sometimes."[11]

Musial had managed to hit .304 in the 1944 World Series, but he always found it difficult to hit in championship games when white-shirted spectators crowded into center field seats. A few years later Musial finally managed to convince the owners that the center field section should be roped off so that hitters could have a dark backdrop to help them see the release of the ball from the pitcher's hand without the distraction of the flicker of white shirts.[12] As mentioned earlier, Musial's knack for seeing and interpreting the emergence of the ball out of the pitcher's hand was one of the keys to his greatness as a hitter. With that edge compromised he tended to underperform in World Series contests.

Major League Baseball made a film documenting the 1944 World Series for the same reason they did so in 1943: to share the climax of the season with the troops fighting the war. The films proved popular with the intended audience as well as with the many nonmilitary fans who got to see them in movie theaters. With the resounding success of the first two films, crude as they were in certain respects, the tradition of World Series films was established and continued after the war and continues to this day.[13] The 1944 film provides a brief glimpse of Musial hitting his home run in game four. Stan's passion to succeed can be observed in this clip as Musial launches himself with a passionate surge toward first base at the completion of his home-run swing, quickly bringing his run to top speed, almost as if he were trying to beat out a bunt. Throughout his career Musial endeavored to take advantage of the extra step down the base line that a left-handed hitter has available to him. Musial felt no need to admire his handiwork after hitting a long drive as so many hitters do these days. In the event the ball bounced off the wall or the right field screen Stan was determined to get as many bases as he could.[14]

In January of 1945 the Donora draft board came calling and Musial entered the Navy, undergoing basic training at Bainbridge, Maryland. In Bainbridge, as well as in Hawai'i where he was assigned to the shipyard at Pearl Harbor, Musial found himself called upon to play baseball for the entertainment of fellow servicemen. In Hawai'i he played in an eight-team league staffed largely by major-league players. After a season of several games a week for a large audience of sailors, Stan played in October for a crowd of 26,000 in what the Navy called it's "little world series." The armed forces audience loved to see home runs. Noting this, Musial changed his batting stance and moved closer to the plate so that he could more frequently pull inside pitches over right field walls.[15] Musial claims that these alterations "proved to be an important step in [his] evolution as a hitter."[16] After his return from the war Musial became much more of a home run hitter. Though his year in the service lost Musial a peak statistical season, the frequent exhibition games kept his body in shape and his baseball skills well-honed.

When Musial's father fell gravely ill with pneumonia, his mother appealed through the Red Cross for Stan to be given emergency leave to see his father. After his leave, he was reassigned to Philadelphia and discharged a few months later. Hitchhiking home to Donora along the Pennsylvania Turnpike with a couple of other sailors from his area, Stan was happy to know that he had gotten out in time to play for the Cardinals in 1946 and relieved to find his father out of immediate danger.[17]

In his back-from-the-war spring training of 1946 Musial's good spirits found expression in his developing penchant for magic tricks and other gags. Commenting on clubhouse antics in the 1940s Marty Marion has said that Musial "was always kidding, a jovial person. . . . If you don't like Stan, you don't like anybody."[18] Although regarded by many reporters as taciturn and colorless, Stan, when among friends and fellow players, could find ways to be the life of the party. In 1946 Stan's joking ways included leaving a fake thumb in the grip of teammates willing to risk shaking hands with him. Such parlor tricks—and his genial harmonica playing, which was to become a Musial trademark—were among the means Stan used to keep things light and lively for himself and his teammates.[19] These antidotes to the big-time pressure of major-league baseball enabled Musial to dispense with his tendency toward shyness and find outlets for his mischievously affectionate personality. The genuinely modest, friendly, upbeat, factual manner with which he dealt with reporters' questions—and, especially, his unwillingness to complain, make excuses, or say negative things about others—frustrated the reportorial desire to stir things up to get a story. Reporters loved or loved to hate sarcastic wise guys like Leo Durocher. About all they could report with regard to Musial was how well he did his job. Stan's sense of humor, growing out of his wise determination not to take himself too seriously, was seldom noted by journalists, most of whom equated the colorful with the controversial.

One spring-training development that was no joking matter for Stan was a fall he suffered in some sandy soil at St. Petersburg's Waterfront Park, which resulted in strained ligaments in his left knee that were to bother Stan, off and on, for the rest of his career. The bad condition of the field was the result of it having been used as a military drill practice field during the war.[20]

The Cardinals were favored to win the pennant in 1946, despite their having come up short in 1945, but there were problematic downturns for some of the team's former core players. Johnny Beazley returned from the war with a sore arm and never recovered his former prowess. The great-fielding and clutch-hitting center fielder Terry Moore was having trouble with his legs and was not the swifty he once had been. Manager Southworth was gone to Boston to accept a better salary from the Braves and had been replaced by Eddie Dyer. Musial felt that one of the Cardinal's greatest losses going into the season of 1946 was Walker Cooper who Breadon had sold to the Giants. As had happened previously with the unloading of Johnny Mize, the Cardinals had given up a major talent and gotten little in return. Although Breadon claimed that he had to get rid of Cooper because the big catcher didn't get along well with Dyer, the real reason appears to be that he had been annoyed by the salary wranglings of both the Cooper brothers—he had already gotten rid of brother Mort in 1945. Musial always felt that Walker Cooper, the best catcher in baseball at the time, would have continued to contribute to the Cardinals long-term success. Cooper's strong right-handed bat was important to keeping teams from piling on the left-handers, as they tended to do when Musial and Slaughter were the primary power hitters on the team. Possibly even more important than Walker Cooper's hitting prowess were his efforts on the field as a team leader and masterful handler of the pitching staff. The lack of this great catcher did not stop the Cardinals in 1946, but Musial felt this loss was the primary cause of the team's not running away with the race in 1946 and one of the reasons for the team's failure to repeat in subsequent years.[21]

Breadon's tightfistedness also led to Cardinal players being targeted for acquisition for the Mexican leagues by the big-spending Pasquel brothers. Of the Cardinals choosing to fly south to Mexico, the biggest loss was Max Lanier, who had won his first six starts for the Cardinals before running after the Mexican money. Musial was heavily courted by the Pasquel's and there was the famous June 6th meeting where Alfonso Pasquel spread out on Musial's bed at the Fairgrounds Hotel in St. Louis five $10,000 cashier's checks, telling Stan to consider that money a bonus on top of the $125,000 they would pay him for five years of play. The astounded Musial, who was getting paid $13,500 by the Cardinals at that time and still carried with him vivid memories of his family's Depression-induced dire straits, told Pasquel that he had to give the matter some thought, but ultimately he yielded to the advice of Eddie Dyer who got to the core of Stan's feelings on this matter by pointing out that Stan would not be happy turning his back on his contract with his own country's big leagues. Playing in the majors was such a dream come true for Stan that he could not bear the thought of giving it up, despite his considerable need for more money to support his family. Though the Cardinals apparently made no direct counter offer to help Musial resist the Mexican temptation, he was called into Breadon's office in August and awarded a $5000 raise. In the midst of a season that was proving to be profitable for the Cardinals, Breadon clearly wanted to lock in the allegiance of his greatest star.[22]

Dick Sisler, son of the former Browns star, was expected to amply fill the Cardinals' needs at first base in 1946. When Sisler failed to live up to that expectation, Eddie Dyer left Musial a not too subtle hint by planting a new first baseman's mitt in Stan's locker. Stan dutifully began taking fielding practice at first base even though it was a position he had never liked on the very few occasions he had played there up to that point in his career, and, without a word of complaint, he ended up playing three-fourths of the games in 1946 wearing the oversized first baseman's glove. As it happened, the June night when Stan first undertook the first base responsibilities in a major-league game was also the night that featured a return to the Cardinal clubhouse of the playing of a recording of "Pass the Bisquits Mirandy"—the silly, pseudo-hillbilly song by Spike Jones that had inspired the Cardinals in 1942. Doc Weaver, the Cardinals' trainer, and Dr. Hyland, their physician, had managed to get a copy of the tune from a local radio station and it's inspirational twang was blaring in Stan's ears as he readied himself for his new position. Somehow all the signs seemed to be pointing in the right direction and the Cardinals began to win more consistently and found themselves inching up toward the league-leading Dodgers. The pressure of infield play was never much to Musial's liking, but he became good at it, and the new challenge did not seem to negatively affect his hitting.[23]

A postseason 1946 article by Donald Drees in *Baseball Digest* on "Iceman Musial" placed special emphasis on Stan's "ice-in-the-veins" knack for not letting pressure hinder his performance. Following the emerging practice of describing Musial as lacking the colorful antics of previous stars like Hornsby and Ruth, Drees declares that Musial's "color is only in his crisp, machine-like rocket hitting; his gazelle-boy running; his determined slides; his efficient fielding." He quotes Stan as admitting that he does not ordinarily suffer from the emotions that plague other players. He quotes Musial as saying he doesn't "get that thrill that makes fellows howl with delight or dance or do a handspring. I can get into the spirit of the gang and act up, but I know I don't feel it like they do." The Musial aloofness to delighted emotions carries over to the anxious emotions, as Musial is shown declaring a lack of concern even in his first World Series game in 1942: "It was a feeling different from the ordinary game, but I know I wasn't nervous or jittery or high-strung. At least I don't think I was."[24] In later interviews Musial would stress the importance of concentration to his success as a hitter. His legendary coolness seems to have been a result of his determination to concentrate on the task at hand. His famed modesty appears to have had a practical advantage for him as a hitter: he would take nothing for granted, and allow nothing to sway him from hitting as well as he could. Jumping up and down was for others to do. Stan just wanted to keep the hits coming.

Musial's ability to keep cool in moments of crisis came in handy during an off-field transportation adventure the Cardinals faced in May of 1946. Desperately needing to get the starting team quickly to Cincinnati to avoid forfeiting a game, Cardinals' traveling secretary Leo Ward chartered a DC-3 aircraft. It was a time when passenger air travel was far from routine. The risky trip became even riskier when the plane ran straight into a dark wall of storm clouds and had to emergency land about fifty miles from Cincinnati. A group of decrepit old taxis were recruited to take the team the rest of the way. The taxi that Musial's group found themselves in had a hood that kept popping up and blocking the driver's view. The driver suggested that one of the passengers ride on the hood to hold it down. Stan took charge of the situation volunteering to drive if the driver would ride on the hood. With his teammates gripping their knees in white-knuckled anxiety, Musial, who could not stand the idea of having to forfeit a game, barreled down the road behind a police escort with his head sticking out the side window to see where he was going.[25]

The steady play of the Cardinals kept edging them closer and closer to the league-leading Dodgers. Of particular help was a four-game sweep of the Dodgers by the Cards in Brooklyn in mid-July in which Musial contributed many key hits. This is the series in which the nickname "Stan the Man" emerged as a by-product of the dismayed acknowledgment by Brooklyn fans of the devastation Musial, in particular, was wreaking on Dodger pitching. In one game in which Musial contributed four hits, Bob Broeg asked Leo Ward what a large faction of Brooklynites had been chanting every time Stan came up to bat. They had, it turns out, been shouting in lamentation, "Here comes the man! Here comes the man!" Broeg's article on this odd tribute is the point of origin for the practice of referring to Musial as "Stan the Man." Musial enjoyed the name, much as he had always enjoyed hitting at Ebbets Field, the scene of a number of his most heroic performances.[26]

The Cardinals played well in the closing days of the season, winning twenty-three of their last thirty-one games, but Brooklyn finished strong, too.[27] The Cardinals and the Dodgers came into the last week of the season neck and neck and then ended with identical records. A playoff would be needed to determine the National League champion. A best-of-three series would be played to settle the matter. Having won the coin toss, Leo Durocher elected to let the first game be played in St. Louis so that the second two games would be in Brooklyn. Durocher was delighted with himself for setting it up this way because it would give the Dodgers the considerable advantage of two home games rather than one. Unfortunately for this theory the Cardinals won the first game and then went on to win the second one, too, bringing the playoffs to an end without need for a third game. It would be the Cardinals against the Red Sox in the 1946 World Series.[28]

The Red Sox were twelve games ahead of the second-place Detroit Tigers at the close of regular play, and they were heavily favored to defeat the Cardinals whose season had been uneven in comparison with the Red Sox's surprisingly dominant year. Howie Pollet pitched a fine opening game at Sportsman's Park, despite an aching back, but the Cards were beaten 3-2 by a Rudy York home run in the tenth inning. Musial helped the Cardinals' cause in the first game with an

RBI double, but, for the most part, this World Series was to be a disappointing one for the stars of their respective teams, with Musial hitting only .222 for the seven games and Ted Williams only .200.[29]

Williams was stymied, in part, by the "Boudreau shift" the Cardinals employed. This strategy modeled after one employed against Williams by Cleveland's Lou Boudreau. Marty Marion has described the shift: "I stayed at shortstop. Kurowski moved over to the right side. He and Schoendienst were over there. Ted didn't try to hit the ball my way. Bunting was against his code. He wanted to challenge everybody, try to hit the ball through there."[30] With the close right field wall in Sportsman's Park, the Cardinals had a particular reason for wanting to encourage Williams to poke the ball to the left side.[31]

Williams was also hampered by the masterful performance of the Cardinals' left-handed, screwball pitcher Harry Brecheen, who threw a six-hitter in the second game to shut out the Red Sox 3-0. Williams admitted in a newspaper column to his difficulties with Brecheen, "Brecheen's pitches look nice to hit at, but when you try to hit him the ball just isn't where you think it's going to be." When the Series moved to Boston for three games, Boo Ferris returned Brecheen's favor by shutting down the Cards 4-0. When Williams contributed to that third-game effort by bunting for a hit, Boston newspapers screamed in large headlines, "TED BUNTS!" [32]

Being down two games to one and playing in Boston did not discourage the Cardinals who won the fourth game emphatically twelve to three. Slaughter, Kurowski, and Garagiola each had four hits. With only one hit to his credit Musial was disappointed, once again, by his World Series performance. When the Red Sox won the next six to three, handing the sore-backed Pollet his second loss of the Series and placing the Sox within one win of the championship, things were not looking good for the Redbirds, especially with Enos Slaughter leaving the game with an elbow injury. Because of the risky nature of the injury, Slaughter was considered unlikely to play in the last two games, but trainer Doc Weaver worked on Slaughter with cold and hot packs, and Enos refused to consider staying out of the action. Working through the pain he contributed a key hit in support of Brecheen's 4-1 game six victory.[33]

The stage was set for one of the most celebrated seventh games in World Series history. With the score tied at three in the eighth Slaughter singled. With two out and Harry Walker at the plate, Slaughter broke for second in hopes of making something happen. When Walker singled, Slaughter—who was not, it should be remembered, a fast runner—decided that he was not going to stop at third no matter how the play developed. Ignoring third-base coach Mike Gonzalez's frantic signals for him to stop, Slaughter barreled around third. Taking the relay from the outfield, short stop Johnny Pesky had his back to the infield, and was not told by his teammates that he should throw home, surprised to find Slaughter steaming toward the plate. By the time Pesky re-cocked his arm and threw, Enos was sliding across with the big score. When questioned afterward by reporters about his risky decision to defy common sense and keep running, Slaughter answered, "I just had a hunch I could make it and I was willing to take the rap if I didn't."[34]

The dramatic ninth inning offered Harry Brecheen, brought in as a reliever with one day's rest, a chance for more heroics, and he stifled a Red Sox rally and earned his third victory of the Series. It was a satisfying triumph for Musial and for all the Cardinals. No one could have guessed, at that point that the Cardinals, who had been for twenty years one of the most successful teams in baseball, would have to wait almost twenty more years, to the year immediately after Musial's retirement, for their next visit to the fall classic.

NOTES

1. James Giglio, *Musial: From Stash to Stan the Man* (Columbia: University of Missouri Press, 2001), 82–83.

2. Peter Golenbock, *The Spirit of St. Louis: A History of the St. Louis Cardinals and Browns* (New York: HarperCollins), 257.

3. Giglio, *Musial*, 84.

4. Stan Musial and Bob Broeg, *Stan Musial: "The Man's" Own Story as Told to Bob Broeg* (New York: Doubleday, 1964), 77–78.

5. Golenbock, *The Spirit of St. Louis*, 256.

6. Musial and Broeg, *Stan Musial*, 76–79.

7. Golenbock, *The Spirit of St. Louis*, 257.

8. Musial and Broeg, *Stan Musial*, 79.

9. Ibid., 80–81.

10. Ibid., 81–82.

11. Golenbock, *The Spirit of St. Louis*, 263.

12. Musial and Broeg, *Stan Musial*, 81–82.

13. *St. Louis Cardinals Vintage World Series Film* (*1943, 1944, and 1946*), DVD (Major League Baseball, 2005).

14. Among the players active as I write this in 2006, Ichiro Suzuki of the Seattle Mariners is one of the players exhibiting a fully Musial-like passion for exploiting that extra step. On the contemporary Cardinals, David Eckstein, though a right-hander, is among the current practitioners of the don't-pause-to-watch-the-flight-of-the-ball philosophy. Both these players are of the hustling lead-off-man type. It is among the keys to Musial's success that, although he was a slugger who batted third or fourth in the lineup during his prime, his passionate desire to make advances on the base paths, especially in his younger

years, gave him the mental set of a lead-off guy. As much as anyone on the club, it was Musial with his passionately adept base-running that earned the Cardinals of the 1940s "The St. Louis Swifties" nickname.

15. Giglio, *Musial*, 97–98.

16. Musial and Broeg, *Stan Musial*, 83.

17. Ibid., 84–85

18. Golenbock, *The Spirit of St. Louis*, 253.

19. Musial and Broeg, *Stan Musial*, 86.

20. Jerry Lansche, *Stan "The Man" Musial: Born to Be a Ballplayer* (Dallas, TX: Taylor, 1994), 71.

21. Musial and Broeg, *Stan Musial*, 86–87.

22. Ibid., 89–91.

23. Ibid., 90–93.

24. Donald Drees, "Ice Man Musial." *Baseball Digest*, November 1946, 17–22.

25. Bob Broeg, and Jerry Vickery, *The St. Louis Cardinals Encyclopedia* (Chicago, IL: Contemporary Books, 1998), 51.

26. Musial and Broeg, *Stan Musial*, 92–93. The nickname served Musial for the rest of his life as a self-identity marker. After I mailed him a few questions for this book, his secretary replied by e-mail. The reply arrived as an e-mail from "Stan the Man." The nickname was, in 2006, still serving as his moniker. It had, by that time, become something of a corporate logo.

27. Golenbock, *The Spirit of St. Louis*, 374.

28. Musial and Broeg, *Stan Musial*, 94–95.

29. Lansche, *Stan "The Man" Musial*, 80–84.

30. Golenbock, *The Spirit of St. Louis*, 376.

31. Musial and Broeg, *Stan Musial*, 95.

32. Lansche, *Stan "The Man" Musial*, 81.

33. Musial and Broeg, *Stan Musial*, 97–99.

34. Ralph Knight and Bob Broeg, "Country Keynotes the Cards." *Saturday Evening Post*, May 17, 1947, 174.

Musial displaying his famed concentration on the task of hitting. *National Baseball Hall of Fame Library, Cooperstown, NY.*

GREAT YEARS AS ALMOST CHAMPS

As a result of his achievements in the mid-1940s Stan Musial was a hot property, and he was determined to get a raise in pay. He had become the National League equivalent of such American League stars as Ted Williams and Hank Greenberg whose salaries towered over the $18,500 Musial earned in 1946. In fact, the salaries of Williams and Greenberg were about four times that much, and, to add insult to this injury, Breadon told Stan that his salary in 1946 had actually remained at $13,500, because, in Breadon's view, the additional $5,000 was a later bonus rather than a permanent boost in pay. Musial pointed out that both amounts were in his contract for that year, and he had to pay income tax on all of it. Musial declared his intention to hold out for a minimum of $35,000. After much haggling back and forth, Stan finally took the field for $31,000. Stan was proud of having stood his ground against his tightfisted boss and was to say later that this was "the most significant salary boost I ever received."[1]

Musial's disappointing hitting in the early part of the season coincided with other Cardinals failings and 1947 left the team in a considerable hole. It turned out that Musial's problems were due largely to an infected appendix. This misery was compounded by a similarly problematic pair of tonsils. The Cardinals' trainer, Dr. Robert Hyland, wanted to operate immediately, but also provided the option that treatments could temporarily prevent the offending body parts from getting worse so that surgery could be put off for the duration of the season. Musial opted, not surprisingly, to have the temporary treatments for the infected areas and continue playing. The ministrations of Dr. Hyland enabled Stan to gain strength and recover his hitting prowess.[2]

In 1947 the Cardinals' chances, as was often to be the case over the years, rose and fell depending on Stan's performance. "As Musial goes, so goes the Cardinals" became a common saying amongst the fans and observers of the Redbirds. As Musial gained strength over the course of the season, his average gradually climbed to .312 by the end of the season, despite his having languished below .200 during the early days of the summer; likewise the Cardinals' standing in the League rose from the cellar to near the top as the season and Stan progressed.[3] It was, however, third baseman Whitey Kurowski, as much as Musial, who carried the Cardinals in 1947. Though his average was slightly less than Musial's at .310, Kurowski led the Cards in on-base percentage, slugging percentage, home runs, and RBIs. The Cardinals failed to catch up with the Dodgers before time ran out on the pennant race, but prospects for 1948 appeared to hold promise for Musial and his team.

The success of the Dodgers in 1947, and in a number of years to follow, owed much to the genius of Branch Rickey who joined the Dodgers after being fired by Sam Breadon. Breadon had unwisely decided he could get along just fine without the expensive and argumentative services of Branch Rickey. Thus Brooklyn's hopes were aided by the attention Rickey paid to the improvement of the Dodger farm system at a time when Breadon was trying to make ends meet by selling off what had formerly been an ample supply of Cardinals talent. At one point, journalist, J. Roy Stockton embarrassed Breadon at a public banquet by accusing the Cardinals' owner of cutting "the baloney too fine."[4]

One of Rickey's most important Dodger innovations was his breaking of the color line by means of his recruitment of Jackie Robinson, who began his major league career with the Dodgers in 1947. Rickey understood that the post-World War II political climate that had seen surging black populations and therefore surging black political influence in big cities like New York made it ridiculous to restrict the opportunities of black people, especially in view of how of valiantly they had fought for their country during the war. Although there was an idealistic side to Rickey's use of Jackie Robinson, it was also a brilliant move in both competitive and economic terms. There was pool of black talent untapped by white Major League Baseball, and, perhaps even more importantly from Rickey's point of view, there was a huge audience of black baseball fans in New York and the other cities where the Dodgers played. Rickey was confident that the interest of black fans could be shifted from the Negro Leagues to an integrated Brooklyn team. White fans, too, were showing up in large numbers to pack the seats. More rapidly than many expected, white fans in Brooklyn learned to appreciate the Dodgers' exciting integrated team. Robinson, especially, proved to be an audience multiplier, especially on the road, where Robinson's presence on the field was good for a significant boost in the box office, even in stadiums of teams that were not competitive in 1947. Attendance could not go up all that much in the modest-sized Ebbets Field in 1947 over the capacity crowds that had turned out to watch the pennant-contending Dodgers in 1946, but in other parks the Jackie factor boosted Dodger income for Rickey in a big way. In Chicago, for instance, the appearance of Robinson in the lineup led to the Cubs setting an attendance record of 46,572 fans. The crowds that turned out especially to root for Jackie Robinson was so enthusiastic in the Windy City that some felt it gave the Dodgers something akin to a home-field advantage there.[5]

Rickey's cleverest and perhaps least admirable strategy was his failure to compensate the Negro League teams from whom he acquired talent. Hiding behind the dubious contention that the black teams did not truly own their players in contractual terms that he needed to respect, Rickey simply stole from these teams whatever players he wanted. Rickey understood that the purloined teams would not want to compromise the situations of Jackie Robinson and the rest by raising a fuss.[6]

In any case, Rickey's great experiment was a smashing success due to the way Jackie Robinson rose to the challenge with his superlative athleticism, tremendous courage, drive to succeed, innovative play (especially with regard to how he ran the bases), and willingness to endure and rise above racially motivated abuse. Rickey's enhancements of the Dodgers and Breadon's unloading of Cardinals talent were to spell the end of a Cardinals era and usher in a decade in which Musial's continued superstardom was to be more often than not the only unmitigated success in which a Cardinals fan could fully rejoice.

Controversial articles by *The New York Herald Tribune* suggested that the Cardinals' players were plotting to strike rather than play against Robinson. Over the years emphatic testimony contradicting that rumor have been put on record by Musial, Red Schoendienst, Terry Moore, Enos Slaughter, Marty Marion, and many others, but the legend, as tends to happen with legends, persists. Ford Frick's comment that "The St. Louis club accepted Robinson better than most," has often been quoted by Bob Broeg as evidence that the Cardinals do not deserve the vilification they received in the New York City press and in some sports books and documentary films influenced by the anti-Cardinals coverage that emerged in 1947. The intense rivalry between the Cardinals and the Dodgers, which had been a central narrative in National League baseball during the 1940s, probably contributed to the desire of New York reporters to make the Cardinals the chief villains in the story of the reluctance of players to accept integration. Perhaps the New York writers were embarrassed by how resistant the Dodgers themselves had been to accepting their new teammate and were anxious to assert that their longtime nemesis, the Cardinals, were worse. In any case, Musial, who had had black teammates in high school, was never seen as a participant in any resistance to integration. In fact, one reporter wrote an absurd account suggesting that a vicious fistfight between Musial, the pro-integration Northerner, and Slaughter, the anti-integration Southerner, caused the hospitalization of Musial. The hospitalization cited by the reporter was, of course, the result of Musial's appendicitis.[7] After the last game of 1947 Musial immediately went under the knife and divested himself of his appendix and his tonsils.

Under Dr. Hyland's care Musial finished strong in 1947 and helped the Cardinals approach the Dodgers, but the Brooklyn team was too far ahead and playing too well to be overtaken. The Cardinals finished second, five games behind the Dodgers. It would be the first of three second-place finishes in a row for the formerly mighty Cardinals, who had seemed close to invincible in the mid-1940s.

A change in management for the Cardinals proved to be inevitable in view of the declining health of Sam Breadon who was dying of cancer and was anxious to spare his widow the task of deciding what to do about the Cardinals. Much criticized by players for his thrifty ways Breadon must be given a share of the credit for what the Cardinals achieved during and continuing after his partnership with the redoubtable Branch Rickey. Under his command the Cardinals developed into a winning venture, gaining six World Championships and nine National League pennants. To make sure that the Cardinals would be in good hands and remain in St. Louis without risk from the inheritance taxes, Breadon worked out a deal with Robert Hannegan, former U.S. Postmaster General, and Fred Saigh, a St. Louis businessman and lawyer. Hannegan, who also suffered from ill health and was not to live much longer, was to sell his share of the organization in 1949. Not knowledgeable about baseball, Saigh, who owned the Cardinals until 1953, was to be associated with the downturn in the club's competitiveness in the early 1950s. With their finishes of second in 1948 and 1949 and third in 1951 and 1952—the Saigh-owned Cardinals were only completely disappointing in 1950 when they fell to fifth place, but, even in that season, the Cardinals were in the thick of the pennant race until a late-season collapse. One of the primary reasons for the continuing residence of the Cardinals near the top of the National League standings during the late 1940s and early 1950s, despite a lack of the depth they had previously possessed, was the presence at the heart of their lineup of arguably the best player of that era, Stan "The Man" Musial.

Negotiating with Musial for his 1948 salary Hannegan argued that Stan should play for the same $31,000 he had earned the previous year. Though Stan's hitting spree at the end of the season had gotten him up over .300 once again, Musial's sickness-hindered performance had been statistically below his normal level. Confident and well aware of how much the club was depending on him, Stan did not agree. Eventually the matter was settled when Hannegan promised a performance bonus if Musial had a good year. As a result $5,000 was later added to Stan's contract.[8]

The 1948 season would prove to be Musial's best. He exercised vigorously during the winter and was determined to come back strong. In fact, he was so strong coming into spring training that his bats felt light in his hands, and he decided to change his grip, moving his hands down to the knob, giving more power to his swing with no loss of control. At twenty-seven years of age Stan felt himself at the top of his form and ready for anything. He had gained maturity and developed patience at the plate and seldom swung at bad pitches. He had learned how to interpret the nature of a pitch by carefully observing the way the ball looked just after it left the pitcher's hand. Ted Williams and others have expressed a preference for guessing what pitch would be thrown, but Musial claims he did not have to guess because he could usually judge how fast a pitch was coming and based on that information could determine which of that pitcher's repertoire was on the way and how it might break. A knack for judging the speed of the incoming pitch and a well-developed awareness of what sorts of pitches each pitcher threw and at which speeds were key to Stan's uncanny ability to be ready for what was coming.[9] In 1948 Musial combined his natural athleticism with his well-developed knowledge of the pitchers and mastery of his own technique and had a career year at the plate.

At the start of the season Musial was happy that manager Eddie Dyer had returned him to right field, his preferred position, but he soon found himself switched to left field to accommodate Enos Slaughter's desire to return to right. The slumping Slaughter also liked that field best and felt it would help his hitting to play there. Though disappointed, Musial registered no complaint and kept on hitting. He was also to put in time in center field and at first base as needed as the season progressed. More than ever the Cardinals needed to depend on Musial in 1948. Injuries devastated the Cardinals' infield—Marty Marion had to miss ten games, Red Schoendienst fifty, and Whitey Kurowski sixty-one.

Brooklyn's Ebbets Field provoked some of Musial's best hitting throughout his career, and this was particularly the case in 1948. In one series in Brooklyn, Stan hit .733 by making eleven hits in fifteen trips to the plate. His barrage included four singles, five doubles, one triple, and one home run. He had two hits in the first game, four in the second, and five in the third. Leo Durocher commented that, "I've seen some great hitters in my time, but I've never seen a hotter hitter over a three-day period than Musial was in this series. Time and again our pitchers would get ahead of him. They'd get two strikes on him. Then the agony would start. He'd foul off three or four good pitches. Then our fellow would make a mistake—and away it went!"[10] Ebbets Field fans had considerable reason to keep groaning, "Here comes The Man again."[11] Altogether, in the eleven games the Cardinals played in Brooklyn in 1948, Musial batted .522.[12] Before one game in Ebbets Field, Dodger pitcher Preacher Roe stuck his head into the visitor's clubhouse to announce that he had come up with a way to get Musial out—walk him on four pitches then pick him off first.[13]

It was a stellar hitting season for Musial in every place he played. He had five-hit games on four separate occasions, matching the single-season record set by Ty Cobb.[14] In one of his most remarkable performances he went into a game against the Braves at Braves Field toward the end of the season at a time when the Boston team was the hottest team in baseball with an eight-game winning streak on the line. It was a big game for both teams. Winning this game would have clinched the pennant for Boston and ended whatever slim chance the Cards might have had for catching up with them. It was one of those occasions during Musial's career when he showed himself capable of playing at a high level while injured. Doc Weaver had tightly bandaged both of Musial's wrists because of injuries in previous games. Stan had jammed his wrists while making a diving catch in the outfield and then he was further damaged by a bruising hit to the hand by a Carl Erskine fastball. Hoping to have success at the plate against the formidable Warren Spahn, Musial decided to dispense with caution and accept the pain. He ripped off the tape before coming to bat in the first inning. Because taking a full swing was painful, he decided to try to just poke the ball over the infield and on Spahn's first pitch he managed to loop a single into left. In his next at bat in the third inning he swung harder and slashed a liner over the leftfielder's head for a double. His wrists were throbbing with pain after that, but, in his next time up, with sarcastic former teammate Red Barrett facing him in relief in a jokingly taunting manner, Musial thought, "To hell with the wrists," and jumped on a change-up and bashed a home run, pulling it into the right field seats. With his wrists now throbbing with pain, Musial was determined to get his fifth hit. The next Brooklyn reliever, Al Lyons, was throwing him nothing but balls so Musial reached for a far outside pitch and smacked it past second baseman Eddie Stanky for a single. It was realized later that Musial had accomplished his painful feat of hitting with a remarkable efficiency that kept the use of his injured wrists to a minimum. He had only swung the bat five times during the game, producing a hit with each swing.[15]

Despite Musial's great year in 1948 the Cardinals managed only a second-place finish. But Stan's best season was a wonder unto itself. Often during that season he seemed to be threatening to hit .400, and he might have managed that had it not been for a scattering of injury-related slumps that brought his numbers down from time to time. He finally ended up with a league-leading .376. He also lead the league in base hits (230), runs scored (135), runs batted in (131), total bases (429), doubles (46), triples (18), and slugging percentage (.702). The only major hitting area in which he did not take the crown was in home runs, but—surprisingly, in view of his tendency not to dominate in the home run department—his thirty-nine homers fell just one dinger short of tying Johnny Mize and Ralph Kiner for the lead in that category as well.[16] Had Stan not been deprived of one homer by a rained-out game he might have won "the triple crown" as champ of the three major categories—average, homers, and RBIs.[17] His most amazing display of hitting earned him his third Most Valuable Player Award.

It was a personally difficult off-season for Stan, whose autumn was devoted to tending to his rapidly declining father, who died just before Christmas in 1948.[18] Adding to the complicated nature of that time was the decision of the Musials' to put down roots in St. Louis by buying a large house in the southwestern suburbs of their new home city. Though this transition had long been contemplated, the move was suddenly urgent because Stan wanted to get his parents out of Donora, which suffered catastrophic smog in October of 1948. The fatal clouds that Donora had endured over the years probably shortened Lukasz's life, debilitated as he also must have been by his years of exposure to pollution within the mill and his sometimes heavy consumption of alcohol outside of it. Among the advantages to permanently settling in St. Louis in 1948 was that it would accommodate the wish of son Dickie to attend school year-round in St. Louis. Ironically, though Stan was not told about it at the time, Hannegan had tried to sell him to the Pittsburgh Pirates right at the very moment that Stan was settling into his new home because Hannegan and Saigh were in bad need of cash for the ball club.[19] It was later revealed that Hannegan's attempts to close a deal to sell Musial for $250,000 fell through largely because Hannegan failed to reach the Pirates GM by phone at the crucial moment.[20] Ultimately Hannegan sold star pitcher Murray Dickson, a deal that, it could be argued, cost the Cardinals the 1949 pennant. Though Dickson had only a 12–14 record for the last-place Pirates, he undermined the Cardinals' chances in a big way by winning against them five times. Furthermore, Dickson's 3.29 ERA for the season indicates he would have been a strong contributor to the effort.[21] The sale of Musial would, of course, have been even more devastating for the team's chances and would have given rise to a storm of protest from fans.

The contract Musial signed with Hannegan paid him $50,000 with the addition of $5,000 more in the event the Cardinals attracted more than 900,000 paying customers to the stadium. Stan rejected Hannegan's initial offer of $45,000 plus $5,000 bonus for every 100,000 in attendance over 900,000. Stan later realized that he had outfoxed himself by not accepting that offer, which, as it turned out, would have earned him $70,000 as a result of the Cards' record-setting attendance of 1,430,676.[22]

Before the 1949 season Musial became fast friends with the owner of a restaurant he and his family frequented. In response to Stan's questions concerning business opportunities, Biggie Garagnani offered to make Stan a partner. Having just expended his savings to buy his house, Musial had to say he could not afford to put up his half of the money. Generously, Garagnani suggested that Stan's half be generated out of the profits. Thus was born the landmark St. Louis business, Stan Musial and Biggie's Restaurant. The restaurant provided Stan with the reassuring knowledge that his family would have financial stability even in the event that his career was shortened by injuries. Musial's success as a businessman, while still a player, laid the groundwork for his life after his playing days. Stan's frequent evening visits to the eatery to fraternize with customers also helped him to blossom as a public personality. He came to appreciate "how warm people felt" toward him and was able to become comfortably adept at the art of interacting with adoring strangers, which was to hold him in good stead over the years.[23] Few celebrities are able to come across, as Musial did, as genial and sincerely friendly. Stan's widely commented on "niceness" contributed to his popularity with fans he met face to face, especially in St. Louis, where he became a beloved figure, though it irritated some out-of-town reporters, especially in New York City, who were in search of controversy and edginess to add bite to their stories.

Though Musial started the 1949 season strong, he soon fell into a slump that he was later to attribute to his decision to strive for more home runs. After he had finished with thirty-nine homers in 1948, it occurred to him that he could hit even more if he would swing for the short right-field fences of several National League Parks, including Sportsman's Park. Trying to swing too hard and aiming to pull pitches that he would normally have punched to left field, Musial's average plummeted.[24] Seeking the emphatic impact of the big bomb, Stan was not crouching as much as was his norm, and he began to press and overstride. All these flaws were compounded as he lost his rhythm and a bit of his confidence. By the end of May, however, Musial realized his mistakes and was able to become himself again. His strong finish was a major factor in the Cardinals almost managing to win the pennant.[25] As was often the case in his career, strong performances against the Dodgers in Ebbets Field featured prominently in Musial's rise to the occasion. In a June series in Brooklyn Stan had eight hits in thirteen times at bat. In the first game in the set he had two homer runs and a single off Preacher Roe to help the Cards to an important win.[26]

Enos Slaughter also had a slow start in 1949. Slaughter's slump was so bad that he was benched for a time, but he eventually returned to form and contributed mightily in the second half. The return of some of the players who had jumped to the Mexican league—Max Lanier, Lou Kline, and Fred Martin—also perked up the Cardinals' performance.[27]

The importance of radio to the Cardinals' situation as the most popular baseball team in a number of Midwestern, Western, and Southern States was underscored when a Radio Appreciation Day was held at Sportsman's Park for a double-hitter in which the Cards swept the Reds. In 1949 Cardinal broadcasts were officially available in Missouri, Illinois, Kentucky, Tennessee, Iowa, Arkansas, Kansas, and Oklahoma. Stations in Mississippi and Indiana were added in 1950 and Texas in 1958.[28] In a number of other states, as well as in Canada and Mexico, antennas were stretched to pick up Cardinals' baseball. The Cards lost some of their glamor as they failed to win a pennant throughout the 1950s, but their fan base remained large.[29]

There were some odd turns of events that went against the Cardinals in 1949. In one game against the Giants, Nippy Jones hit a two-run homer for the Cardinals only to see it disallowed because umpire Jocko Conlan had declared a balk on pitcher Adrian Zabala just as the pitch was thrown. The rules were later changed to give a team the option of refusing such balks in situations such as this, but in 1949 there was no choice and the Cardinals had to accept a 3-1 loss despite having scored three runs. The Cardinals fell short of the pennant by losing in a frustrating fashion two sets of games to two of the weakest teams in the league—the Cubs and the Pirates. Ironically, ex-Cardinal Murray Dickson pitched one of the Pittsburgh victories.[30]

Over the entirety of his career Musial hit well at Forbes Field, but, through the end of 1949, playing in front of the many Donora folks who came to see him play the Pirates there had seemed to cause Musial to press too hard and not perform at his best. He had hit only .255 at Forbes Field during his spectacular 1948 season, and he was struggling to hit .200 in 1949. But Musial was not the only Cardinal underperforming at the end of what had been an exhausting season.

The series against the Cubs was particularly exasperating. In one game, the Cardinals left twelve men on base while losing 3-1 to "nothin'-ball" pitcher Bob Chipman whose left-handed "lollipops" the Cardinals hit hard again and again without managing to score runs. The Cardinals' fade at the end of the 1949 season resulted in a much-lamented second-place standing, finishing one game behind the Dodgers.[31]

When the dust had settled, Musial could look back on an outstanding season in which he led the league in hits, doubles, triples, and on-base percentage. His

.338 batting average and his thirty-six home runs put him second in those two categories.[32] Stan was, however, "sick at heart" over his team's near miss and rode the train back to St. Louis, replaying in his mind some of the many lost close games that might have been won.[33]

NOTES

1. Stan Musial and Bob Broeg, *Stan Musial: "The Man's" Own Story as Told to Bob Broeg* (New York: Doubleday, 1964), 101–102.

2. Ibid., 104–105.

3. Ibid., 106–108.

4. Peter Golenbock, *The Spirit of St. Louis: A History of the St. Louis Cardinals and Browns* (New York: HarperCollins, 2000), 375.

5. William Marshall, *Baseball's Pivotal Era: 1945–1951* (Lexington: University Press of Kentucky, 1999), 148–149.

6. Ibid., 130–131.

7. Golenbock, *The Spirit of St. Louis*, 381–385.

8. James Giglio, *Musial: From Stash to Stan the Man* (Columbia: University of Missouri Press, 2001), 162–163.

9. Mark Newman and John Rawlings, "Man to Man." *Sporting News*, July 28, 1997, 10–11.

10. Ray Robinson, *Stan Musial: Baseball's Durable "Man"* (New York: Putnam, 1963), 75–76.

11. Musial and Broeg, *Stan Musial*, 92–93.

12. Robinson, *Stan Musial*, 76.

13. Musial and Broeg, *Stan Musial*, 113; Joseph Stanton, *Cardinal Points: Poems on St. Louis Cardinals Baseball* (Jefferson, NC: McFarland, 2002), 34.

14. Giglio, *Musial*, 164.

15. Musial and Broeg, *Stan Musial*, 116–117; Giglio, *Musial*, 166–167.

16. John Grabowski, *Stan Musial* (New York: Chelsea House, 1993),12–13.

17. Giglio, *Musial*, 167.

18. Musial and Broeg, *Stan Musial*, 112. The comment on the death of Lukasz Musial appears as a caption to a picture on an unnumbered page following page 112.

19. Giglio, *Musial*, 168–169.

20. Bob Broeg, "The Man Reveals Near Miss as '48 Bucco." *St. Louis Post-Dispatch*, April 6, 1963.

21. John Snyder, *Cardinals Journal* (Cincinnati, OH: Emmis Books, 2006), 371.

22. Musial and Broeg, *Stan Musial*, 122.

23. Ibid., 120–122.

24. Ibid., 123.

25. Giglio, *Musial*, 174.

26. Musial and Broeg, *Stan Musial*, 124.

27. Giglio, *Musial*, 175.

28. Snyder, *Cardinals Journal*, 375.
29. Stanton, *Cardinal Points*, 27.
30. Snyder, *Cardinals Journal*, 374–375.
31. Musial and Broeg, *Stan Musial*, 128–130.
32. Snyder, *Cardinals Journal*, 372.
33. Musial and Broeg, *Stan Musial*, 131.

Musial and Schoendienst were great friends as teammates and both continued to play important roles in the Cardinal organization in their postplaying days. *National Baseball Hall of Fame Library, Cooperstown, NY.*

ALREADY AN OLD-TIME GREAT

Musial of the 1950s was an institution of sorts. Expectations that he would always be super were high and, until the falling off to a .255 average in 1959, he always delivered. To the sports-writing establishment Stan's routine superstardom and smiling demeanor gave dismayingly scant opportunity for the elements of tension, suspense, and surprise they felt they needed to make their discussions of an athlete "newsworthy." This state of affairs led to articles with titles like "Musial—as Usual."[1] The routineness of Musial's superstardom, in combination with his modest and friendly manner, did, however, lend a unique aura to his celebrity. As one reads over the great quantity of articles written about Musial for newspapers and magazines all over America in the 1950s, one senses that the writers came to understand how appealing to their baseball-fan readers was Musial's unusual yoking together of niceness and greatness. He seemed already to be a hallowed resident of the Hall of Fame, even as his long career had barely reached its halfway point.

Perhaps the definitive statement concerning the hero/saint reputation that had already adhered to Musial in the early 1950s can be found in, "What Stan Musial Means to the Cards," an article by Cardinals' owner, Fred Saigh, which was published in *Sport* in 1952. Saigh comments at length on the specialness of Musial, describing Stan as a genuine hero, "Who gives you everything he has every inch of the way," and leads an admirably "untainted personal life" with "no scandal, no bad taste, no bitter controversy." Speaking from his "employer's-eye view," Saigh declares that Musial worship accounts for a large portion of the Cards attendance at home, as well as in the many parks on the road where Stan is uniquely revered by fans of the opposing teams. Saigh makes special mention of how highly The Man is regarded in the Polo Grounds and Ebbets Field where Musial's hitting has done so much damage to New York hopes. To underscore the superlative nature of Stan's value, Saigh asserts that were Brooklyn to try to trade for him they would have to offer six of their star players. With seemingly sincere hyperbole Saigh indicates that he would consider nothing less than Brooklyn's "two best outfielders, its two most valuable infielders, its first-string catcher and a front-line pitcher."[2]

In 1950, it appeared that Musial had a shot at hitting .400. With his average at .442 in early June questions about that possibility began. Musial pointed out to reporters that June was too soon for that sort of talk and declared that such thoughts would only be worth considering if he reached September with an average in that range. Injuries proved to be a big part of Musial's story in 1950, and Stan himself commented that the damage he suffered may have "reduced my chances" to achieve .400.[3] With Musial, however, it is often difficult to gage the particular effect of injuries on his batting statistics because of the frequency with which he hit surprisingly well when his body was under stress. An awareness of an obstacle or limitation often seemed, in the short term, to intensify Stan's concentration and to increase, at least for a game or two, his ability to deliver.

His first big injury came in April when he lost his footing in soft dirt in Pittsburgh. Musial probably should have take more than a few days off to allow his strained ligaments to heal, but he anxiously returned to the lineup after only a few days off. This brief layoff had one nice upside for Stan in that it provided him with some unusual mid-season moments of closeness with his nine-year-old son Dick who was, at the same time, recovering from an emergency appendectomy. Surprisingly, Stan's worries about his knee seemed to help his concentration at the plate, and his average stayed high. His next "freak injury" happened in June when, while playing first base, he tried to spear an errant throw with his bare left hand and the ball tore a deep gash between his second and third fingers. Needing to cushion his hand with a pad, Stan lost some points on his average, and then lost more points when his continuing problems with his knee forced him to wear a brace.[4]

Musial's desire to help his team through passionate, extra-effort fielding, which had led to his early season hand injury, was evident again in September when Stan almost made a spectacular play in a vain attempt to fend off a Cardinal defeat. Trying to rob the Pirates' Jack Phillips of a walk-off grand-slam home run, Musial leapt high against the eight-foot wire left-field fence at Forbes Field. Briefly knocked unconscious by his collision with the fence, Musial lay on the ground while everyone waited to see whether he had made the catch. When pitchers in the Pirate bullpen retrieved the ball and held it up, the umpire declared the home run.[5]

Despite falling short in what might have been his best chance to break through to the magical .400 plateau, Musial had a fine statistical year in 1950, leading the league in batting average at .346 and slugging percentage at .596. He finished second in hits at 192, doubles at 41, and total bases at 141. He hit 28 home runs, while driving in 109 runs and scoring 105.[6]

A highlight of Musial's hitting performance was the thirty-game hitting streak he had in July, which, surprisingly, ended on a day when almost everyone else on the Cardinals had a hit in a 13-3 shellacking of the Dodgers. At the end of the game the Dodgers tried out a marginal relief pitcher to see what he could do. Billy Loes—an arrogant, nineteen-year-old, bonus-baby righthander—was brought into pitch as Musial was coming up for his last at bat. Pee Wee Reese and Jackie Robinson asked Loes if he knew that the batter had a long hitting streak going. Loes reportedly replied, "Yeah, and I'm going to throw one right down the middle to him." Reese and Robinson laughed, but Loes did exactly that, and Musial, perhaps overanxious because of his desire to keep his string of hits going, was unable to take advantage of a perfect hitter's pitch and grounded into a force out to end the streak.[7] Musial had not quite equaled the longest Cardinal hitting spree, the thirty-three-game streak that Rogers Hornsby had in 1922. Albert Pujols was to equal Musial's thirty-game streak in 2003.[8]

Despite Musial's outstanding play, the 1950 season had been a major falling off for the Cardinals. Though they had lingered in first place as late as July 24, they were to end up in fifth. The last time the Cardinals had been that low was in 1938, when they finished sixth. The Cardinals were a team of veterans—no one was younger than twenty-seven—and it appears they ran out of steam late in the season. Manager Eddie Dyer could see that his services would no longer be desired, and he resigned. Dyer had managed the Cardinals since 1946, but, with exception of that first year, had not managed to bring a championship to St. Louis. His team had put together a winning record again in 1950, but it was clear Fred Saigh wanted to try someone new at the helm.[9]

The new manager for 1951 was Marty Marion, whose playing career was nearly over due to back and knee problems. Also considered for the job was Johnny Keene, a minor league manager for the Cardinals at Rochester, who would later get his chance to manage the Big League club and figure in important ways in the situations of Musial and the Cardinals in the early 1960s.

As a result of the Cardinals poor showing in 1950, Saigh expected some of his players to accept pay cuts or do without raises. Musial, however, was coming off an outstanding year and was pleased with the salary Saigh had in mind for him. A base salary of $75,000 with a $5000 attendance clause meant that Stan would be making at least $80,000—a $25,000 raise from the previous year. Saigh warned Musial that his raise could be affected by regulations put in place by the federal Wage Stabilization Board, an esoteric entity created in response to economic uncertainties related to the Korean War. Aside from the question of whether or not all the money would be paid, Stan was pleased to note that the offered salary made him the highest salaried player in the National League—quite a rise in stature and prospects from his impoverished minor league situation just ten years earlier.[10]

The Cardinals were hot to start the year and were in first place with an 11-5 record on May 7, but they cooled off after a snowy road trip to the Northeast during which most of the team's starters were incapacitated by a virulent flu epidemic. Thirteen of the team's players were out of action for at least a day. Several were out for more than a week. At the worst point, the sickly squad was beaten down seventeen to three by the Giants. Despite the strong showing they were to make later in the season, the Cards were never able to overcome the deficit they fell into during their bout with the epidemic.[11]

The Reds were able to take advantage of the Cardinals' weakened condition in Cincinnati and hoped to compound their advantage by insisting on making up a rained out game with an immediate double header rather than putting off the make-up game till later in the season as was the more typical practice. This did not entirely work out for them in the second game, however, as a still severely ill Musial, who had been sunning himself in the bullpen in hopes of recovery, offered to try to contribute as a pinch hitter. Dragging himself to the plate and looking like he could barely lift his bat, Stan unexpectedly put the Cardinals ahead and on the way to victory with a three-run home run, surprising the disbelieving Reds manager, Luke Sewell, who had stayed with a right-handed pitcher because he had assumed Musial, who had failed to hit the ball out of the infield during batting practice, would not constitute a threat.[12]

Stan was pleased to have received the most votes from the fan's All-Star poll, 14,428,383, and he lived up to their expectations in the All-Star contest itself, delivering a single and a home run.[13] The homer came at the expense of Ed Lopat, who had informed Preacher Roe, the evening before the game that he had figured out how to pitch to Musial. As Musial's big hit landed in the upper right field stands, Roe, who was sitting in the National League bullpen, leapt to his feet and shouted to Lopat that he had already figured out how to pitch to Musial that way.[14]

Despite their winning ways at the end of the summer, the Cardinals were not able to catch up to the Dodgers and Giants, and finished in third place as the Giants won the pennant by means of Bobby Thompson's shot heard round the New York newspapers. Marty Marion was fired as manager, despite how well the Cardinals played outside of their flu-tormented slump. Musial did not agree with the decision to give his friend the boot, commenting that "Most of us felt Marty Marion had done well enough to be given another chance." Saigh appears to have been particularly upset about all the close-game losses the Cards had suffered at the hands of the Dodgers. With the history of rivalry between the two teams, it was galling for the owner that Brooklyn had taken the season series eighteen of twenty-two games. Saigh was also peeved because Marion loved to hang out at his St. Louis home at every opportunity and did not spend much time in the clubhouse, thus making it hard for Saigh to have regular contact with him.[15] Marion's frequent changes in the lineup—trying out five-second basemen and four first basemen in the first half of the season—was criticized by some sports writers as damaging to the teams "cohesion." Musial, for instance, was moved back and forth between infield and outfield at various points.[16] Saigh seems also to have felt that Marion's relaxed and easygoing manner made him insufficiently inspirational as a leader.[17] As his next manager he selected the fiery and aggressive Eddie Stanky, who belonged to the Leo Durocher school of conspicuous aggressiveness. Stanky's nickname was "The Brat."

It had been a frustrating season for Saigh in several respects, including the difficulties of competing for press attention in St. Louis with the owner of the Browns, the infamous Bill Veeck, who pulled off some of his most famous stunts in 1951, including the bringing to bat of the midget Eddie Gaedel.[18]

Musial's hitting goals for the season included his hope that he could win his fifth batting title and that he could become, thereby, the first player to win two batting titles in a row in the National League since Rogers Hornsby had done it in 1925. The speedy Richie Ashburn of the Phillies, whose adeptness at getting bunt hits Musial seems to have both envied and resented, was his principle rival, but Stan brought it off, leading the league with a .355 average. He also contributed thirty-two home runs, making him the only Cardinal slugger in a lineup notably lacking in power.[19]

Musial did not receive his $25,000 raise for 1951 until 1952, and then only because Stan struck up an acquaintance with Maurice Tobin, the Secretary of Labor, at a baseball dinner in Boston. Tobin and Musial happened to be seated at the same table and after much discussion of baseball matters, Tobin listened with interest to Stan's mention of the restriction that had been unfairly applied to his salary. Tobin encouraged Stan to come to Washington and when he did the matter was quickly resolved. When Saigh pointed out that the extra pay would largely be lost to taxes, Stan declared that he "Didn't care. Now, at last, I was officially an $80,000-a-year ball player."[20]

Stan's emphatic pride in his pay seems to have resided more in the satisfaction at being highly valued than in a need for a sizable raise. With his business interests thriving and likely to continue to do so, Stan did not feel the need to milk his baseball pay as a hedge against the postcareer poverty that many other professional athletes needed to worry about. Musial indicated to Saigh over the course of the winter that he did not expect a raise for the 1952 season. Aware of Stan's attitude on that point, Saigh staged Musial's contract signing as a public event that received extensive press coverage. Called into Saigh's office to finalize and sign the contract, Stan found himself surrounded by reporters and faced with the offer of a contract all filled out except for the amount of the salary. With the cameras rolling all around them Saigh asked Stan to write his own ticket, saying only that, "Anything short of your owning the club tomorrow morning is all right with me." Amazed by the stunt, Stan at first tried to resist the circus atmosphere by asking to put off his decision, saying he wanted to be last to sign so that it would be clear everyone else on the team had gotten an adequate offer, but, pressed for an on-the-spot decision for the media, Stan finally responded that he would sign his 1952 contract under the same terms as he had for 1951. Saigh had cannily counted on Musial's wanting to be seen as a good guy. When a reporter called Saigh a "Helluva fine crap shooter," Saigh was able to support the Stan-as-nice-guy image by saying he had counted on Stan's "character."[21]

Spring training came as somewhat of a release from anxiety for Stan who had been shuttling back and forth between Donora and St. Louis because of the serious illness of his mother.[22]

Just before the 1952 season the irascible Ty Cobb contributed an article to *Life* magazine attacking what he felt was the lackadaisical play of most major league stars.[23] Cobb remarked that the hustling play of only two contemporary players, Phil Rizzuto and Stan Musial, could be seen as equal to the performances of the "old-time greats" like himself. In an interview he gave after the appearance of the article, Cobb expressed particular disdain for the vaunted prowess of Joe DiMaggio, comparing Joltin' Joe unfavorably as a hitter to George Sisler of Cobb's era. Praising Musial as the sort of player "who will score from first on a single," play "as hard when his club is way out in front of a game as he does when they're just a run or two behind," and dive for a shoestring catch in an exhibition game "as if the World Series depended on it." Cobb credited Musial with having "the power of Napoleon Lajoie," "the stamina of Eddie Collins," and the steadiness of "Honus Wagner."[24] Cobb further commended Stan for his willingness to play multiple positions. Although Cobb's comments were obviously not a balanced or fair analysis, his praise of Musial seemed to many to be perfectly true. Though

Stan's modest demeanor would not allow him to fully assent to this praise, he clearly relished this high praise from an important commentator and subsequently struck up an acquaintance with Cobb and exchanged letters with him from time to time.[25]

Eddie Stanky, likewise, was high in his praise for the team effort evident in Musial's gracious acceptance of assignments at all three outfield positions as well as at first base. Stanky himself was lauded for his handling of the Cardinals in 1952. Although the team once again finished third, they won seven more games than in the previous year, and those eighty-eight wins proved to be the highest victory total for any Cardinals team in the second half of Musial's career. Stanky certainly lived up to his feisty reputation, getting into frequent and sometimes uproarious arguments with umpires. In one game in Cincinnati, "The Brat" so provoked plate umpire Scotty Robb that a shoving match ensued. When the league fined Robb more than Stanky, the distressed umpire resigned in a huff.[26]

It was another strong season for Musial at the plate. Though Stan's .336 average was lower than in some other years, he was happy to have won his third batting championship, easily besting his nearest challenger, Frankie Baumholtz of the Cubs, who batted .325. As a publicity stunt, Musial was brought in from the outfield to pitch to Baulmholtz in the first inning of the final day of the season. Musial, who jokingly tossed the pitch in softly, was not pleased to be involved in what he felt was an undignified gag. In the spirit of the occasion the left-handed Baumholtz switched to hitting right-handed. When Solly Hemus fumbled a soft grounder, the awkward occasion was brought to a sloppy conclusion with Baumholtz reaching first base on an error.[27]

With the goal of 3,000 lingering as a somewhat secret hope, Stan was delighted to have gotten his 2,000th hit. He got this big hit off Phillies' pitcher Curt Simmons. Musial's numbers led the league in several categories—in total bases (311), doubles (42), hits (194), runs (105), and slugging percentage (.538); but Stan was disappointed that his ninety-one RBIs were a falling off from his usual level.[28]

Over the course of Musial's long career there were a number of occasions where attentions to his unique batting stance led to declarations by various observers and players that attempts at imitation of that illimitable stance were unwise, to say the least.[29] Contrary to this trend, was Stan's mentorship of Peanuts Lowrey in 1952. Lowrey teasingly complained during spring training that he should be able to hit as well as Stan in view of the fact that both of them were equal in having two eyes, two arms, two legs, and one head. Stan replied by going into his batting stance and declaring, "You haven't got this" and then wiggling his hips as he always did to loosen up at the plate. Jokingly determined to put this advice to use, Lowrey wiggled before his next two times at bat and got hits both times, leading him to declare that he would now be a "seat-wiggler" for life.[30] Apparently this worked fairly well for Lowrey in 1952. There is no clarity about whether or not he continued to wiggle in subsequent seasons.

After Fred Saigh was convicted in January of 1953 for federal income tax evasion, he was pressured to sell the Cardinals by National League President Ford Frick. Saigh always maintained he was an innocent victim, and he made a persuasive case that this was so in an interview he gave to Peter Golenbock shortly before his death in 1999. Saigh remained a die-hard fan of the Cardinals throughout the rest of his life. Saigh apparently could have made a substantially larger profit had he sold the team to groups in Houston and Milwaukee who were anxious to bring the prestigious franchise to their towns, but he was determined to keep the team in St. Louis. Finally, several concerned citizens persuaded August Busch and his beer company Anheuser-Busch to agree to buy the Cardinals. It is probably the most fortunate decision Busch was ever to make. The Anheuser-Busch association with first the Cardinals and later with other sports activities has been key to the company's prosperity.[31] Golenbock contends that Fred Saigh's greatest contribution to the Cardinal legacy was his determined effort to keep the team in St. Louis and that Cardinal fans should erect a statue in tribute to Saigh, without whose unselfishness, "the rest of Musial's career might well have been in either Milwaukee or Houston."[32]

Musial was anxious to begin the Busch era in Cardinal baseball with a successful year. Perhaps he may have been too anxious. Though he had clusters of good games from time to time, Stan found himself suffering through a discouraging slump during most of the early weeks of the 1953 season. An upside to this perplexing downturn was the outpouring of concern and good wishes Stan received by mail from many of his devoted fans. Good luck charms and gratuitous advice were arriving from all directions. Everybody and his kid brother seemed to think he knew how Stan could get back on track. J. Roy Stockton, sports editor of the *St. Louis Post Dispatch* offered an interesting and, for Stan, an alarming theory. In his regular column in the paper Stockton attributed the following statement to a "knowledgeable" player: "I hope I'm wrong, but I've always believed that when Musial started to slip as a batter, he'd slip suddenly and with a terrific crash. Look at him and compare him with another good hitter, say, Enos Slaughter. Batting isn't a very complex operation for Slaughter. He just stands up there with his bat poised and, when he likes a pitch, he swings." The unidentified source supposedly went on to say, "But it isn't that way with Musial. Look at him. He goes through all sorts of motions batting. He takes an unusual stance, sort of winds himself up for each swing and throws his entire body into the business of swinging the bat." Stockton's expert went on to speculate that Stan might never again be able to get his timing right because of the complicated nature of his batting pro-cedure.[33]

It seems likely, though Musial and Broeg do not say so, that the theorist was Stockton himself who might have put his half-baked analysis into the mouth of a fictitious player so that he would not be going on record as suggesting that the prowess of the beloved Stan the Man might be a thing of the past. Though buoyed by the continuing support of his fans, Musial was not without fears. Stockton's column was not, of course, the first instance of negative speculation about the viability of Stan's batting stance and style. Such comments had come hot and heavy during Musial's early days in the majors before his relentless success at the plate silenced them. In response to the Stockton theory, Musial conceded that his timing might have been temporarily thrown off by the unusually large number of rainouts, which prevented the Cardinals from playing as steadily in the spring as they would normally have been able to do. Most specifically helpful to the correction of Musial's difficulties was the opportunity manager Stanky set up for the Cardinals' coaches to compare Musial's at bats from previous seasons with careful observation of some of his current plate appearances. It was discovered that Stan had been overstriding by a foot or more during his slump. The use of film, Stanky knew, had helped Gil Hodges come out of a slump in a previous year, and, as it turned out, this innovative use of motion pictures was a big help to Musial as well. Correcting his stride and adjusting his stance somewhat to bring it more in line with his previous best practice contributed to Stan's going on a tear in mid-June. Starting on June 17, Stan's batting revived remarkably, as he swatted twenty-four hits in forty-three times at bat to raise his batting average from .251 to .303 in the space of only twelve games. In a one-week road trip through Pennsylvania and New York he went nineteen for twenty-seven and drove in twelve runs.[34]

With his second half surge Stan was able to get his number up to a Musial-like level with a batting average of .337, one point higher than his 1952 league-leading average, with thirty homers and an even 200 hits. It was the sixth time he had achieved the 200-hit level. With his fifty-three doubles he led the league in that category for the seventh time. He also lead the league in walks with 105 and his first-time win in that category shows that Musial had exhibited patience at the plate despite the frustrations of his early season slump. The rise to a high average was particularly satisfying in this season in which doubters had assailed the viability of his style of hitting and his stance at the plate. Stan professed feeling a special gratitude to the many fans who had mailed him their words of support and continued to applaud him in the ballpark while he was suffering through his difficulties in April and May.[35] During a Fourth of July double-header against the

Cubs at Wrigley Field, Musial passed Rogers Hornsby as the all-time career hit leader when he rapped his 2,111th hit. Though Stan led the Cardinals in most hitting categories, his roommate, Red Schoendienst, managed to surpass him for the team batting average lead. Red's .342 hitting performance was the best of his career. Red was edged out for the league title, however, by Dodger Carl Furillo's .344.[36]

Despite strong play in many phases of the season, the Cardinals finished in a third-place tie with the Phillies, and Auggie Busch had his first taste of how hard it would be to move his company's new possession in the direction of a major league championship.

In 1954, Musial signed for $80,000 for the fourth season in a row, but this time he was signing with Busch and company. Stan was asked in a preseason interview about his long-term career prospects in view of his arrival at the ripe old baseball age of thirty-four. When a reporter mentioned that Stan was now 777 hits from his dream goal of 3,000, the usually modest Musial predicted that he would make it to 3,000 hits, saying that he expected to be able to play at least three or four more years at "top speed." How much that goal meant to Stan was evident in several of his remarks, including his indication that with the 3,000-hit total in sight he would want to keep playing, even if his average began to reside consistently below the .300 mark. He was admitting that joining the 3,000 club would compel him to keep swinging, even at the risk of undermining his high career batting average, which had long been his proudest professional possession. Stan's confidence in his potential for career longevity was, he claims, in part a result of his feeling that he had inherited his father's hardy durability. Despite the wear and tear of extremely hard work and the bad effects of alcoholism and other health challenges, Lukasz had always remained trim and fit and his hair hardly admitted a hint of gray, and his son felt he had inherited a toughness from the tough old man.[37] It is interesting that Stan attributed his on-going prowess to his father's genes, but it could be that the training in physical exercise that Lukasz emphasized in Stan's younger years had more to do with The Man's knack for staying in shape than did the traits passed-along with the paternal DNA. It should also be noted that Stan's long-lived and vigorous mother's hereditary transmission was probably at least as advantageous as his father's. [38]

Stan's status as the grand old man of the Redbirds was underscored when the only man senior to Stan, Enos Slaughter, was unceremoniously released by the team that had been his home for sixteen years. Encountering each other in the stadium parking lot after Slaughter had received the bad news, both Musial and Slaughter burst into tears.[39] Wearing the birds-on-the-bat uniform of one of baseball's most successful and popular teams was a badge of honor these two veterans had shared since 1941. Slaughter had loved being a Cardinal, and so, too, Musial realized, did he. Stan had become, for himself as well as for others, the quintessential last, great Cardinal. He was the lone remnant of the often glorious Cardinals of the 1940s. During St. Louis' often dreary and always pennant-less 1950s, fans could cheer Musial in a double way, as a current star and as a remembrance of the great teams of the past.

The Cards, who finished sixth in 1954, were a hard-hitting team with largely pathetic pitching, aside from the stellar shutout mound performances of Harvey Haddix, before an injury reduced his effectiveness. Slaughter's replacement in the outfield, rookie Wally Moon, was a big contributor to the team's hitting statistics in support of a too often losing cause.

But it was still Stan who was the main man as he amply proved in one of the most remarkable one-day displays of hitting in baseball history on Sunday, May 2, 1954, in a double-header played against the Giants at Busch Stadium. In the first inning of the first game Stan walked. In the third, he caught hold of a big, slow Johnny Antonelli curve and lifted it onto the roof in right. In the fifth, Antonelli threw Stan an unhittable low inside pitch, but, keeping his hands close to his body, he managed to golf it high and far, depositing in on the right field roof for a two-run homer. In the sixth, Stan lined an overhand curve from relief pitcher Jim Hearn to right for a single. In the eighth, with the game tied six to six and two men on base, Stan was concentrating on making solid contact in hopes of bringing in at least one run, but, as it turned out, he connected so solidly that he planted another homer on the roof to give the Cards a three-run lead. Stan excitedly shared the moment with his wife over the phone between games. It was Stan's first three-homer game in the majors, and he was delighted to have finally done it.

In the second game, Don Liddle, pitching cautiously, gave Stan a first inning walk to the vociferous displeasure of the crowd, anxious to see if Musial could put another one out of the park. In the third, Musial hit a Liddle fastball "as hard" he claimed "as any that day," but it was hit to the deepest part of the park, and somewhat against the wind, and Willie Mays hauled it in at the wall in right center. In the fifth inning, however, Stan blasted a Hoyt Wilhelm curve entirely over the right field pavilion and onto Grand Avenue. This was a rare feat of power and loft because a homer of that sort would have to clear not just the pavilion itself but also the screen at the back of the wall intended to keep homers from endangering pedestrians, cars, and windows across the avenue. Stan was especially proud of his fifth home run of the day, which he hit in the seventh inning, because it came off a hall-of-fame quality knuckle ball from Wilhelm. A knuckler is a slow pitch that requires the batter to supply the power, but Musial managed to hit this one over the pavilion in right center and, again, onto Grand Avenue for his longest dinger of the day. Eddie Stanky, coaching third at the time

Stan hit his fifth dinger, commented on the surprise of seeing Stan, who usually ran the bases with an expression of grim determination, rounding second base and heading toward third, laughing out loud with the sheer joy of his unexpected feat. Facing Larry Jansen in the ninth and eager to try for homer number six, Stan popped up to the first baseman. Stan's performance was record-setting. After the game, reporters were quick to inform him that no one had ever hit five homers in a double-hitter before. Stan was amazed to hear this and was especially surprised to hear that Babe Ruth had never even hit four homers in a double-header. In 1972, Nate Cobert would become the second person to hit five home runs in a double-header, but, as of this writing, Stan's record of twenty-one total bases for a double-header still stands. It is interesting to note that Colbert, who grew up in St. Louis, was in the stands at Busch the day Stan had his five-homer double-header. Thrilled at what he managed to do on this auspicious day, Stan was amused to find himself brought down from the clouds by the skepticism of his thirteen-year-old son, who remarked, "Gee, Dad, . . . They must have been throwing you some fat pitches today."[40]

Musial was remarkably potent with the long ball early in the 1954 season with twenty home runs in just his first fifty games. His distance clouting even showed up in a home-run-derby fund-raising exhibition contest held in Cleveland in July, which Musial won by slugging seven homers in ten chances. Because his pace was ahead of what Babe Ruth's had been in 1927, Stan was faced with questions from reporters about the possibility of besting Ruth's sixty-homer season. Stan laughed off that thought repeating again and again that he was just a singles hitter who sometimes hit home runs. Indeed, Musial's long ball numbers fell off in the second half of the summer, though Stan kept hitting well. The reduction in Stan's power could be related to the ferocious heat in St. Louis in August, with the temperature reaching 113 degrees during one daytime contest. Still, Stan finished with thirty-five homers, a fine total for any season. His average also stayed high at .330, though he was to fall short of the hitting crown this time.[41]

The formidableness of Stan's long hits in 1954 stimulated an unusual strategy that recalls the shift employed against Ted Williams in the 1940s. Biddie Tebbetts, the Cincinnati manager, on two occasions directed his shortstop to become a fourth outfielder leaving only the third baseman, Bobby Adams, to cover the left side of the infield. The first time the Reds tried this, Musial, determined to get the power shot his team needed rather than the base hit they were willing to concede, struck out. The second time they tried this, Musial went for the hit, driving the ball hard to the left side, unfortunately right at Adams. Commenting on his successful ploy Tebbetts joked that "I couldn't put anyone up there on the right field roof . . . so I was determined Musial wouldn't hit one between my outfielders for two or three bases."[42] Any infielder playing against Musial in his prime would have been happy to move back further on the grass. Stan's prowess as a line-drive hitter with power made him a most worrisome presence at the plate. Anyone who ever saw The Man spraying vicious line drives in every direction during batting practice would not relish the prospect of standing in front of him with nothing but a glove for protection. Warren Spahn put it succinctly, "Once he timed your fastball, your infielders were in jeopardy."[43]

The crowning emblem of Musial's transcendent all-time-great-player-who-is-also-a-nice-guy fame came with the appearance on the cover of the May 1, 1954 issue of the *Saturday Evening Post* of a painting by John Falter. This oft-reproduced and truly iconic image depicted an expressionless and implicitly saintly Musial, in full uniform beside the Cardinals' dugout, signing autographs for five appreciative young boys.[44] A classic example of baseball art, Falter's illustration partakes of the sort of shared-national-sentiment feeling that adhered to many of the pictures for the cover of that magazine by Norman Rockwell and, yet, there is a lack of overt sentiment to Falter's dryly painted picture that makes it seem less sentimental than a typical Rockwell painting. Falter seems more interested in the reportage of a truth than any sort of artificially heart-warming tale telling.[45] As we shall see, Bob Broeg and others were to promote the idea that this inspirational image should become the basis for a monument to Musial. The shifting of this project toward the awkward, but widely beloved, monument of Musial-at-the-bat that was finally erected is an interesting development in the cultivation of the Musial legend that will be discussed later.[46]

NOTES

1. Charles Dexter, "Musial—As Usual." *Baseball Digest*, September 1951, 5–10.

2. Fred Saigh, "What Stan Musial Means to the Cards." *Sport*, July 1952, 12–14, 57–58.

3. Stan Musial and Bob Broeg, *Stan Musial: "The Man's Own Story as Told To Bob Broeg* (New York: Doubleday, 1964), 134.

4. Ibid., 133–134.

5. John Snyder, *Cardinals Journal* (Cincinnati, OH: Emmis Books, 2006), 383.

6. Jerry Lansche, *Stan "The Man" Musial: Born to Be a Ballplayer* (Dallas, TX: Taylor, 1994), 113.

7. John Carmichael, "Musial's Streak Ends the Hard Way." *Baseball Digest*, October 1950, 61–62; Musial and Broeg, *Stan Musial*, 137.

8. Snyder, *Cardinals Journal*, 384.

9. Ibid., 382–385.

10. Musial and Broeg, *Stan Musial*, 139.

11. Snyder, *Cardinals Journal*, 387.

12. Musial and Broeg, *Stan Musial*, 140.

13. Lansche, *Stan "The Man" Musial*, 114–115.

14. Musial and Broeg, *Stan Musial*, 143.

15. Ibid., 144–145.

16. James Giglio, *Musial: From Stash to Stan the Man* (Columbia: University of Missouri Press, 2001), 189.

17. Musial and Broeg, *Stan Musial*, 144–145.

18. Bill Veeck with Ed Linn, *Veeck—As in Wreck* (New York: Putnam, 1962), 11–23.

19. Musial and Broeg, *Stan Musial*, 139, 144.

20. Ibid., 146–147.

21. Fred Saigh, "What Stan Musial Means to the Cards." *Sport*, July 1952, 13–14, 57; Musial and Broeg, *Stan Musial*, 147.

22. Musial and Broeg, *Stan Musial*, 148.

23. Ty Cobb, "The Greatest Player of All Time Says: 'They Don't Play Baseball Any More.'"*Life*, March 17, 1952, 136–138, 141–142, 144, 147–148, 150, 153.

24. Lansche, *Stan "The Man" Musial*, 118; Giglio, *Musial*, 192.

25. Musial and Broeg, *Stan Musial*, 151.

26. Ibid., 148–149.

27. Snyder, *Cardinals Journal*, 396.

28. Musial and Broeg, *Stan Musial*, 152–153.

29. Joseph Stanton, *Cardinal Points: Poems on St. Louis Cardinals Baseball* (Jefferson, NC: McFarland, 2002), 33; Glen Singer, "Stanley Frank Musial (A Paean)." *Elysian Fields Quarterly*, 23(4), 2003, 70.

30. Musial and Broeg, *Stan Musial*, 152.

31. Snyder, *Cardinals Journal*, 397–398; Peter Golenbock, *The Spirit of St. Louis: A History of the St. Louis Cardinals and Browns* (New York: HarperCollins), 395–398; David Halberstam, *October 1964* (New York: Random House), 1994, 17–23.

32. Golenbock, *The Spirit of St. Louis*, 396.

33. Musial and Broeg, *Stan Musial*, 154–158.

34. Ibid., 157–158.

35. John Grabowski, *Stan Musial* (New York: Chelsea House, 1993), 45–46; Musial and Broeg, *Stan Musial*, 159.

36. Snyder, *Cardinals Journal*, 397–401.

37. Musial and Broeg, *Stan Musial*, 161.

38. Margaret Carlin, "Musial's Mother Cried . . . When He Quit Baseball. *The Pittsburgh Press*, September 15, 1963.

39. Musial and Broeg, *Stan Musial*, 161.

40. Musial and Broeg, *Stan Musial*,160–163; Lansche, *Stan "The Man" Musial*, 130–131; Bob Broeg, *The Greatest Moments in St. Louis Sports* (St. Louis, MO: St. Louis Historical Society Press, 2000), 98.

41. Musial and Broeg, *Stan Musial*, 164–167; Snyder, *Cardinals Journal*, 408.

42. Musial and Broeg, *Stan Musial*, 167.

43. Lansche, *Stan "The Man" Musial*, 129.

44. Michael Ruscoe, ed., *Baseball: A Treasury of Art and Literature* (New York: Hugh Lauter Levin, 1995), 167.

45. Snyder, *Cardinals Journal*, 407–408; Stanton, *Cardinal Points*, 40.

46. Bob Broeg and Jerry Vickery, *The St. Louis Cardinals Encyclopedia* (Chicago, IL: Contemporary Books), 87; Giglio, *Musial*, 280–282. Although Broeg considered a "mockup" by St. Louis illustrator Amadee Wohlschlaer as the prototype for the projected monument, the design and Musial's autograph-signing stance were clearly derived from Falter's painting.

Musial in 1958 receiving his seventh and final Silver Slugger Award for his winning of the 1957 batting championship. The symbolic silver bat is being presented to Stan by National League President Warren Giles. *National Baseball Hall of Fame Library, Cooperstown, NY.*

THREE THOUSAND AND COUNTING

In his autobiography Stan Musial refers to 1955 as the "year of the big minus."[1] It was a falling off for Musial's average, finishing as he did at .319, his lowest mark since his appendicitis-hindered 1947 season. Efforts to extend Musial's games-played streak by keeping him in the line-up without occasional days of complete rest during a typically hot St. Louis summer, was probably not helpful to his average. Nevertheless, Stan's overall numbers were strong, as usual leading the teaming in most hitting categories. He contributed 33 home runs, 108 RBIs, and scored 97 runs and was especially happy to have reached the 2,500-hit milestone in this trajectory toward the 3,000-hit goal.

Among the new names in the Cardinals' stats list was that of rookie third-base man, Ken Boyer, who lead the team in stolen bases. Boyer, who would emerge as one of the leaders of the Cardinals in the post-Musial era, was from a Cardinals-loving family. The Boyer family's regard for the legend of Stan the Man was so high that, when Ken's brother Clete was offered the number six for his Yankee uniform, young Clete was reluctant to presume to wear Stan's number until Mickey Mantle persuaded him that Stan would not mind. Having grown up in a hotbed of Cardinals fandom amidst the foothills of the Ozark Mountains in southern Missouri, Ken and Clete were among the many young ball players of the late 1950s and early 1960s who regarded Musial with something akin to awe.[2] Mantle, too, had been a Musial devotee in his youth, having grown up in the Cardinals' territory known as Oklahoma.[3]

The 1955 minus was bigger for the Cardinals than it was for Musial with the team finishing in seventh place with sixty-eight wins and eighty-six losses. This was the poorest showing for the Cardinals since their 65–89 sixth-place record in 1924 and lowest position in the standings since 1919. Bob Broeg mentions that a sportswriter distant from St. Louis called this Redbird team "the best seventh-place club in history," but such talk offered scant consolation to Gussie Busch who had the displeasure of seeing his supposedly great franchise plunge toward the bottom of the National League. Not surprisingly Eddie Stanky, whose cantankerous antics were never popular with St. Louis fans, was fired early in this dismal season and was replaced with former Cardinal Harry Walker. After the season Walker was also fired and replaced by Fred Hutchinson. Walker's efforts as a minor-league manager and a major-league coach were to continue to be valuable to the Cardinals organization, but his brief 1955 tenure as leader of the big-league squad was hampered, Musial felt, because the 1955 team was held back by the inexperience of its younger players and the off years of its older players. Some observers felt, too, that Walker had overworked and exhausted the team during the worst dog days of summer by subjecting them to extended drills on fundamentals. It seems likely, however, that the hard work of that sort paid dividends in the future great performances of developing talents such as Boyer.[4]

Another greatly regretted minus for the Cards in 1955 was the loss of their inspirational and eccentric trainer, Doc Weaver, to a heart attack. A big, jovial man who had first come to the Cardinals at the request of his former Ohio Wesleyan football buddy, Branch Rickey, Weaver had earned fame in the 1940s for his "double-whammy" curses on opposing players, and his marshaling of momentum by his endless replaying of the Spike Jones' recording of "Pass the Bisquits Mirandy," and various other musical oddities, which had served as the background noise to some of the Cardinals' greatest successes. Weaver had probably also extended the careers of Cardinal stars such as Marty Marion and Whitey Kurowski, whose disabilities had been remedied by the crucial assistance Doc Weaver's magical hands could deliver. Marion, in gratitude, had given Weaver a set of bronze bookends molded to resemble Doc's large and tender hands. Weaver's passing away was another of the many ways an era was being left further behind as the increasingly Cardinal-unfriendly 1950s ground forward.[5]

The 1955 All-Star game proved to be an exciting moment for Stan and his fans. The game was tied 5-5 in the twelfth inning when Musial, who had not been swinging well in earlier innings was the leadoff hitter against hard-throwing 6'6" Frank Sullivan of the Red Sox. As Musial got into his stance at the plate he exchanged a few words with umpire Bill Summers and catcher for the American League Yogi Berra. All three agreed that they were tired and wanted to call it a day; and then Musial made it happen by smacking the first pitch high up into the right-field bleachers at Milwaukee's County Stadium for a walk-off home run. It was a satisfyingly bright moment in a dark season as Musial rounded third base to find most of his fellow National League All-Stars gathered to greet and congratulate him on his opportune blast. Musial had been hitting below .300 at the All-Star break and had not been elected as starter on the team, but Leo Durocher had put Stan into the game early in the action. Durocher commented later that Stan "owed me that one ... he owed me one ... after hitting so many against me, including five in one day."[6]

In 1956, Gussie Busch's frustrations at Cardinal failings led him to hire Frank Lane as his general manager. This provocative and controversial personality had earned the nicknames "Trader Lane" and "Frantic Frank" because of the penchant he had shown in his former job in the White Sox organization for swapping, selling, and buying personnel at a breathtakingly rapid rate. Though given free reign to make whatever deals he wanted, Lane entered the season declaring that six of his players—Musial, Schoendienst, Boyer, Virdon, Moon, and Haddix were "untradable"—but in the first couple of months of the season he dealt away half the guys on that list, including beloved Cardinal and close Musial friend Schoendienst and had set his sights on trading the biggest name on the list, The Man himself, to the Phillies for their star pitcher Robin Roberts. When Biggie Garagnani, Stan's restaurant business partner, heard about the pending deal, he tried to contact Busch to protest the idea and raised a fuss with every Anheuser-Busch administrator he could manage to reach by phone. Garagnani went so far as to declare to one brewery official, "I'll bet you $10,000 Stan won't go to Philadelphia. He'll retire. So you'll have no deal, no Musial either, and a lot of embarrassment." Garaganani's intervention got the attention of the big boss and the trade did not go through. When Biggie told Stan what he had heard and what he had done, the surprised and upset Musial indicated to his partner (and to the many reporters who asked him what he would have done) that retirement from baseball would, indeed, have been a real possibility under such circumstances, but, upon reflection, Stan speculates in his autobiography that, with his 3,000-hit goal hanging just about within sight, he probably would have decided to swallow his pride and pack his bags for Philly. Quitting baseball when he was still hitting well, Stan had to admit, would not have been easy for him to do.[7]

And Stan was hitting well in 1956, despite several slumps that kept his average down to .310, but he lead the league in RBIs with 109 and hit 27 home runs.[8] Highlights included his noting on his fifteenth anniversary in the major leagues that he had accumulated 2,766 hits. With his goal of 3,000 in mind he declared to reporters that he thought he would probably play only two more years. That would have him retiring after the 1958 season; little did he know that he would have one of his better years in baseball in 1962 and would not hang up his spikes for good until the end of the 1963 season. Another big 1956 moment for Stan was the All-Star game where—just as the stadium press box was announcing over the loudspeaker that the Ted Williams' homer in the previous half inning was his fourth career All-Star homer and had tied him with Stan Musial for the all-time record—Musial came up to bat and blasted the first pitch into the stands, forcing the announcer to shift gears in midsentence and say, "Sorry, Mr. Musial has just untied the record." Finally, Stan was voted the winner of the first Player-of-the-Decade award as the result of a poll of ten-year players, managers, scouts, reporters, broadcasters, umpires, and club owners conducted by *Sporting News*. Delighted by the selection, Musial and others pointed out that part of the reason he was selected over DiMaggio, Williams, and Feller was that those stars were more identified with an earlier era, while Musial's prime years had fallen largely within the decade under consideration. Musial's modesty about his ranking in relation to DiMaggio and Williams did not, however, diminish the considerable satisfaction he felt at being singled out as the best of the best.[9] Furthermore, this vote for Musial over his fellow members of the Great Triumvirate, at a time when the achievements of all three were fresh in the minds of voters who had seen them play, is an interesting development for those who would like to argue that Musial was, indeed, the best of the three.

Amid the accomplishments of 1956 there were, however, a few less auspicious turns of fortune for Stan. After a fly ball fell in front of him that his manager felt a younger man would have caught, Hutchinson moved him in to play first base, commenting that Musial "doesn't cover the ground he used to." This was one of the first times anyone had mentioned that age might be becoming a factor in the play of Musial. Though he denied it at the time, Musial seems to have been stung when he was moved from third to fifth in the lineup during one of the several slumps he suffered from in 1956.[10]

The most dismaying day of the year for Stan was August 22, when, in addition to being hitless at the plate with two strikeouts, he made two damaging errors, muffing a ground ball at first early in the game and then making an aberrant throw to second on what would have been a crucial double play. Regarding Stan as one of the causes of the Cardinals' 5-3 loss to the Dodgers, some fans did what no St. Louis fans had ever done before. For the first time in his career Musial was booed by the hometown fans. The next day, in response to this unprecedented singing of boo birds to the great Musial, a group of fans took out a large ad in *The St. Louis Globe-Democrat* newspaper to criticize the bad behavior of what they saw as a miscreant minority:

A PUBLIC APOLOGY TO STAN MUSIAL

For the thousands of us who were shame-faced by the thoughtlessness of a few spectators at Wednesday's game, please accept our apologies. We are certain that even now those who took part in the demonstration regret their actions. For to you, Stan Musial, we owe our gratitude for giving us many years of fine sportsmanship and superb play. St. Louis and the nation will always acclaim you as the Greatest Player of Our Era. We look forward to seeing "the Man—the Best Man," for years to come.

Sincerely, TEN OF YOUR MILLIONS OF ADMIRERS[11]

Among the lowest points of the season for Stan was the trading of his roommate and close friend Red Schoendienst; it was one of the worst of Frank Lane's many unrestrained bad dealings for the Cardinals. Although Lane was later to get some credit for helping to build The Big Red Machine in Cincinnati, his moves in St. Louis in 1956 are difficult to justify. The team was leading the league with a thirteen to six record and began to go downhill in response to the demoralizing fire-sale nature of Lane's moves. Several of the discarded players—including Schoendienst, Bill Virdon, and Jackie Brandt—were to become stars on teams who would successfully compete against the Cardinals. His moves, generally, did not even seem to have a coherent building-for-the-future logic to them when one considers that he often exchanged promising younger players for marginal veterans.[12] A team that began the season looking like a contender ended the year in a discouraged fourth place with a losing record of seventy-six wins and seventy-eight losses.

In the interim between seasons, Busch served notice that he expected Frank Lane to come through or go away, "I expect the Cardinals to come close to winning a pennant in 1957—and 1958 is going to have to be a sure thing—or Frank Lane will be out on his ass."[13] Though 1958 would not work out well, Musial's great play in 1957 propelled the team close to the place Busch had in mind for them.

In January of 1957, a fund-raising dinner on behalf of a cancer charity was billed as a Musial tribute and featured the coming together of all of Stan's various major-league managers—except for Billy Southworth, who had a conflicting event and could not make it. Remarks on Stan and his achievements were made by Eddie Dyer, Fred Hutchinson, Marty Marion, Eddie Stanky, and Harry Walker. Busch used the occasion to announce that Musial's number 6 would be retired after his playing days were over. This honor was a particularly flattering distinction because it marked the first instance of a retired number in the history of the franchise. Stan was especially pleased with the emphasis in remarks made by Stanky and Walker on his (Stan's) career-long tendency to run as hard as he could out of the box. In commenting on the remarks of his former managers, Stan makes explicit his belief that his all-out-running approach was doubly advantageous in that it helped the team to win at the same time that it boosted his personal statistics:

> I do believe that going all-out brings its individual rewards as well as its team benefits. For instance, if a batter breaks away from the plate at full speed, he'll often get the extra base that eludes him if he waits until rounding first base to shift into high gear. It's too late at that point to realize that a long single might have been a short double.[14]

At least one trade Lane made in preparation for the 1957 season was very helpful to the Cardinal's best hitter. The acquisition of Del Ennis from the Phillies and the insertion of that strong-hitting outfielder into the cleanup slot in the lineup, right after Musial, resulted in lessened tendency to pitch around Stan, who took advantage of the opportunity presented by his seeing a greater number of good pitches than he had in some recent previous seasons. Stan batted a remarkable .434 in spring training and then burst into the regular season with four for four in the first game of the summer.[15] In addition to hitting 24 home runs and gathering 105 RBIs, Ennis became a good friend and roommate to Stan—remedying, somewhat, the comradeship void left behind by the departure of Schoendienst. It also helped Musial and Ennis that emerging-slugger Boyer was batting fifth.[16]

Stan attributed some of his early success in 1957 to a "secret" change in his approach at the plate. He had been troubled for several years by the increasing use against him of the slider, which, because its speed was not much different from a fast ball, sometimes caused him to get less than the best part of the bat on the ball, even when he was able to make last-second adjustments. He explained that he had decided that, if he "couldn't beat the slider, [he] would join it" by means of "cutting down the degree of [his] stride." Although this strategy would "leave the outside of the plate unprotected for a well-controlled fastball," Stan felt that few pitchers would be able to "thread three straight strikes across the outside corner"; furthermore, he theorized that, if he did not make his change in strategy too obvious, it would not be detected by the opposition who would continue to fear Stan's past tendency to slam outside-corner fast balls into left and left-center field. This change in stance worked quite well for Stan for much of the season, but resulted, he felt, in a late-season slump when opposing pitchers finally caught on to his secret. Shifting back to his usual stance brought him back into sync and enabled him to close out the year hitting well.[17]

Musial's sometimes troubles against the slider seem to have been due to his reliance on observing the speed of the pitch as a means to determining how a pitch would behave. Unlike Ted Williams, who admitted to being a "guess hitter," Stan always claimed he usually "knew" what pitch was coming because of his ability to remember each pitcher's arsenal and judge which type of throw was headed his way by means of judging its velocity. Concentration, Stan always contended, was key to this knack, and he felt that the slumps he endured from time to time were usually caused more by failures of concentration than by mistakes of physical execution.[18] The great role played by concentration in Musial's mastery at the plate could explain why he was sometimes able to hit with such extraordinary effectiveness when injuries and limitations held him back physically, while adding an edge to his determination to concentrate and succeed.

Stan had mixed feelings about one of the statistical high marks he reached in 1957. In mid-June, Musial surpassed Gus Suhr's National League record for consecutive games played. There was much press attention when Musial played in his 824th consecutive game, and former-Pirate Suhr sent a congratulatory telegram, but several commentators, and Musial himself, were dismissive of the achievement. All one had to do to keep such a streak alive was to show up and play an inning or two. Despite the praise heaped on Musial's durability in 1957— similar to the even bigger fuss recently made over Cal Ripkin's breaking the much larger American League record of Lou Gehrig—showing up for work seemed to Stan a minimum expectation rather than a major achievement. When an injury forced an end to Stan's streak at 895 games, he was not particularly displeased to end his streak of consecutive appearances at 895. Musial felt that taking a day off now and then could enable him to play better and help his team more.[19]

He was, however, very unhappy to be in danger of missing multiple games at a time when the Cardinals were threatening to have a successful season. The injury came in a late August game against the Phillies when Stan tried to adjust his swing during a hit-and-run play in order to drive the ball behind Wally Moon who was breaking toward second base. In his effort to pull a curve ball that was high and slightly outside the strike zone Stan awkwardly wrenched his swing and dislocated his shoulder, fracturing a bone and suffering some muscular tears. When Musial insisted upon returning to the lineup after only a fourteen-game absence, he could throw the ball only with difficulty, but, in his typical concentration-enhanced-when-injured manner, he raised his batting average and helped the Cardinals make a race of it by slapping hits to all fields, getting sixteen hits in thirty-one chances in September. After the Braves clinched the pennant, Hutchinson told Stan to rest the last few games and give some rookies a chance to show their stuff.[20]

On the brink of his thirty-seventh birthday, Musial was delighted to have won his seventh batting crown with a .351 average. He was proud, too, of having driven in 102 runs out of the 171 times that runners were presented to him in scoring position. His twenty-nine homers were not bad either, especially considering he could not swing with power in any of his September at-bats. *The Sporting News* named him National League Player of the Year. The old man was, all the sports pages were pleased to declare, still The Man.[21]

It was a restorative season for the Cardinals' reputation with a second-place finish and many exciting high points. Frank Lane was full of praise for what he called "a heroic ball club, a bunch of guys who wouldn't quit." Lane, however, knew his days with the Cardinals were numbered, and, when, after much diligent sending out of inquiries, he was able to secure an offer from the Cleveland Indians, he submitted his resignation to Busch in November. Bing Devine was appointed as his replacement as Redbird general manager. Devine was already an eighteen-year veteran of the organization.[22] Devoted to the Cardinals and well-respected by players and the baseball world generally, Devine would endeavor mightily to bring the Cardinals to the championship level.

Devine, anxious to reward Musial for his excellent season and flush with revenues from the team's strong 1957 attendance, asked Stan what he felt his salary should be. When Stan expressed a wish to get paid at least as much as the highest-paid player in the National League, Ralph Kiner of the Pirates, who had been earning $90,000, Devine readily agreed to sign Stan for $91,000. By indicating that he wanted his salary to be the highest in the league Stan had started a corporate-pride thought process in the Cardinals' business office that came to fortunate fruition for Musial when Devine called to tell him that the Cardinals had decided to make him the first $100,000 man. Apparently the publicity value of that round figure was suggested to the management team by Bob Broeg.[23]

As the 1958 season got underway, Stan was well aware that he was only forty-three hits away from his goal of 3,000. He declared a desire to "get them in a hurry because—who knows?—I might get hit by a cab." One reporter raised the prospect of another impressive record: If Musial could win his eighth batting title, he would tie Honus Wagner's National League record. Stan agreed that such a development would be great but indicated that one more title would be nowhere near the thrill of reaching 3,000.[24] "I want the 3,000th hit more than anything else in my life," he declared early in the season, "Nothing that ever happened to me before will equal the moment I make that hit. I won't be able to relax until I do."[25]

Stan's focus on the 3,000-hit goal had been a running theme in his conversations with his long-time chronicler and confidant Bob Broeg since the day when Musial hit number 1,000 in 1948. Broeg teased Musial that 1,000 was nothing compared with the 3,152 total that Paul Waner had reached in 1945. Stan was intrigued to learn that only seven other players besides Waner—Ty Cobb, Cap Anson, Honus Wagner, Tris Speaker, Napoleon Lajoie, and Eddie Collins—had reached the elusive 3,000-hit plateau.[26] Stan's passionate pursuit of this goal was reinforced by a conversation he had with Hall of Famer Al Simmons, whose one great regret about his career was his falling short of 3,000 hits. Simmons greatly regretted all the times early in his career when he had taken days off by pretending to be sick and in other ways neglecting to go for every single hit in the days when hits came easy to him. Falling short of the goal by only seventy-three hits, Simmons bewailed all the ways he had wasted his early opportunities.[27] Striving to avoid Simmons' regret had become a preoccupation for Musial and, as the goal came into sight in 1958, he had his eyes locked on that prize. Stan's high statistical performances over the course of many years may have, in fact, been at least partially due to the way he steeled himself year in and year out to not let any possible hit get away from him. Broeg says Musial urged him to keep mentioning the possibility of 3,000 hits to keep his motivation level high even when he was suffering through the hottest summer days, even when the Cardinals were languishing low in the standings, and even when he might have wanted to rest, for a moment or two, on his laurels.[28] As his hit total climbed over the years, the relentless Musial's craving for hits remained insatiable, and, in 1958, all that hard work was about to be rewarded.

At the outset of the 1958 season Musial was on a tear. In the Cards' opening road trip to the West coast to play against the Giants and Dodgers he hit over .500 despite the unfriendly-to-left-handed-hitters nature of their temporary ball parks. Keeping in mind how hard it would be for him to hit homers in those parks, Stan contendedly slapped line-drive singles and doubles in every direction. Proud of his ability to adapt to whatever circumstances he might face, Stan comments in his autobiography on how frustrated other left-hand hitters, notably Duke Snider, were by the unfair dimensions and breezes of those unkind facilities.[29]

Anticipating that Stan would get his 3,000th hit by May 11, Stan's partner Biggie Garagnani staged a celebration at their restaurant following the doubleheader that concluded a Cardinals homestand. Though he contributed five hits in the two games, Stan was still shy of the mark on the evening of the party. The affair was attended by more than 300 notables—including the Governor of Missouri, the Mayor of St. Louis, and the President of the National League.[30]

Next up for the Cardinals was a two-game series against the Cubs so it seemed likely Musial would get the big hit in Chicago. Stan and Lil were accompanied to Chicago by their longtime Donora friends Frank and Molly Pizzica. In the first game in the Windy City, Stan managed to get his 2,999th hit, a double, which left him at the brink with one more game to play against the Cubs before a return to St. Louis for another home stand. Stan mentioned to coach Terry Moore his wish that he could get the next hit back home in St. Louis in front of his many St. Louis supporters. Hutchinson and Moore talked it over, and it was decided that Stan would sit out the second Chicago game unless he was needed as a pinch hitter.[31]

That night, before the Musials and the Pizzicas were to have dinner at the hotel restaurant, Molly Pizzica could not be found and Stan and the rest of the group searched anxiously for her in the hotel, in the surrounding streets, in the nearby movie theaters, in the hospitals, and in all sorts of other nooks and crannies. The police were called. At last the search was suspended till morning. Stan had only been asleep a few hours when the phone rang. It was Molly demanding that Stan tell her where her husband had run off to. When the facts about the previous evening were finally made clear, it turned out that Molly had gone to take a nap in her room before dinner and had somehow gotten off at the wrong floor. When the elevator operator found the stout, elderly woman struggling to make her key work in the door of a room that she insisted was hers, he let her in with his key. Of course, the room looked exactly like her actual room. Falling deeply asleep after the hectic day, she awakened in distress at what she thought was the inexplicable disappearance of her husband and friends.[32]

The thoroughly unrested Musial was happily taking a nap in the visiting bullpen at Wrigley Field when, in the sixth inning, Hutchinson signaled from the dugout that he wanted Stan to come in as a pinch hitter for pitcher Sam Jones. The Cardinals were trailing three to one; they had a runner in scoring position at second base; and their best hitter was needed. A roar went up from the small crowd when Musial's name was announced and he trotted in from the bullpen to get his bat. Understandably the Cubs pitcher, Moe Drabowsky, worked carefully, not wanting to be a name in the history of Musial's record book. With the count two and two Drabowsky beautifully laced a curve ball on the outside corner. Though fooled by the pitch and off balance, Musial, in typical Musial fashion, was able to recover and drive the ball down the left-field line for an RBI double. Stan had reached 3,000 hits in his sixteenth season. (It had taken Ty Cobb seventeen seasons to reach that mark.).[33]

The umpire, Frank Dascoli, secured the ball for Stan's collection, and Hutchinson brought in a pinch runner. Before leaving the field Stan stopped at the box behind the Cardinals dugout where his wife and the Pizzicas were cheering for him and gave Lil a big kiss. One of the photographers later asked him, "Stan, do you know that blonde who kissed you out there?" He had to admit that he did. An impromptu press conference continued in the clubhouse through the end of the game, which the Redbirds finally won five to three for their sixth win in a row.[34]

That evening's train ride from Chicago to St. Louis was always to remain one of Stan's favorite baseball memories. The festivities began with a steward bringing Musial a large cake with "3,000" written in numerals on top in red frosting. To add to the merriment, Stan bought a bottle of champagne for winning pitcher

Sam Jones, which was quickly consumed by all. When the train reached the station at Clinton, Illinois, a crowd of more than fifty people were chanting, "We want Musial! We want Musial!" The crowd cheered wildly when Stan emerged to greet them and sign the various things they thrust at him. When the train pulled into the state capitol of Springfield an hour later a raucous crowd of more than one hundred serenaded him with "For He's a Jolly Good Fellow." After the train got underway again, Stan, happily exhausted by all the adulation, fell asleep, seated in the parlor car, with family and friends chattering all around him. Meanwhile, back in St. Louis, a crowd had been gathering for hours, so when Stan's train pulled in after 11 P.M. there were more than 800 people packed into Union Station. A platform was found where Musial could address the throng. "I never realized that batting a little ball around could cause so much commotion!" Stan declared, and then went on to remark, "I know now how Lindbergh must have felt when he returned to St. Louis." A jokester in the crowd shouted, "What did he hit?"[35]

The Cardinals continued the celebration with a party in June to which were invited many celebrities and the four still-living members of the 3,000-hit club. Tris Speaker and Paul Waner were able to come; Napoleon Lajoie and Ty Cobb could not make it and were sent their commemorative plaques by mail. Stan's teammates presented him with a silver bowl and a plaque displaying a warmly appreciative message:

> To Stanley Frank Musial, an emblem of esteem from his teammates. An outstanding artist in his profession, possessor of many baseball records; gentleman in every sense of the word; adored and worshipped by countless thousands; perfect answer to a manager's prayer. To this, we, the Cardinals, attest with our signatures.[36]

Among the gifts that Musial most enjoyed receiving was a special state license plate provided by Missouri Governor James Blair emblazoned with the magic number "3,000." Stan proudly displayed this honorifically numbered plate on his car for many years. In later years, as more players, with the benefit of longer seasons and no loss of time to war service, reached the 3,000 plateau, the distinction lost some of its transcendent glamor, but, for Stan, his thrilling double on May 13, 1958—the culmination of many years of pointing toward 3,000— and the surprisingly glorious train ride that followed were always remembered fondly.

Unfortunately, the Cardinals as a team did not continue to play well and they closed the season tied for fifth place and only three games above rock bottom. This downturn cost Fred Hutchinson his job even before the end of the season. Coach Stan Hack was asked to serve as manager during the closing weeks and then

Solly Hemus, a former Cardinal with no managerial experience, was appointed the manager for the upcoming 1959 season. Musial was disappointed by this turn of events because he had great respect for Hutchinson and felt that the manager deserved another chance.[37]

Perhaps because of a letdown following all the celebrations Stan's hitting declined somewhat as the year progressed, but it was, nonetheless, another distinguished year for The Man and, when the dust had settled, his batting average stood at .337. The winding down of the season was, however, not with out its difficulties for Stan. He was hampered in September by a pulled leg muscle, but a larger problem was how overtired he had become by the end of the season. This weariness seemed related to his lack of power at the end of the summer. He hit only one home run during the closing two months of the season, and his RBI total for the season was down to sixty-two, the lowest number he had ever put up in that category.[38]

In view of how exhausted Stan found himself in October it was not a fortunate development for him that Busch had accepted a proposal for a postseason trip to Japan for a series of games against a Japanese All-Star squad. Musial asked to be excused from the trip, but the sponsors in Hawai'i and Japan indicated that the Cardinals had been invited largely because they were the team of the renowned Stan Musial. Though Lil was six-months pregnant she went with him, and they had a festive time.

The recreational aspects of the October trip that grandly concluded Musial's momentous 1958 were enjoyable, but Stan's continuing weariness and the continuous eating and drinking opportunities that were impossible to refuse took their toll on Stan's readiness for the 1959 season. He subsequently avoided making excuses for the falloff in his performance in 1959, but it needs to be said that the activities of his autumn and winter of 1958–1959 were a considerable strain at a time when Stan was badly in need of recuperative rest from the physical challenges of a particularly demanding season and the emotional roller coaster involved in his finally achieving the long-striven-for 3,000-hit goal in the midst of some down years for his team. Feted, banqueted, and shown all around by their gracious hosts, the Musials and the rest of the Cardinals contingent enjoyed their Japanese experience, while also managing to play good baseball in the exhibitions.

Some accounts of the Cardinals' sojourn across the Pacific seem to suggest a vacation junket involving only a few lightly contested games, but the truth is that the Redbirds were faced with an unusual October–November miniseason of more than twenty games, involving extensive travel and unusual venues, playing conditions, and after-game events. Adding to the intensity was the circumstance that the Cardinals were under the direction of an ambitious new manager, and Solly Hemus was determined to make a statement concerning his abilities as a honcho by means of winning as many games as possible. Hired by Busch primarily because his gung-ho style seemed to promise improvement in the focus of the underachieving Redbirds, Solly wanted to make the most of this highly publicized postseason showcase to prove that he could make these birds fly as high as their boss expected.

The comments of Red McQueen, the sports editor of *The Honolulu Advertiser*, who reported on the Cardinals in Honolulu and then joined the entourage in Japan are suggestive of the nature of this transoceanic adventure. McQueen—who was clearly a Yankee aficionado and not inclined to think favorably of the St. Louis team—mentioned repeatedly in his series of columns about the trip his expectation that the Cardinals would not fare well in Japan. McQueen felt that the Japanese All-Star squad put together to face the Redbirds would prove far more formidable than the individual regional teams thrown against the Yankees and Dodgers during previous goodwill tours. McQueen referred approvingly to the opinion of Japanese journalist Fujio Nakazawa, who theorized that—in view of the four losses suffered by a presumably superior-to-the-Cardinals team like the Dodgers—the loss of at least five games could be expected for the Cards. Infuriated by the implication that the Cardinals were not in the same class as the Yankees and Dodgers, Solly Hemus indicated to the more than fifty reporters assembled for the press conference at the Tokyo airport where Nakazawa offered his insulting supposition that he expected his team to be better than previous visitors. "Goodwill or not," Hemus declared emphatically, "we did not come here to lose. We'll be all out in every game and I'll be disappointed if we lose two games." Wally Yonamine, who would be playing for the Japanese squad, predicted, however, that "sheer fatigue" would probably cause the Cards to drop at least six games against the carefully chosen Japanese stars.[39]

Rising remarkably to the occasion and the demands of their frenetic manager, the Cardinals managed to win all but two of their sixteen games in Japan and all of the games they played in Hawai'i, Manila, and Korea. It was an achievement that made demands on all Cardinals. The many younger players on the team were trying to secure a favorable assessment with regard to the coming season, but Musial, too, was trying his best. Yoshio Tanaka, manager of the Hanshin Tigers commented on the Cardinals superior effort:

> "Even under adverse ground conditions, they stole bases as on October 25 in Tokyo. They are not conserving their energy; they give their all. Even Musial, when he rapped a triple, ran hard. There is no loafing on the field. In previous tours by major leaguers, even when a triple

was possible, a player would be satisfied with a double. . . . There are a few things we can learn from the visiting team."[40]

Yetsuo Higa, the Honolulu businessman who put together the Cardinals tour, as well as the previous tours by the Yankees and Dodgers, remarked on the Redbirds' good showing:

> Of all the major league teams that have come to Japan, the Cardinals hustled the most, taught the Japanese more about baseball and made the best impression on the Japanese fans, on and off the field. Above all they have done, the Cardinals have set a precedent that all American baseball clubs should follow when they come to Japan in the future: Go all the way—or don't go at all.[41]

Musial's celebrity status placed special sorts of stress on him in Japan. Several commentators noted how disappointed Japanese fans were that Musial, the superstar, although hitting over .300 in the Japan series, did not seem as superhuman as they had expected. In particular they were disappointed that he hit only two home runs in the sixteen games. "I don't hit that long ball any more," Stan declared to one reporter early in the series, "but I'm going to do my best to please the fans." Later in the trip Stan mused, "I wish I had been here when I was younger." Though not finding himself able to fully live up to the sky-high expectations of his Japanese admirers, Musial was well-received everywhere; as McQueen noted, "He's been a goodwill sensation at every stop. Fans have even rushed on the playing field for Musial's autograph. . . . Worn out from the regular season, traveling and sight seeing, the ancient and honorable Musial may be giving the Japanese a show of base hits. But a few years ago, he would have given them plenty of tape-measure homers."[42] With his fledgling manager urging the team to make a lively showing and Stan wanting to show the Japanese that he deserved his fame, the "ancient and honorable" star depleted his reserves to an unusual degree on the brink of his thirty-eighth birthday.

In retrospect, the concluding festivities of 1958 were to seem a kind of farewell party to the greatness of Stan the Man. In a surprising reversal of the endless paeans of praise that had characterized his 1958 achievements, Musial would have to face, during 1959, an endless array of journalistic speculations about when he would retire. If he were to end his major league career on a high note, Stan would have to find a way to rise from the ashes of 1959, a year that, as we shall see, turned out for him to be the end of a decade in more ways than one.

NOTES

1. Stan Musial and Bob Broeg, *Stan Musial: "The Man's" Own Story as Told to Bob Broeg* (New York: Doubleday, 1964), 169.

2. John Snyder, *Cardinals Journal* (Cincinnati, OH: Emmis Books, 2006), 412–416; Joseph Stanton, *Cardinal Points: Poems on St. Louis Cardinals Baseball* (Jefferson, NC: McFarland, 2002), 50–51.

3. Roger Kahn, *The Era* (New York: Houghton Mifflin, 1993), 244–255; Bob Broeg and Jerry Vickery, *The St. Louis Cardinals Encyclopedia* (Chicago, IL: Contemporary Books, 1998) 78.

4. Snyder, *Cardinals Journal*, 414–417; Musial and Broeg, *Stan Musial*, 172–173.

5. Musial and Broeg, *Stan Musial*, 171–172.

6. Earl Lawson, "Musial Wraps Up Game for Nationals." *Cincinnati Times-Star*, July 13, 1955; Musial and Broeg, *Stan Musial*, 169–170.

7. Joe Williams, "Frank Lane's Plan to Trade Musial Really Irked Man." *Pittsburg Press*, April 11, 1964; Musial and Broeg, *Stan Musial*, 177–178.

8. Snyder, *Cardinals Journal*, 418–419.

9. Musial and Broeg, *Stan Musial*, 179–180.

10. James Giglio, *Musial: From Stash to Stan the Man* (Columbia: University of Missouri Press, 2001), 199.

11. Jerry Lansche, *Stan "The Man" Musial: Born to Be a Ballplayer* (Dallas, TX: Taylor, 1994), 145.

12. Ibid., 141–144.

13. Snyder, *Cardinals Journal*, 429.

14. Musial and Broeg, *Stan Musial*, 183–184.

15. Lansche, *Stan "The Man" Musial*, 147.

16. Giglio, *Musial*, 202.

17. Musial and Broeg, *Stan Musial*, 183–189.

18. Mark Newman and John Rawlings, "Man to Man." *Sporting News*, July 28, 1997; Harry Paxton, "A Visit with Stan Musial." *Saturday Evening Post*, April 19, 1958, 33, 113.

19. Giglio, *Musial*, 203–204; Musial and Broeg, *Stan Musial*, 187–188; Lansche, *Stan "The Man" Musial*, 151.

20. Giglio, *Musial*, 204–205.

21. Musial and Broeg, *Stan Musial*, 192–205.

22. Snyder, *Cardinals Journal*, 428–429.

23. Giglio, *Musial*, 205.

24. Paxton, *A Visit with Stan Musial*, 114.

25. Ray Robinson, *Stan Musial: Baseball's Durable "Man"* (New York: Putnam, 1963), 92.

26. Bob Broeg, *The Greatest Moments in St. Louis Sports* (St. Louis: Missouri Historical Society Press, 2000), 106.

27. Robinson, *Stan Musial*, 92–93.

28. Broeg, *The Greatest Moments in St. Louis Sports*, 106.

29. Musial and Broeg, *Stan Musial*, 196–197.

30. Lansche, *Stan "The Man" Musial*, 156.

31. Broeg, *The Greatest Moments in St. Louis Sports*, 106

32. Musial and Broeg, *Stan Musial*, 199–200.

33. W. C. Heinz, "Now There Are Eight." *Life*, May 1958, 113.

34. Lansche, *Stan "The Man" Musial*, 157–158.

35. Giglio, *Musial*, 208–209.

36. Lansche, *Stan "The Man" Musial*, 160.

37. Musial and Broeg, *Stan Musial*, 202–203.

38. Giglio, *Musial*, 209–210.

39. Red McQueen, "Cards in for Rough Time." *The Honolulu Advertiser*, October 24, 1958.

40. Red McQueen, "Cards Are a Hustling Team." *The Honolulu Advertiser*, November 6, 1958.

41. Musial and Broeg, *Stan Musial*, 204–205.

42. Red McQueen, "Musial Disappoints Japanese." *The Honolulu Advertiser*, November 14, 1958.

A BIG FINISH

With Stan at thirty-eight years of age and underperforming in the early days of the 1959 season, rookie manager Solly Hemus kept him on the bench more and more frequently, thinking that the team's future lay with younger players such as Curt Flood, Bill White, and Gene Oliver who needed to have opportunities to develop. Though this rebuilding-year attitude made sense in certain respects, it was more than a little frustrating for Musial as he watched his team limp to a seventh-place finish while his lack of opportunities prevented him from getting into any sort of rhythm at the plate. Among the oddities of the half-baked Cardinals of 1959 was the presence on the roster of four players—Stan Musial, Bill White, George Crowe, and Joe Cunningham—who would have been best utilized at the first-base position.[1]

Stan's statistical downturn in 1959—his batting average was .255—caused him dismay but not despair. His fierce pride prevented him from even considering retiring after that unfortunate season. He could not allow that disappointing performance to be the conclusion of his career. Furthermore, he felt he knew the major reason for his disappointing performance. He was convinced his downfall had been a failure to stay in shape during the off season, a mistake he had avoided in the past.[2]

There seem to be several reasons for this mistake. The 1958 season had been intense, as we have seen, and Musial had tired toward the end of it. Stan's inclination to relax more totally than usual during the off season was reinforced by manager Solly Hemus's recommendation that Musial take it easy during the winter and play only sparingly during spring training to conserve energy for the season to come. Then, of course, there was the Cardinals postseason trip to Japan. Because Musial was treated royally by his hosts and could not help but consume lots of good food, his weight went up to 187 pounds with the extra poundage settling mostly around his hips and waist. On top of all that Musial was allowed to come late to spring training so that he could stay with Lil for the birth of their daughter Jean.[3]

Stan's days of playing intense basketball games in the high school gym in Donora as a means to keeping in shape in the winter were behind him, but he needed to find alternatives, ways to keep himself at least as physically fit as he had been in his younger years. He could never regain the speed and quickness of his youthful vigor, but he was hoping to attain enough strength and stamina to significantly better his 1959 numbers. He found a guide back to fitness in Walter Eberhardt, the director of physical education at St. Louis University. In the late 1950s, and especially in the winter before the 1959 season, Musial had relied on dietary strategies to keep his weight from going up too much, but he could see that he would need the sort of vigorous regimen Eberhardt had to offer. Exercises and running, running, running got Stan into a new sort of peak condition.[4]

Though Musial and the Cardinals did well in spring training, the start of the 1960 season did not open fortuitously for the Redbirds. Musial found himself questioning the strategies of manager Solly Hemus who Stan felt sometimes made unwise decisions in a panic mode. Hemus believed in his hunches, but his against-the-grain decisions seemed too often to lead to losses.

Musial rode the bench frequently in 1960, just as he had in 1959. Stan's distressing relegation to the sidelines culminated for him in a special management meeting that was held at Auggie Busch's Grant's Farm estate where Musial—in the presence of Busch, vice-president Dick Meyer, and general manager Bing Devine—was "gently" informed by Hemus that the Cardinals would be going with a younger, mostly Musial-less, lineup. Though upset by this news and its pompous delivery much more than he was willing to show, Stan professed to accept it like a "good soldier," but he did not let the moment pass without expressing for the record that he felt strongly that he "could still help the ball club."[5]

Musial understood that emerging star Bill White was the best guy to play first base, but he was convinced he could contribute in his old position in left field. It frustrated Stan to see the Cardinals stumbling along, losing game after game, with only slight hitting production coming from its various left fielders while he cooled his heels on the bench. Though Stan did not overtly express anger toward his manager, it must have been upsetting, as Ray Robinson puts it, for "one of the handful of men in history to stroke over 3,000 hits" to be "told by Manager

Solly Hemus, a man with a tissue-weight lifetime batting average, that he could no longer hit curve balls the way a big-leaguer should."[6]

Knowing how Musial felt about not having the opportunity to show he could still play, Bob Broeg, in his role as Musial's confidant, told Danny Murtaugh, manager of the Pittsburgh Pirates, that Musial might consider finishing his career in his original hometown. Although the Pirates were to go on to capture the National League crown and the World Series in 1960, the issue was very much in doubt throughout the season. The Pirates felt that a resurgent Musial could be just the edge they needed. As frustrated as Musial had become with his treatment by Hemus, giving up wearing the birds-on-the-bat Cardinal uniform was not something he wanted to do, but he would have accepted the move if it meant that he would be given at least one more real chance at a productive season. As the situation unfolded, the Pirates finally decided not to pursue the acquisition unless Musial was given his unconditional release. They professed to be unwilling to steal Musial from Bing Devine, but their primary reason for holding off may have been an unwillingness to take on Musial's large salary—especially considering the risk involved. How could they be certain, after all, that Hemus' doubts were not justified?[7]

Meanwhile Musial did not allow his ride on the bench to cause him to fall out of shape—spurred on by his resolve to be ready as well as by the example and advice of veteran journeyman reserve, George Crowe, whose hard work in practice helped him keep his edge as a reliable pinch hitter and part-time starter. Running daily wind sprints in the outfield and exercising regurlarly, Musial was determined to do well when called upon. Still, had not injuries to other players reduced Hemus' left-field options, Stan might never have been given a sustained opportunity. Stan had begun to form a resolve to quit after the midseason All-Star break if he had still not gotten back into the lineup by that time. But, lacking alternatives, Hemus decided to try starting Musial in left, and Stan rose to the occasion, batting close to .500 over a three-week period and getting his average for the season up to .300 by the All-Star game.[8]

Underscoring Musial's revival was his selection by National League manager Walter Alston as a sentimental-favorite, last-minute addition to the roster. In the first of the two All-Star Games held that year Musial came through with a pinch-hit single, as the Nationals won the game 5-3. In the second All-Star contest Musial blasted a home run to the third deck of Yankee Stadium, a major thrill for Stan who had not played in "The House That Ruth Built" since the 1943 World Series. Stan's success in the All-Star Games reminded many, including Stan, of the remarkableness of his long career. For instance, Casey Stengel, manager of the American League All Stars, was led to recall the early days of Musial's emergence.

Stengel recounted how Stan "almost took the leg off a my first baseman" the first time a Stengel team encountered Musial in 1941.[9]

In the second half of the 1960 season, the Cardinals woke up, inspired perhaps by the revitalized Musial, and were suddenly a factor in the pennant race, at times challenging the Pirates for the National League crown. Great performances by Cardinals pitchers—in particular by starter Ernie Broglio and reliever Lindy McDaniel—were crucial to the Redbird rebound, but it often seemed that Musial's heroics were the major factors in key games. Stan helped beat the Pirates three times in August with home runs at a stage in the pennant race when it looked like the Pirates might not be able to sustain the potential greatness of their season. Stan recalled feeling a certain "coolness" coming from some of his Donora friends in response to his damaging blows to Pittsburgh hopes.[10]

When the dust settled on the season, however, the Cardinals had fallen back to third place and Musial's average had tailed off somewhat to end at .275; but, for Stan, the second half of the 1960 season had been an important recovery of his stature as a hitter to be reckoned with. It seemed to many of Musial's fans and friends that he had reached the perfect point to call it quits. Why not retire with his second-half-of-1960 return to greatness lingering as his farewell to the game? It made sense that he did not want to end on the sour note of 1959, but surely ending after a season that had a strong finish would constitute a satisfying and dignified context for his retirement. Stan seriously considered that option. He could certainly get by without his baseball salary because of the prospering of his business ventures, but he ultimately could not bring himself to quit yet. He felt strong and fit and confident that he could have a better overall season in 1961 than he had had in 1960, and he was determined to give that possibility a try. He also had the backing of the Cardinal's management, which was well aware of the continuing box office appeal of Stan the Man.[11]

Stan's confidence that he would put up better overall numbers in 1961 than he had in 1960 proved correct. Playing in a little more than 60 percent of the games, Stan had seventy RBIs and averaged .288 while hitting fifteen homers and twenty-two doubles. The disappointing performance of the Cardinals' pitching staff kept the team out of contention. Solly Hemus' proclivity for panicky innovations tended to make matters worse, and Busch, frustrated that baseball success was continuing to elude his most determined efforts, fired Hemus just before the All-Star break.[12]

Johnny Keane, one of Hemus' coaches in 1961 and a long-time minor-league manager in the Cardinals organization, took over as manager of the Cardinals. Musial and the rest of the Redbirds were pleased about this change. Keane's good judgments about his players and his experienced grasp of the essential elements involved in managerial decision-making would, the players felt, enable him to fare far better than his predecessor had.[13]

In one of his most interesting performances in 1961 Musial demonstrated, once again, his odd knack for performing at his best when hampered by a painful ailment. In a game in San Francisco he was suffering intense pain due to an abscessed tooth he would have to have removed shortly after the game in an unusual midnight dental appointment. Additionally, on that night he also suffered from a pulled leg muscle and a cold that kept him awake the night before. Though suffering from all these disadvantages, Musial went out and got two hits, both of them homers. One of the homers was a grand slam. His seven RBIs for the contest made it one of the most productive outings of his career, the most he ever got in a single game, thus demonstrating, once again, Musial's surprising knack for concentrating better "when he isn't feeling up to par."[14] Stan's various triumphs over physical challenges speak to the issue of his consistency at the plate over the course of his long career.

Looking toward 1962 it was clear that Musial would play at least one more year. Johnny Keane told Stan to work hard on his conditioning over the winter so he could be ready to play in more games than he had in 1961. Musial was happy to undertake that challenge. Keane's confidence that Stan could be extraordinary again for at least one more round was just the stimulus number 6 needed to make that hope become a reality. Miraculously, he made Keane's prediction come abundantly true by turning himself into a new version of superstar Stan the Man. Not the same as the youthful version to be sure, but super, nonetheless. So enthusiastically did Stan pursue getting in shape that he managed to achieve his rookie playing weight of 175 pounds, but he then found he needed a little more weight to stay strong and maintained himself at about 180 pounds for most of the season. He found his better condition and reduced poundage paid off in many ways. He found, for instance, that he could slide better than he had in recent years and even managed to be quick enough to steal a few bases.[15]

Musial's iconic status was underscored when KMOX advertised their coming season of radio broadcasts by publishing a large photo of Stan and captioning it with references to him as the ultimate Cardinal, the symbol of the St. Louis team. Johnny Keane made clear his preseason expectations for Stan by announcing that he was expecting Musial to start at least one hundred games and hit at least as well as he had the year before. Stan jokingly predicted that budding star center fielder Curt Flood would get lots of exercise—flanked as he was to be by forty-one-year-old Musial on one side and thirty-nine-year-old Minnie Minoso on the other.[16]

Repeatedly asked when he would be retiring, his standard response was that he would continue playing as long as it was still fun and he felt he was still helping his team to win. "I don't want to sound corny," he remarked at one point, "but baseball has been so much a part of my life for so long that I'd miss it terribly. I never imagined it would be so hard to quit. Year after year it's always been the same. I feel no older and I can't wait to start spring training." One reporter commented in 1962 that to understand the importance of baseball for Musial "you'd have to see Stan in spring training, where the formalities are less restrictive than in league competition, to appreciate the zest he has for the sport. If he isn't swinging a bat, he's playing catch ball. If he isn't running in the outfield, he's shagging flies. A stranger would take him for a rookie, striving to catch the manager's attention. To Musial the work was pleasure."[17]

The Cards and Musial got off to a spectacular start in 1962 with the team surging to six straight victories and Stan hitting at a .458 clip. Neither could continue at quite that high level, but, surprisingly, the team was to fall off more than Musial. Stan was to stay in contention for the batting crown all season, and, though several slumps kept him from holding onto the .350+ pace that he maintained for most of the season, he ended with an impressive .330, in third place behind Tommy Davis and Frank Robinson for the league batting championship. No modern player had hit for such a high average in the over-forty bracket. Cap Anson's performance in the 1890s was the last time anyone as old as Stan had hit so well.[18]

At times during the 1962 season it seemed the only thing that could keep Musial from the batting crown would be a failure to get him enough at bats to qualify, but Keane managed to balance giving Stan sufficient rest with getting him into enough games. Had if not been for his scattering of slumps, Musial's numbers in 1962 could have been even more astonishing.

Musial's slumps in 1962 tended to arrive on the occasions when he was on the brink of breaking records—a circumstance that suggests he cared deeply about records and felt pressure when they came into sight, even though he usually downplayed their importance when asked about them by reporters. Especially exciting and unsettling for Musial was the tying and breaking of Honus Wagner's National League record of 3,430 hits. Growing up in Donora, Stan had revered Wagner for his longtime stardom for the Pittsburgh Pirates. To pass the marks of the renowned "Flying Dutchman" was a highly emotional dream-come-true.[19]

After the hot start to his season Stan found himself batting around .400 and just one hit away from tying Wagner's record, and then, with cameras poised all around him to record the big moment, Stan fell into a zero-for-thirteen slump, dropping his average fifty points until he finally got his 3,430th hit off Juan Marichal in San Francisco. Following that, Stan endured a zero-for-eight streak before he got the record-breaking blow off Ron Peranowski in Los Angeles.[20] The press coverage of Musial's quest for the Wagner record sometimes fused with various sorts of attempts to assess the importance of Musial to baseball, and America in general. A *Time* magazine article entitled "A Saint with Money" chatted about how Musial had the "most of everything" and went on to list many of his records and career totals. The article quoted Leo Durocher's remark that "there is only one way to pitch to Musial—under the plate" and then went on to say that Musial refutes the most infamous Durocher-ism, as he is "the living proof that nice guys do not necessarily finish last."[21] Back in St. Louis, Lil missed the radio coverage of Stan's record breaker because she had fallen asleep during the long ball game that lasted past midnight in the central time zone. She joked that she might be "too old for this game," which is meant for "young people like Stan."[22]

Johnny Keane noted how much breaking the Wagner record meant to Stan, commenting that it "is the first time I've ever seen Stan show emotion in all the years I've been with the club." Keane helped Stan more than once during this big year by being attentive to The Man's state of mind. One day in Cincinnati Stan was frustrated at popping up at a crucial moment in which a hit or a long fly could have given his team a chance to win the first game of a double hitter. Knowing that Musial's frustration was heightened by the prospects of the two days he would have to wait for a chance to redeem himself, Keane broke with what had been the usual pattern and played Stan in the nightcap. Putting a hand on Stan's shoulder Keane declared, "You're playing the second game, Stan ... and you'll get four hits." Musial did not quite fulfill that prophecy, but he was delighted with the three hits he did get and greatly appreciated his manager's perceptive support.[23]

Stan broke Mel Ott's longstanding record for runs when he scored his 1,860th run. The breakthrough brought attention to one of the often overlooked aspects of Musial's talents. From the start of his major-league career he had always been a great runner of the bases. He had been one of the fastest of the "St. Louis Swifties," but, even as he lost his speed to age and injuries he remained a cunning and opportunistic base runner, usually able to judge when he could grab an extra base and often willing to try. This underestimated knack became especially apparent to some commentators when the no-longer-speedy Musial stole two bases in 1962. Stan got the biggest kick out of the base swipe he accomplished in a game at Wrigley Field attended by his son Dick, a fleet young man whose sports were track and football and who happened to have taken a break from his studies at Notre Dame to come over to Chicago to see his Old Man play. Though Stan also hit a home run in that contest, all his son wanted to talk about after the game was his father's unexpected mad dash for second base.[24] Stan in turn was proud of his son who graduated in June of 1962, becoming the first member of the Musial clan to earn a college degree. Musial's oft-professed yearning for a college education for himself was evident in the surprising timing of Stan's receiving an honorary doctorate from Monmouth College the day after his son's cap-and-gown ceremony.[25]

With the terrific first half Stan had in 1962 it was a forgone conclusion that he would be selected for the All-Star Game, which was held in Washington, DC. While in the nation's capitol, Musial, who had campaigned for President Kennedy, was delighted to be invited to visit the White House, where he and Kennedy shared their joke that, though Musial and Kennedy were close in age, one was considered surprisingly old for his sports prominence while the other was considered surprisingly young for his governmental elevation. When Kennedy jokingly tried to pin Stan down about his retirement plans, Musial responded like a politician, saying he had not yet made that decision.[26]

Among Stan's hitting highlights in 1962 were the four consecutive home runs he slugged at the Polo Grounds just before the All-Star break. The last three homers were in one game, and this time his wife, who had missed his previous three-homer-games for various reasons, was in the stands to see all three of Stan's circlings of the bases.

Stan set new records frequently in his last two seasons. The records that meant the most to Stan were those associated with players, such as Wagner, who he had admired in his youth. For instance, he got a big kick out of breaking Mel Ott's National League RBI record, particularly since he did it by means of a two-run homer off a tough-to-hit young pitcher named Don Drysdale. His surpassing of Ty Cobb's major league record for total bases was another thrill. In commenting on his one-record-after-another progress though his concluding seasons Musial responded to reporters in his typically modest way, repeating often his notion that he had been a "lucky" man to have had so many healthy seasons.[27]

A "Stan Musial Day" was staged in New York City by the Mets. It was highly unusual for an opposing player to be honored in that way. It was, in fact, the first time it had happened in the eighty-year history of the Polo Grounds—but it was a heartfelt tribute on the part of a city where Musial had accomplished some of his most remarkable feats. It was the city whose Brooklyn fans had made him The Man. Congratulatory messages came from far and wide. President Kennedy's message told Stan that, "You make us all believe that life really begins at forty." The plaque given to Musial on behalf of the Mets by Casey Stengel was an interesting document for a number of reasons: "The New York fans, through the Mets, salute the greatest player of his generation for over two decades. Stan Musial of the St. Louis Cardinals has enhanced the prestige of the National League both on and off the field."[28] This salute would seem to fly in the face of the Joe DiMaggio's routine insistence, frequently made in New York contexts, that he be referred to as "the greatest living baseball player." It does not seem likely that Mets would have intended their tribute to Musial as primarily an anti-Yankee or anti-DiMaggio gesture, and, of course, DiMaggio's generation could be interpreted as slightly earlier than Musial's, but the festivities were certainly a declaration that the Mets, who had brought National League baseball back to the Big Apple, wanted to lay claim to New York City's great tradition in the senior circuit by conspicuously celebrating the NL's most revered superstar.

Musial, who had always loved playing in New York, was deeply moved by the tribute and found it difficult to overcome his emotions and speak to the crowd that evening. He declared: "I especially want to thank the Mets for bringing National League baseball back to New York."[29] It had, furthermore, been a difficult several days as he tried to gather his family in New York for the festive moment. Difficulties with lodgings and transportation caused him anxious moments. Because of how little sleep he had gotten before the game, Keane wanted to let him rest on the bench for the entire contest. But, with fans steadily chanting, "We want Musial," the manager had no choice but to bring him in as a pinch hitter. Amidst all the commotion, the Mets pitcher could not get the ball over the plate and was roundly booed by the New York crowd as he issued a walk on four pitches to Musial, who was then taken out for a pinch runner and given a resounding send off by the crowd.[30]

Musial seriously considered retiring on the very high note of his 1962 triumphs, but he could not bring himself to quit because he "was having too much fun hitting," especially when manager Johnny Keane and general manager Bing Devine were enthusiastically urging him to continue. In a historically curious development eighty-one-year-old Branch Rickey, brought in as a consultant by Busch, publically and repeatedly called for Musial to retire. In his prime Rickey had made a habit of selling or trading expensive stars when they were in their prime or slightly past it so as to leverage their value in the open market. It had always been a canny strategy and sometimes worked out well enough when Rickey's farm system was producing a surplus of talented players, but this sell-off-the-best-guys philosophy had often infuriated fans and players. Musial himself always claimed that the early unloadings of such stars as Johnny Mize, Walker Cooper, and Harry Walker had prevented the Cardinals from extending the dominance that their 1940s excellence might have made possible. Rickey's unsolicited pronouncements concerning what he felt was the necessity of discarding Musial created genuine problems for Bing Devine. Rickey had a hard time accepting that Devine, who had long ago been one of his office boys, was now a boss whose authority Rickey would have to yield to. Busch finally put the matter to rest by declaring his support for Devine and Devine's belief in the value of keeping Musial on the field.

"Since when do you ask a .330 hitter to retire?" Busch responded, when beset by reporters.[31]

Musial was excited about the Cardinals' prospects for 1963 and agreed with Devine's decision to trade for talented veterans like Dick Groat and George Altman in hopes of short-term success rather than subscribing to the rebuilding-year strategy advocated by Rickey. Groat, especially, proved essential to the Cards' strong performances in both 1963 and 1964; he challenged for the batting championship in 1963 and provided the sort of stability and leadership at the short-stop position that the Redbirds had long lacked. The Cardinals started the regular season strong, helped by excellent pitching—with Ray Washburn, Bob Gibson, Ernie Broglio, and Curt Simmons all looking impressive—before falling into several slumps, but Musial was feeling his age and often found himself unable to rise to the occasion. In particular, he seemed a liability in the field where he was finding it hard to get to fly balls he would have easily pocketed in his days as the Donora Greyhound.[32]

At the plate he was troubled that "he just wasn't able to concentrate" as he had been able to in his prime. Too often he was taking called third strikes that he would have recognized as hittable and swung at in his younger days. Doctors commenting on his situation suggested that his eyes might have lost their focus or his reflexes gone rusty. He disliked remarks by reporters to the effect that his many business and family concerns may have distracted him, but he had no answer to such charges other than to admit that, yes, he was getting older and aging was taking a toll in ways that were undeniable though hard to identify in any specific way. One family matter that seems to have distracted him more than a little was the difficult pregnancy of his son's wife and the anticipation of the birth of his first grandchild, which finally happily happened in mid-September. After hearing that good news Stan passed out cigars and then went out and hit a two-run homer against the Cubs. It happened that the game at which Stan was handing out cigars was prefaced by a brief alumni game involving retired Cardinals stars. When the aging versions of Joe Medwick and Terry Moore shouted, "Hey, Gramp, you belong with us," all Stan could manage by way of reply was a laughing, "Next year!"[33]

Injuries hampered Musial's performance on a number of occasions. A badly pulled muscle behind his right knee, suffered in June, was followed by a ruptured blood vessel in the same knee the next day. His problematic knee kept him in and out of the lineup for the better part of a month and made it difficult for him to maintain his timing and confidence at the plate.[34]

Facing an annual where-are-we-now meeting with Bing Devine, Musial came to the difficult decision and informed Devine that he was ready to announce that 1963 would be his last year. Stan wanted to make the announcement in

St. Louis and to tell his teammates first. Devine suggested Stan divulge his decision at the Cardinals' annual mid-August picnic at Gussie Busch's Grant's Farm. Stan reflected afterward that the high emotions of the occasion might have been accentuated by the gloomy, rain-soaked nature of that afternoon. In response to Stan's announcement Ken Boyer spoke for his teammates as he thanked Stan for being "an inspiration, the leader who's won for us" and went on to call Stan "the greatest player who ever put on a uniform." Other responses were in a similar vein with the Cards' traveling secretary Leo Ward remarking that "watching Musial hit" has been one of the best parts of his job and Johnny Keane stating that his "greatest thrill has been putting on the same uniform as Stan Musial." Endeavoring to gain some positive leverage out of the sad moment, Musial declared that he would "like to go out on a winner. Our 1942 club was farther behind and won." He went on to say, "I've dreamed for a long time of playing in one more World Series. I think we still have a chance to do it." These inspirational sentiments do not seem to have had any immediate impact on the slumping Redbirds, but in September the Cardinals were to catch fire and almost make Musial's wishful thinking a reality.[35]

An unexpected effect of Musial's announcement was that the rest of the season came to be a nationwide farewell-to-Stan party. Deeply moved by the many expressions of appreciation in opposing ballparks as his team proceeded through its road trips, Stan found concentration hard to come by, remarking, "Whenever there was a ceremony bidding me good-bye, I didn't hit a lick."[36]

Completing a three-game sweep of the formerly red-hot Phillies at the beginning of September, the Cardinals suddenly felt confident and went on a rampage, winning nine in a row and then, after one loss to the Pirates, went on to ten in a row. This amazing stretch drive that saw the Cardinal win nineteen out of twenty was the most remarkable streak Musial had witnessed since the beginning of his major league career. It seemed a reinvention of the amazing comeback of 1942 that enabled the Cardinals to catch and best the hard-driving Brooklyn Dodgers of those days. In the 1963 version of the big comeback the Cards were chasing the Dodgers, just as they were in 1942, but this time the Los Angeles version of the team did not succumb to the Redbird rush. The Cardinals' surge ended in the closing days of the season when they were swept three in a row by Sandy Koufax and company.[37]

Among the delights of the winning streak for Musial was the revival—by Bob Hyland, son of the late Cardinal physician, and Bob Bauman, Doc Weaver's successor as Cardinal trainer—of the grand tradition of inducing Redbirds to play spectacular baseball by means of the exquisitely goofy theme song of 1942 and 1946, "Pass the Bisquits, Mirandy." In order to secure that oddball tune the junior Hyland had to track down Spike Jones in Beverly Hills and persuade him to provide a copy of the dubious classic. Hearing that tune blaring from the clubhouse record player delighted Stan—evoking memories of the long-ago, happy days of his youth when he endeavored to play the slide whistle in the midst of the unlikely combo of Doc Weaver strumming a twangy mandolin, Harry Walker beating on coat hangers, and Johnny Beazley attempting to get the lyrics right in an off-key tenor voice.[38]

Although on the brink of retirement, Musial "felt like a kid," reveling in the pennant-fever happiness of the moment. In the first game of the series, Musial hit the last home run of his career, number 475, and the crowd of 32,444 went berserk, especially since Stan's last blast to the pavilion roof tied the score and seemed to auger a favorable outcome, but the Dodgers carried the day and clinched the pennant a few days later.[39]

Musial had, as he had so often done in the past, performed well against the long-time rival Dodgers with an average of .325 against them for the season, but his overall average for the season had dropped to .255 over the long haul of his wearyingly festive final season. In retrospect it seems likely that his numbers would have been better had he saved the announcement for the postseason and allowed himself to have a more normal summer, but Stan expressed no regrets and declared that he was proud to have finished his career with the 1963 Cardinals, "a club that wouldn't quit."[40]

The last game of the season for the Cardinals, which took place in St. Louis, was turned into a grand farewell party for Stan the Man. Reporters and photographers followed Musial throughout the day leading up to the game. The account of the day by W. C. Heinz for *Life* was to be the most widely circulated. His getting dressed in the locker room had to be restaged several times so that all photographers could get the shots they wanted. While the journalists concentrated on Stan's every move, prankster Sam Jones hovered behind them spraying sneeze powder, which set off a fit of sneezing and watery eyes. When Stan himself began to sneeze, Jones retreated to his locker pretending to stifle his laughter. Every so often Stan would exclaim, "I've changed my mind! I'm not going to retire!" After having finally finished putting on his uniform for the last time and having patiently answered all the rather repetitive questions, Stan withdrew to Johnny Keane's office to review and revise the farewell remarks he had written on index cards. During batting practice, fans cheered Stan's every line drive, and he was asked to autograph bats, balls, and all sorts of other things by players on both the Cardinals and the Cincinnati Reds. One of the Reds players who approached him was a young second baseman named Peter Rose who would eventually surpass Musial's National League hits record.

After circling the stadium in a convertible with his family, Stan began the ceremony by walking to the microphone area in front of home plate. Players for the Cardinals were lined up along one baseline, and players for the Reds along the other. A pair of Cub Scouts bestowed a Scout neckerchief on Stan, which he wore for the rest of the program. A parade of speakers offered tributes. Ken Boyer presented Stan with a ring from the players with number 6 set in diamonds, a gift that Stan especially appreciated because his World Series rings from the 1940s had been stolen from his home several years before. Harry Carey enjoined Stan to "hit one more out on Grand Avenue." Johnny Keane paused at the end of his remarks and choked out, "I try to picture the clubhouse after the game. . . . " and as his voice faltered, Stan bowed his head and began to cry softly. Gussie Busch made the expected announcement about the retirement of Stan's number because, he remarked, "Nobody could do it justice." Commissioner Ford Frick's tribute seemed to have been inspired, in part, by a Wordsworth poem. Frick's felicitous sentences—"Here stands baseball's perfect warrior. Here stands baseball's perfect knight"—were later to be inscribed on the Musial statue. There was a playing and stadium-wide singing of "Auld Lang Syne," and then Stan was awarded a drawing in which he was shown leaning on a bat and signing an autograph for a boy. The drawing was made by *St. Louis Post-Dispatch* cartoonist, Amadee, under the direction of Bob Broeg. The drawing, which was derived from the famous *Saturday Evening Post* cover by John Falter, was meant to be the basis for a bronze statue of Stan for which Broeg and others were endeavoring to raise money.

In his brief, emotional speech Stan thanked his wife and children "for their strong support for a part-time husband and father," and thanked God "for giving me the talent I have and the good health I have been blessed with." He also thanked "baseball" for revealing to him "the opportunity that America offers any young man who wants to get to the top in anything."

The ceremonial nature of the occasion was evident even in Stan's first at bat against big Jim Maloney, the Reds fireballing a twenty-three-game winner. After the first pitch was thrown to Stan, time called and the ball was put aside for delivery to the Hall of Fame. Not surprisingly Stan lost some concentration and struck out looking that first time up, but he made up for it by getting two dramatic hits and contributing significantly to the Cardinals' victory. After being taken out for a pinch runner after his second hit, Stan found more interviewers and cameras awaiting him in the clubhouse. Musial noted to reporters that his concluding game offered an interesting pair with his first 1941 game for the Cardinals, when he also contributed two hits and the team also won three to two. Stan's longtime friend Frank Pizzica reflected on the feelings of the Donora contingent after Stan had left the field. "We just sat there," Pizzica said, "and thought of being associated with someone who's ranked with Ruth and Cobb. I cried today and I tell you unashamedly."[41]

On October 20, a testimonial dinner was held for Stan as the culminating event of what St. Louis Mayor Tucker had declared to be the "Stan Musial Day." The dinner at the Chase Park Plaza Hotel, for which Joe Garagiola was the master of ceremonies, was a fundraiser, sponsored by the St. Louis members of the Baseball Writers Association to raise money in support of the proposed Musial statue. Among the more amusing speakers was Pittsburgh manager Danny Murtaugh who declared with wisecracking vehemence, "I have been looking forward to this day for many, many years. If I'd known Stan was waiting for money for a statue, I'd have donated it years ago."[42]

Stan knew that he was to be a vice president for the Cardinals as part of what the future would hold, but exactly what that job would entail and what sort of future he might have as a baseball executive was not at all clear. He was confident, however, that his businesses would support his family. He faced the future without the financial anxieties that beset many retiring athletes. He hoped, nevertheless, that he might be able to contribute in some genuine way to the Cardinal's future success.[43]

NOTES

1. John Snyder, *Cardinals Journal* (Cincinnati, OH: Emmis Books, 2006), 436–437.

2. Stan Musial and Bob Broeg, *Stan Musial: "The Man's" Own Story as Told to Bob Broeg* (New York: Doubleday, 1964), 211.

3. James Giglio, *Musial: From Stash to Stan the Man* (Columbia: University of Missouri Press, 2001), 240.

4. Jerry Lansche, *Stan "The Man" Musial: Born to Be a Ballplayer* (Dallas, TX: Taylor, 1994), 170.

5. Musial and Broeg, *Stan Musial*, 211–214.

6. Ray Robinson, *Stan Musial: Baseball's Durable "Man"* (New York: Putnam, 1963), 165.

7. Bob Broeg, "Stan Musial's Fight to Keep Playing." *Sport*, April 1963, 29–31, 84–86.

8. Ibid., 84–86.

9. Musial and Broeg, *Stan Musial*, 217–218.

10. Ibid., 218–220.

11. Giglio, *Musial*, 242–244.

12. Musial and Broeg, *Stan Musial*, 221.

13. David Halberstam, *October 1964* (New York: Random House, 1994), 106–118.

14. Musial and Broeg, *Stan Musial*, 222.

15. Ibid., 222–223.

16. Lansche, *Stan "The Man" Musial*, 179–180.

17. Robinson, *Stan Musial*, 168.

18. Lansche, *Stan "The Man" Musial*, 188.

19. Wagner resembled Musial in being a nice guy as well as a super player. See Bill James, *The New Bill James Historical Baseball Abstract* (New York: Simon & Schuster, 2001), 591–592.

20. Lansche, *Stan "The Man" Musial*, 181–182.

21. "A Saint with Money." *Time*, May 25, 1962, 53–54.

22. Broeg, "Musial's Fight to Keep Playing," 85.

23. Musial and Broeg, *Stan Musial*, 224.

24. Robinson, *Stan Musial*, 173–174.

25. Musial and Broeg, *Stan Musial*, 227.

26. Robinson, *Stan Musial*, 184–185; Giglio, *Musial*, 249–252.

27. Musial and Broeg, *Stan Musial*, 226–227.

28. Lansche, *Stan "The Man" Musial*, 186.

29. Giglio, *Musial*, 260–261.

30. Musial and Broeg, *Stan Musial*, 228–229.

31. Halberstam, *October 1964*, 31–34; Musial and Broeg, *Stan Musial*, 233.

32. Musial and Broeg, *Stan Musial*, 234–236.

33. Musial and Broeg, *Stan Musial*, 236–238; Giglio, *Musial*, 268.

34. Giglio, *Musial*, 266.

35. Musial and Broeg, *Stan Musial*, 237; Giglio, *Musial*, 267–268; Lansche, *Stan "The Man" Musial*, 192.

36. Musial and Broeg, *Stan Musial*, 236–237.

37. Gigio, *Musial*, 268; Musial and Broeg, *Stan Musial*, 237–239.

38. Musial and Broeg, *Stan Musial*, 238.

39. Giglio, *Musial*, 268; Musial and Broeg, *Stan Musial*, 239–240.

40. Musial and Broeg, *Stan Musial*, 240.

41. W. C. Heinz, "Stan Musial's Last Day." *Saturday Evening Post*, October 11, 1963, 96–98; Musial and Broeg, *Stan Musial*, 240–243; Giglio, *Musial*, 269–271; Lansche, *Stan "The Man" Musial*, 195–197.

42. Giglio, *Musial*, 272.

43. Ibid., 274–275.

Stan addressing the crowd in the plaza outside Busch Stadium in 1968 at the ceremonial unveiling and dedication of *Musial*, an eighteen-foot-tall bronze sculpture by Carl Mose. *National Baseball Hall of Fame Library, Cooperstown, NY.*

MR. CARDINAL

Musial's knowledge that he would be serving as a vice president for the St. Louis Cardinals after his retirement must have been a comforting thought to him. He avoided, for the most part, the sorts of downfalls many, even wealthy, stars endured once they were off the field. His several successful businesses positioned him well to make the jump to retirement a much less anxiety-arousing transition than it usually is for professional athletes. But, though he was not worried about being able to feed his family and pay for advanced schooling for his children, it would have been difficult for Stan to break off his deep-felt emotional connection to baseball with the abruptness that retirement routinely entails.

The cord to Cardinal baseball that was never cut proved valuable to both Stan and his team. Serving as a living symbol of a great tradition enabled the preservation of his legend in the place in which it was most readily and fully grasped and worshipped. Though often neglected or sidestepped in the grand story of American baseball, as narrated at greatest length by writers with East Coast affiliations, Musial and the Cardinals have nurtured one another in their somewhat solitary bastion on the Mississippi River.

Musial began participating in business meetings for the Redbirds in September of 1963, even before having played his last game. Though no detailed job description for his early position as a Cardinals vice president appears to be available, there was mention in his 1963 player contract of the expectation that he would be making public appearances for the Cardinals for at least thirteen years into the future. From the start it was understood that he would continue to serve as a popular face for the team's promotions. The value of Musial as a commodity in this regard is demonstrated by the more than fifteen hundred invitations to speaking engagements he received shortly after he retired. That striking quantity of requests is one sort of demonstration of how busy Musial could have been in the mid-to-late 1960s if he had allowed himself to respond, even on a small scale, to the demands his popularity and fame generated.[1]

One invitation he did not turn down came from President Lyndon Johnson who wanted Stan to take over as the Special Consultant to the President on Physical Fitness from former football coach Bud Wilkinson who was stepping down from this prestigious, but potentially time consuming, part-time job. The President's Council on Physical Fitness to which Musial's position was attached had been established in the Eisenhower administration in response to the concern that American citizens seemed to be in worse physical shape than European citizens. With the emergence of the Cold War and the call for athletic vigor by the Kennedy administration, there seemed to be some urgency to the cause of fitness. Musial's national familiarity and his well-publicized reliance, late in his career, on a concerted off-season program to keep himself viable as a topnotch athlete made him an ideal candidate for the post. His miraculous comeback from over-the-hill washout to reborn superstardom in his penultimate season seemed the most eloquent sort of testimony concerning the efficacy of fitness.[2] President Johnson, noting the symbolic importance of Musial at the time of the appointment, remarked, "There are few men who have served as American heroes with such dignity."[3]

The job was mostly a volunteer effort whose small monetary compensations were seen as beside the point, and, as a largely figurehead director, Musial could not easily exert leadership in the context of the volunteer council over which he had no real authority, but, as a bully pulpit for the advocacy of fitness and as a visible position from which he could network with important people in American sport, business, entertainment, and governmental circles, it was a very attractive proposition, and Stan seems to have enjoyed it immensely. The Cardinals were happy to approve this multitasking on the part of their new vice president in view of the additional prominence it gave him as a spokesman for sport in general, while still remaining a spokesman for the Cardinals in particular. Though he may not have been able to do everything he might have liked for the fitness program by the time he finally resigned in 1967, he was able to point out in his final report several areas of gain in the popularity of the program and the participation in it by state, city, and private organizations. President Johnson remained appreciative of Musial's efforts throughout, though some members of the government complained that Stan too often gave priority to his baseball obligations when multiple enterprises competed for his attention.[4]

His new Washington connection did not, in fact, deter Stan from participating in the activities of the Cardinals organization during the Redbirds' 1964 season, a tumultuous and surprising season which would culminate with the team winning its first World Series since 1946. Many reporters would ask Stan, after the Cardinals secured the 1964 championship, if he did not regret his retirement the year before. Musial's reply to such queries was a firm denial that there was anything to regret. Had he not retired, Stan reasoned, Bing Devine would not have traded for Lou Brock, the crucial missing piece of the puzzle that made them a championship team. With typical modesty Stan repeatedly explained that a 1964 Cardinals with a Musial instead of a Brock in left field could not have gone all the way. Although this view makes complete sense, in view of the sensational contributions of Brock, Stan must have realized that there could have been scenarios where the Cardinals acquired Brock without discarding Musial. Stan's emphatic answer provided him with an effective way to fend off the too often repeated question, but there must have been some moments in which he thought about how satisfying it would have been to have been on the field for one more championship season.[5]

Stan was deeply appreciative of what Bing Devine had accomplished in putting together the team that won it all in 1964. Besides pulling off one of the greatest trades in baseball history by dealing a soon-to-fade Ernie Broglio to the Cubs for the previously underappreciated Brock, Devine had also acquired such crucial contributors as Curt Flood, Bill White, Dick Groat, and Julian Javier and brought up from the minors such essential people as Mike Shannon and the remarkable veteran rookie knuckleballing reliever Barney Schultz. Busch's misguided decision to fire Devine just before the Cards heated up and began their drive for the pennant led to the unfortunate postseason resignation of Johnny Keane and much resentment toward Busch on the part of the players; however, the decision to fill the managerial vacancy for the following year with Stan's old friend Red Schoendienst, who had been serving as a coach for the Cardinals and was universally liked and respected by the players, resolved the discontent. Certainly Musial, from his vantage point on the sidelines, was delighted that Red would be helming the team in 1965.[6]

Before the issue was decided in 1964, Stan greatly enjoyed many aspects of his retired status. For instance, he was able to witness such spectacles as the Indianapolis 500 and the Kentucky Derby. He could not have even considered attending such events during his more than two decades as a professional baseball player, and the chance to do such things was a welcome development.[7] The freedom to have a life beyond baseball during the warm-weather months of spring, summer, and early autumn offered many welcome opportunities.

Stan was, however, a hardworking guy, as he always had been. Back in 1955 Ogden Nash had speculated in "The Tycoon," a poem on Musial written for *Life* magazine, that "The business life of Mr. Musial/ is, to say the least, unusual./ First base, outfield, restaurant, bank,/ all are home to Stanley Frank." Nash concluded his paean to Stan's multitasking by saying, "no one grudges success to Stan,/ good citizen and family man,/ though I would love to have his job—/ one half tycoon, one half Ty Cobb."[8] Energetically tackling the challenges of his several jobs Musial saw no problem in the large number of his commitments. Because his responsibilities for each job were flexible, he felt he could coordinate them in such a way that all could be handled at the same time without difficulty. Musial explained his rather overly optimistic view of this strategy to a reporter: "The only thing that makes it possible to do two or more jobs at once is that I can coordinate them. As vice-president of the Cardinals, I'm not tied down to their office in St. Louis. My job during the baseball season is to scout talent, sign players, help young hitters, and make public relations appearances. I can fit that in with my travels around the country."[9] This balancing act could, however, have its complications. For instance—after Musial said no to an invitation to participate in a sports parade in Bloomington, Minnesota because of St. Louis obligations—it was discovered by a member of the chamber of commerce of that town that Stan had actually come to the town on that day to scout a college baseball player. Though Musial was, indeed, preoccupied with Cardinal business on that day—the Bloomington official was not happy with Stan's handling of the matter.[10]

Despite the multiple demands of his duties as a businessman, baseball executive, and fitness program director—Stan endeavored to travel with the Cardinals as often as he could. Following the game from the stands offered comforts of relaxation, hotdogs, and beer that he had formerly had to avoid. In the midst of his hectic schedule, Stan was having a great time, but it became evident that he was overextending himself when he collapsed while watching a Cardinal game at Busch Stadium on September 1, 1964. He suffered from uncontrollable vomiting and was briefly disoriented. He was diagnosed as having viral enteritis and was said to be suffering from dehydration and exhaustion. Ironically, considering that he was the point man for a physical-fitness initiative, Stan had allowed himself to fall somewhat out of shape physically after his retirement, and his indulgence in stadium food and his employer's beverage appear to have taken their toll. After his recovery from this distressing incident, Stan strove to return to healthier habits to lead his fitness mission more fully by his own example.[11]

After the Cardinals defeated the Yankees in the seventh game of the World Series to gain the 1964 championship, a celebration was held at a new Musial and Biggie's Restaurant that Stan and company had opened recently in a prime location near Forest Park. Stan was pleased that Cardinals sportscaster Jack Buck, addressing the assembled Cardinals staff and boosters, spoke in praise of the great efforts of Bing Devine, calling him the primary builder of the victorious team. Musial admired Buck's courageous saying of what everyone was thinking in that regard, especially since Buck was only Harry Caray's side man in the broadcast booth in those days and was by no means secure in his position if Busch had decided to take umbrage at his remarks.[12]

The Cardinals new general manager Bob Howsam was later to be a big success in Cincinnati, and has been given some of the credit for helping build the Big Red Machine there, but in St. Louis his aloof, no-nonsense style was not popular with the players and others—following, as it did, the reign of the more personable Devine. With the players and the fans, however, the hiring of Red Schoendienst covered a multitude of sins. Though he had never managed before, Red was a familiar and respected figure as a player and coach. On the same day as the announcement of Schoendienst's hire, Branch Rickey, who had supported Howsam's preference for filling the management slot with Charely Metro, was dismissed from his role as a consultant for the Cardinals. Rickey's role in the downfall of Bing Devine was a lingering gripe with Busch, who was glad to be free of the irascible Rickey's influence. Though the Cardinals did not perform well in the first two years of Schoendienst's tenure, Busch stuck with the likable redhead, and he was to go on to have the longest term as manager in Cardinals' history, serving through the summer of 1976. Musial's friend and longtime roommate weathered the storms of Busch's frustration over the Cardinals' underachieving performances during his first two seasons at the helm, as the Cardinals finished seventh in 1965 and sixth in 1966.[13]

In 1966 the Cardinals departed from their longtime home in old Busch Stadium (a.k.a. Sportsman's Park) to make their way down to the banks of the Mississippi River to take up residence in the new Busch Stadium—one of the many round stadiums built in the 1960s and 70s to accommodate both baseball and football. In each of the last twelve games in the old stadium living legends of that old ballpark's distinguished past were honored, one honoree for each game. Musial was, of course, one of those honored, as were Jesse Haines, Joe Medwick, Frankie Frisch, Chick Hafey, Dizzy Dean, Terry Moore, Johnny Mize, Enos Slaughter, Marty Marion, Red Schoendienst, and George Sisler. Sisler was the only representative of the St. Louis Browns, the team that owned the park for much of its history.[14]

As a senior vice president for the Cardinals during 1964, 1965, and 1966– Musial was able to contribute to discussions preliminary to management decisions, expressing his opinions concerning proposed trades and other matters. For instance, Stan witnessed Howsam's vacillations over the proposed trade of Ray

Sadecki to the Giants for Orlando Cepeda. Musial's many years of conversation with Stoneham made him aware that Stoneham, too, would be touchy about such a deal and that the arrangement would be likely to fall through if Howsam asked for more than an even swap. Despite Cepeda's questionably healed knee and the rumors that he had been a difficult personality in San Francisco, his potential superstardom made him worth the risk in the view of Musial and others. In particular, Musial and Schoendienst advocated taking the risk because Cepeda's potential greatness could make up for what had been lost in the offense and the defense when Bill White had been traded.[15] Musial and the rest of the pro-Cepeda faction saw their recommendation result in the acquisition of a central figure of a championship team in the making. Stan's participation in such discussions familiarized him with the business of running the ballclub so that when Howsam, aware that Busch was on the verge of firing him, secured a job with the Cincinnati Reds, and the boss asked Stan to replace Howsam as general manager—Musial felt ready to say yes to the proposition without a moment's hesitation.[16] Just before he officially became general manager, Stan was able to express his support for picking up another important piece of the puzzle, Roger Maris. Frustrated with the Yankees and New York City, Maris had been set to retire when the trade to the Cardinals emerged as a possibility. Though the trade was officially Howsam's last deal, Musial "showed a Midas touch when he pulled the trigger in a deal for Maris." Had Musial not persuaded Maris that the Cardinals and St. Louis would treat him well Roger might have decided to go ahead with his original plan and retire.[17] Bob Gibson felt that Musial had made a "bold move" to secure Maris despite the reservations expressed concerning him.[18]

A number of journalistic pundits were skeptical about Musial's chances for success as a general manager. Shirley Povich of the *Washington Post* speculated that Musial's nice guy tendencies could make him easy prey for the ruthless executives on other teams. She pictured them "rubbing their hands at the prospect of doing business" with Stan.[19] Some wondered why Stan would even consider taking on this problematic task, especially considering the modest salary of $35,000, which seemed all the more problematic in view of Busch's decision to continue the policy he had started with Howsam of not giving his baseball executives a contract of any sort. One commentator states the situation this way: "The question of the month in baseball: Why did Stan Musial, headache-free and independent, take the general managership of the Cardinals. He is not a 9-to-5 guy, and even his friends, which number 1,863,467 at last count, say he isn't tough enough."[20]

Jimmy Cannon addressed a column to Musial, twisting Stan's nickname to call him "The (Lonesome) Man." Cannon argued that Stan would not be able to be himself anymore. The famous columnist patronizingly declared that Stan would have a hard time understanding that he would have to hurt people to survive as a

GM. Cannon suggested, somewhat between the lines, that Stan would eventually be expected to fire his best friend Red and might not have the stomach for the task.[21] Dick Young's column reported a conversation with Musial in which he confronted Stan on the toughness issue, asking him directly if he would be able to fire his good friend. Stan rightfully dismissed the question as premature, indicating his belief that Red was the Walter-Alston-type manager and would be likely to last a long time in the job. Stan's prediction, of course, came true.[22] Stan's good friend Bob Broeg, not surprisingly, predicted success for Stan and Red; however, Stan may have been surprised to read Broeg's mention that Stan's lack of talents in the areas of "articulation and pronunciation" could cause him problems in the public arena. No doubt Broeg had in mind continuing as Musial's ghostwriter and Boswell as his friend moved onward and upward.[23] Despite Broeg's concerns for Musial's public speaking tools, Stan seemed to experience no obvious difficulties of that sort as he made the rounds of press interviews concerning his appointment. Hardly intimidated by the doubters, Stan asserted on several occasions that Busch had wanted him to take the job right after he retired as a player: "I could have had the general manager job three years ago. . . . Gussie Busch would have given me anything I wanted, but I didn't think I was ready for the job at the time."[24]

Stan's wife, Lil, saw his rise to the top job in the Cardinals organization as an important fulfillment for her husband: "What has impressed me most, I think, is coming from a small town and going out into the world. And Stan going from a baseball rookie to a world figure as he is today." To explain Stan's knack for doing well in his many pursuits, Lil credited Stan's patience and independence of judgment: "Stan won't yield to pressure. He makes up his own mind when he's ready. I've learned to wait." Laughing about the the surprising nature of this new executive development in Stan's career, Lil confessed that Stan's capacity for ascendency seemed to be boundless: "Wonders never cease with this man of mine. . . . I hope you'll have to interview me again ten years from now—when Stan has become baseball commissioner."[25] Family expectations took another interesting turn with regard to Stan's mother who felt her boy should insert himself back into the Cardinals lineup as a player. Now that he's the boss, Mary Musial reasoned, he should be able to play whenever he wants. Stan had to explain to his mom that it would not look good if he asserted his authority in that way, and, besides, he had enough to do fielding his position in the front office.[26]

Musial reveled in once again having a key role to play in the Cardinal campaign. He suited up for spring training, delighted to be putting on his old number 6 uniform again. Working out with the players, offering batting tips when asked, and engaging in the chat and camaraderie of the clubhouse, he was able to contribute to the team's relaxed and optimistic demeanor. Had his manager been someone other than his old friend Red, this down-on-the-grass general managing might not have been workable. Stan was, however, careful not to usurp any fraction of Schoendienst's role. He felt comfortable to be out there on the training field as both a friendly participant and an observer of the team's progress. His dual careers as ballplayer and businessman made it relatively easy for him to think in business terms while in the midst of tossing the ball around. It is not something a Howsam or even a Devine could have done, but everyone involved seems to have appreciated Stan's positive presence in the midst of the preseason drills and calisthentics. His salary discussions with players had all been reasonable and generous. He did not give away the factory, but he also did not force players into special pleadings by lowballing his offers. Players appreciated Stan's no nonsense preference for talking immediately about what might be the fairest figure. Musial did, however, sometimes feel hard pressed because of his lack of knowledge of baseball law. Fortunately, the institutional memory of his office staff often came to his aid and, whenever he felt particularly at a loss, Bing Devine, who had was then working as the general manager for the New York Mets, was always willing to field Stan's telephoned questions. Stan was happy with the team he had on the field and made only one major trade in his tenure in the business office, acquiring Jack Lamabe from the Mets to enhance the pitching staff after Bob Gibson suffered a broken leg. Fortunately for Stan and the Redbirds, the emergence of Nelson Briles as a starting pitcher during Gibson's period of recovery, served to keep the Cardinals in the pennant race and the Lamabe insurance was not as crucial as it had seemed to be.[27]

Some commentators theorized that Busch and his minions conceived of the Musial-Schoendienst pairing as a short-term solution to bring fans to the ballpark, with the idea in mind of capitalizing at the ticket window on the immense popularity in St. Louis of these two Cardinal legends; however, Red's selection proved to be a wise move that helped a topnotch group of players realize their potentional.[28] Discussing the nature of his collaboration with his friend the general manager, Schoendienst noted that Stan refrained from visiting the clubhouse too often for fear of impinging on the manager's domain, but kept in constant touch, offering his sharp-eyed observations in a helpful way. Red explained that he could rely on phone calls from Stan "often before a game and always afterward.... Stan has patience, knows the game and we talk about it. He might see something and tell me what he's seen or ask about something."[29]

The close relationship of Schoendienst and Musial made for ease with regard to many matters of consequence for the advancement of the team's chances, including such important improvisations as Red's decision to convert Mike Shannon from a right fielder to a third baseman. Stan thought well of the idea because he trusted Red's instincts. He supported Red's and Mike's determination to make this idea work. Manager and infielder-in-the-making spent long hours in one-on-one sessions, Schoendienst swatting ground ball after ground ball at the much bruised but undeterred Shannon. With Maris, Flood, and Brock firmly established in their positions, Shannon knew he was not likely to get much playing time in the outfield. Mike stopped more balls with his chest than his glove in spring training, but he was a tough, dedicated athlete who had been a football star in college. He had a rocket for an arm and no fear of line drives, both key attributes for a third baseman, and he was determined to secure a meaningful place on the team. This innovative move kept Shannon's big bat and enthusiastic attitude on the field, and he managed to became a solid defensive third baseman.[30]

The Musial-Schoendienst partnership benefited from the mature intelligence of many of the players on the squad. As Nelson Briles has explained it, "Red was the best manager for that ball club, because he was dealing with veterans. He was dealing with players who had won a series in '64, and so they knew what winning was all about. These guys had five, six years of major league experience and so what Red did, what was so important, he stayed out of the way. . . . He let Brock and Flood do their game. Curt would take pitches deep into the count to let Brock steal, and they had their own hit-and-run. They had defensive things they did. Same thing all the way through the lineup. And that was a huge plus."[31]

There was a quiet effectiveness to Musial's general managing that paralleled the low-key good judgments of Red as field manager. The acquisition of Lamabe appeared problematic at first as he failed to do well in his early outings, but ultimately he proved valuable to the team, primarily as a reliable relief pitcher. Musial's success as a wheeler-dealer lay, however, most conspicuously in his decisions *not* to make deals that were on the table at various points before and during the summer of 1967. For instance, in the closing days of the Howsam era, Stan opposed two proposed trades for stars whose contributions could not possibly have made up for the key younger players who would have been lost. Other teams had their eyes on the Cardinal's young talent, but Musial was not going for it. He refused to support a deal that would have sent Nelson Briles, Steve Carlton, Bobby Tolan, and Alex Johnson to the Cubs for Billy Williams; and voted against a swap that would have shipped out Briles, Carlton, Shannon, and Phil Gagliano in exchange for Cincinnati's Leo Cardenas, Gordie Coleman, and Joey Jay. Stan was no Trader Lane and had no desire to be. His belief in the Cardinals' roster as it stood at the outset of his general managership jived perfectly with Schoendienst's supportive demeanor on the field. The 1967 Cardinals, dubbed "El Birdos" by Cepeda, were a team of strong personalities who knew they were good and lived up to that understanding. The calm, patient confidence of the management team that backed them up was key to the relaxed, determined, unflappable nature of the team that would win 101 games in 1967, finishing ten and a half games ahead of the second placed Giants.[32]

The World Series against Boston was an important fulfillment for a talented squad. Lou Brock and Bob Gibson performed so magnificently that both had to be given cars in honor of their MVP-level contributions. Brock hit .414, stole seven bases, and scored eight runs. Gibson struck out twenty-six in his three complete game victories, while allowing only a total of three runs. Postseason veteran Maris came through with a .385 average and seven RBIs. Javier, who had missed most of the action in the 1964 Series because of an injury, hit .360.[33] An oddity of the 1967 festivities was the hoopla in the Boston newspapers concerning what they called "The Impossible Dream" Red Sox team. The frenzied excitement of the Boston press corps was understandable given the long history of Red Sox frustration and the remarkable fact that the 1967 American League championship arrived in Boston one year after the team's disastrous ninth-place finish in 1966. One of the symptoms of the zeal of the Boston newspapers during the series was the commissioning of various players to supply the papers with their daily thoughts about the action in the form of journals edited by reporters. This sort of thing had been done in the past and continues to be done today, but its intensity in 1967 was fueled by the competitive nature of Boston's major papers, each endeavoring to one-up the others with their press coverage. Carl Yastrzemski's thoughts were "corrected and developed" by Cliff Keene for the *Globe*. Jim Lonborg was filtered through Bill Liston for the *Herald Traveler*. The *Record-American* doubled its pleasure by capturing Dick Williams' musings as handled by Larry Claflin and Tony Conigliaro as rendered by Fred Ciampa. All this half-baked rhetoric from Red Sox personnel about themselves and their prospects angered the Cardinals players at various points and provided them with motivation to answer on the field the sometimes provocative Sox proclamations. Most motivating of all was a declaration by Red Sox manager Dick Williams on the eve of the seventh game that seemed, to the Cardinals, unforgivably arrogant. When Williams declared that he expected Jim Lonborg to win for the home team in the final contest, he was simply giving the Boston press and the public the positive message they were eager to hear in what he must have felt was a witty manner, but the prominent assertion that the next day would bring "Lonborg and champagne," which the *Record-American* displayed as a banner headline and other news media distributed far and wide, gave the Cardinals their rallying cry for the final contest. They famously chanted "Lonborg and champagne, hey! Lonborg and champagne, hey!" with mocking vociferousness from their dugout and later in a jubilantly lively musical rendition in their clubhouse after their victory.[34]

Musial's departure from the general manager position two months after the World Series triumph came as a surprise to fans and especially to the press, some of whom were not persuaded by explanations offered by Busch's office. Musial was later to provide plausible reason's for his "retirement," including the sudden death by heart attack of his business partner Biggie Garagnani, which Stan claimed required him to devote more of his time to his restaurant. Most commentators have taken him at his word that it was his decision to retire after one remarkably successful season as a general manager. Are there any other general managers with a batting average of 1,000? Once again, Stan seems to have knocked the cover off the ball.

There were speculations, however, about whether there might be more story to tell about his departure. *Boston Post* sports writer, Al Hirshberg pointed out that Stan's evident delight in the job and the great satisfaction he had in being able to work with longtime comrade Schoendienst would suggest that Stan's sudden departure might not have been entirely to his own liking.[35] Grim-faced photographs of Stan at the press conference in which he and Devine discussed the transition suggest that the ending of Musial's general managership was not a welcome occasion for him.[36] Giglio cites a comment by Musial that he would someday give a fuller account of the "real story" of his stepping down and points out that Stan never did explain further. Giglio speculates that a problem arose over World Series tickets—apparently Stan oversold them.[37] It seems, however, unlikely that a logistical problem of that sort could have been sufficient to end Musial's reign. Although it is not hard to imagine that a quarrel between the hot-tempered Mr. Busch and the sensitive Mr. Musial could have led to Stan's departure from the top post in the Cardinals office, it is likely that Stan did want to get away from what Bob Broeg called "the long telephone hours of a general manager."[38] It is worth mentioning, too, that the opportunity to avoid being constantly on call must have been attractive, especially as he had a very young daughter, Jean, who would have been glad to see her father more often.[39] Overall, the outcome was greatly to Stan's advantage. He had other ways to make money and a continuing career in the precarious field of general managing could only have gone downhill from the success of 1967. With his brief stint as a general manager universally regarded as a walk-off homer, Stan was able to remove himself from the fray with his stature undiminished. Remaining connected to the Cardinals as a vice president, he was able to settle into the role of Mr. Cardinal without being constantly on the spot for the team's ups and downs. Busch's hiring of Bing Devine as Musial's replacement was widely seen as righting an old wrong. Stan was happy to see his longtime friend, colleague, and advisor returning to the Cardinal camp.[40]

In August of 1968 Musial's status as the iconic figure of St. Louis baseball was underscored with the unveiling of an enormous statue memorializing him as the quintessential Cardinal. This monument to Redbird sainthood is remarkable for a number of reasons, not least of which is the fact that Musial was honored in this distinctive way at such a young age. Only forty-seven years old when the statue was completed and just a few years into his retirement, Stan was already deemed deserving to be regarded as a heroic icon of his team's tradition. He was honored in bronze, in fact, a year before he was even eligible to be considered for the Baseball Hall of Fame. The honor involved in being gigantically bronzed in his adopted city even before his plaque went up on the wall in Cooperstown was not lost on Musial. At the unveiling ceremony Stan joked that he was "feeling 18 feet tall" in reference to how high the redoubtable monument rose; it was a ten-foot figure on an eight-foot base. Deeply moved by the occasion Stan also declared, "I want to thank everyone—for my mother and the Musial family—for making me a Cardinal forever." This moment was a crucial one in Stan's life as he became the definitive Mr. Cardinal, leaving behind to some extent, such other identities as The Boy from Donora. Many of the still living "Cardinals legends" who had played with Stan were invited and many attended. In the presence of his many great colleagues Musial was declared the greatest. A feature of the celebration was a reunion of members of the 1941 team who had been there at the start to witness the emergence of the little-known, recently-regarded-as-damaged-goods rookie who was going to go on to become Stan The Man. The 1941 Redbirds who were able to make it to the party included Johnny Beazley, Walker Cooper, Frank Crespi, Erv Dusak, Harry Gumbert, Ira Hutchinson, Howard Krist, Whitey Kurowski, Eddie Lake, Gus Mancuso, Marty Marion, Steve Mesner, Johnny Mize, Terry Moore, Don Padgett, Howie Pollet, Enos Slaughter, Lon Warneke, and Ernie White.[41]

The idea for a monument to Musial came from his good friend Bob Broeg, who had also become a kind of high priest of Stan the Man, and that renowned nickname was itself the result of the writings of Broeg. Brooklyn fans may have been the first to chant "Here comes the Man, again! Here comes the Man!" But it was Broeg who seized upon the possibilities of the name as a means to celebrate the remarkable baseball potency of this quiet, hardworking, mild-mannered citizen of the National Pastime. Stan, Broeg's passionate advocacy declared, was not just one of the best hitters—he was *the* man. Calling him Stan The Man asserted, in the face of whatever anyone might say in favor of other hitters, that this guy was *the* one we should most admire. Broeg was, of course, not alone in his devotion to Musial. For instance, Bob Burnes, the top baseball writer for St. Louis' other big daily newspaper, *The Globe Democrat*, was also a Musial supporter. Burnes, who had started his career as a beat writer for the Browns, was not close to Musial on a day-to-day basis and not as ambitious to undertake literary projects as Broeg; nevertheless, Burnes was also a steady fan of Musial and his legend. Furthermore, in many of the other cities around the country there were sports columnists with a special affection for Musial, regarding him as the ideal of the star player as nice guy. It may sound reductive or sentimental to say that the enthusiasm for a Musial monument had something to do with a groundswell of support for the human decency allied with traditional notions of good sportsmanship that Stan seemed, to many, to represent, but that was, in fact, what was happening. Since its beginnings Major League Baseball had striven to be acceptable to imperatives of moral rightness; however, as hard as baseball has tried to satisfy the moral standards of those who comment on it from Henry Chadwick through Grantland Rice and onward to George Will and company, it has always fallen short. Though all American sports have fallen short in this way, baseball's case is special because it has tried so hard and so long to gain approval.[42] Stan the Man was an interesting case in which the ideal seemed to have been consummated. Even James Giglio's exhaustive searchings for flaws to balance his praise for Stan with some sort of negativity yielded little "dirt" beyond several slightly embarrassing odds and ends—an obscure financial dispute between Stan's family and Joe Garagiola's family, some grumblings from a few folks in Donora who complained in self-serving ways that Stan should have contributed more money to their projects, some mentions of concerns that Stan sometimes drank and smoked a little more than fans knew, and so forth. If these are the worst things the hardworking Mr. Giglio could come up with, perhaps Stan was, indeed, a saint.[43]

When one considers the underlying moral content to the impetus for a Musial monument, it is not surprising that the original design—apparently the idea of Bob Broeg as articulated in sketches and paintings by a member of Broeg's *Post-Dispatch* staff, cartoonist Amadee Wohlshlaeger—was a translation of John Falter's *Saturday Evening Post* cover illustration into a two-figure composition of Stan signing an autograph for an adoring little boy. The design—which Broeg dubbed *The Man and the Boy* and Wohlschlaeger called *Baseball's Bond*—was unveiled at the retirement dinner for Stan that was billed as a fundraiser for the statue. Broeg's and Wohlschlaeger's notion for a memorial would have celebrated the greatness of the nice-guy ideal as much as it would have celebrated Stan's greatness as a player. In fact, Stan's graciousness to fans would have been the content of the statue's message and Stan's greatness as a hitter would have implicit rather than expressed. Broeg's timing for the launching of the fundraiser was good, poised as it was on the tip of the moment of enthusiastic celebration of the retiring superstar. A significant quantity of funds was raised.

Large bronze monuments are, however, expensive. Money was raised from various public and private sources, but eventually pursuit of the project was taken over by the City of St. Louis and the mayor, Raymond Tucker, appointed a committee, which included himself. After some deliberation the committee decided to support the proposal of Carl Christian Mose, a Danish citizen and a former St. Louis resident, who was a long-time friend of Mayor Tucker. Mose had taught for many years at Washington University in St. Louis. I have seen no statement anywhere to the effect that there was cronyism involved in Tucker's choice of Mose, who was a respectable modernist sculptor whose years in St. Louis had given him some claim to insight into the spirit of the area and who had previously established his status as a "local" professional by doing a bronze sculpture of General Pershing to decorate the exterior of Missouri State Capitol in Jefferson City.[44]

In view of the nature of the Musial statue eventually produced, it is clear that Mose and the committee favored a concept for this public sculpture that would be heroic in nature, a warrior-at-the-bat so to speak. This is hardly surprising when one considers the history of public sculpture in America. A heroic, solitary figure, frequently a general on horseback, has a prestige that a genre scene concept such as *The Man and the Boy* would not have. The committee must have reasoned something along these lives: Why should we settle for a vulgar, Norman-Rockwell-style piece when we can have the equivalent of a heroic-warrior image by giving the public an image of Musial in his famous batting stance. To state it in another way: Why give the public a genre-scene sculpture when they could have something akin to Michelangelo's *David*? Unfortunately, if this is the way they thought, Mose was certainly no Michelangelo. As a modernist, he clearly wanted to get to the essence of Musial's stance without actually giving a fully literal depiction of it; he was not a sculptor who possessed the interest in or the draftsmanship skills necessary for the sort of realistic rendering of the famous stance that the committee and the public probably thought was coming during the several years Mose was at work on his Musial. Physical distance probably kept Mose largely safe from the prying eyes of the St. Louis press. Because the sculptor lived in a secluded area outside of Washington, D.C. while he worked on this piece, Mose had lots of access to Musial who regular visited the national capitol in connection with his fitness-council duties, but he had no reason to expect the inquiries and visits from journalists like Broeg and Burnes, which he probably would have had if he had been available in an area easily accessible from St. Louis.

The most substantial article on the statue's development appeared in a D.C. newspaper. In that article Mose explained to interviewer Steve Gruback that he felt he was going to be able to capture Musial's stance. Seemingly attentive to physical particulars, Mose, who had gotten photographs and measurements of Stan of every imaginable sort, commented on how impressed he was with Musial's twenty-two-inch shoulder span. His remarks, in the widely distributed story, suggested an interest in the mechanics of Musial's body as much as its outward appearance, pointing out that, with his wide shoulders, Stan was "like a wedge. That's where he got the power." Exuding confidence, Mose expressed little doubt concerning the prospects for the success of his statue, noting only the limitation that he might not be able to capture "that little wiggle in Musial's stance" and joking that perhaps putting a motor in his statue would bring that element into the figure as well. Guback, who was probably well aware of Bob Broeg's unhappiness over the change in the design from the man-with-boy to the man-with-bat, pressed Mose on the point of resemblance and reported that Mose confessed that a sculptor's work is, like the work of an umpire, "always open for criticism, particularly from the subject, his relatives or friends." Mose admitted "that's a risk you take."[45]

Criticism of the monumental Musial has not been in short supply. Bob Broeg, who had mounted the campaign for the statue, was more than a little distressed by the outcome. Though his group, the St. Louis chapter of the Baseball Writers Association, remained on board with their large financial contribution to the effort—he was never reconciled to what he called "a sad conclusion," particularly in view of the fact that most of his contributors gave their money on the understanding that they were supporting the making of *The Man and the Boy*. Broeg pointed out, with some justification that as much had been made in the publicity about Mose's dedication to capturing Musial's famous stance, the statue's lack of truth in that regard was a failure to deliver on a promise.[46] Broeg must, however, have been reluctant to say much in public about the matter because of his initial spearheading of the initiative and because to disparage the statue could not be helpful to the Musial fandom Broeg was so dedicated to promoting. He understood that a quarrel of that sort would only be hurtful to Stan and would not change the hard fact of the statue's prominent presence as a landmark at the new stadium.

And landmark it certainly did become. A large percentage of Cardinals fans probably voiced to friends and family on many occasions the familiar phrase, "I'll meet you by the Musial statue." The size and distinctiveness of the statue and the universal awareness in St. Louis of The Man and his monolithic accomplishments resulted in the statue assuming a civic usefulness, its ugliness accepted somewhat affectionately as part of its identity.

Admirers of Mose's design, if there are any at this point, might argue that the complaints about the statue are the result of an unsophisticated public not having the capacity to appreciate public art that is not representational in a detailed way. Certainly that point of view would explain some of the criticism, but it also happens to be the case that attacks on the statue have come from viewers with training in the history of public sculpture.[47] The problem, in essence, seems to be that Mose was not honest with either the fans or himself. With his indulgence in a hulkingly abstracted comment on the legendary potency of Stan's stance, Mose probably wanted to think that he was "capturing" some essential aspect of Musial's stature at the plate, but he should have understood that his work was falling between two stools, unsatisfactory as abstraction and unsatisfactory as representation. By giving the figure the heft he felt it should have, the sculptor distorted the graceful artist at the bat that was Stan the Man into a brutish, caveman-like figure. If Mose's preliminary rhetoric had been less focused on an implied realism of approach, the statue's reception might have been better, but, it might be the case that his rhetoric of realistic rendering was what got him the job in the first place. In the end, Musial fans might have felt caught in a bait-and-switch ploy.

In his remarks at the statue's unveiling Stan thanked "Mr. Mose and the wonderful people in St. Louis," but his remark that he would "like to think of this statue as a symbol of sportsmanship"[48] suggests that the moral anecdote provided by a man-and-boy image would have been more to his liking; certainly nothing about Mose's hunchbacked giant has anything to declare about sportsmanship.

Musial was more forthcoming on his feelings about the Mose statue in conjunction with the authorization in 2004 of a larger-than-life bronze of the original man-boy design for the the Missouri Sports Hall of Fame in Springfield, MO. John Hammons, a wealthy individual, contributed $100,000 to commission popular representational sculptor Harry Weber to make the piece, whose title was changed to *The Boy and the Man*, a reversal of words that enhanced the sportmanship content of the concept. Weber had become the sculptor of record for sports images in Missouri. His projects included the numerous action-oriented sculptures of famous St. Louis baseball players designed for the outskirts of Busch Stadium. Weber's five-foot Musial for that project shows Stan just completing his swing. Other five-foot bronze renderings of Gibson, Brock, Schoendienst, Slaughter, and so forth have also been popular with fans. In a well-publicized 2004 session with Weber in connection with the man-boy design, Musial voiced his complaint about the difficulties he had with Mose back in the 1960s. "He'd made me all bulky.... I tried to get him to change it, but he just never would. So finally I told him, 'Well, just go on and get it done.' He never did get it right." Weber, on the other hand, made a public show of seeking Musial's approval, showing Stan a clay mock-up of what he had in mind. One of Weber's revisions of Amadee's original sketch was to have the boy offering a ball rather than a notebook for signature, and Stan objected to this feature saying that few kids back in the old days had clean balls to devote to such purposes. Wanting to keep that nice round ball in the design, Weber protested that he himself had gotten Musial to sign a ball when he was a kid. Stan, who knew Weber's family, stood firm on the issue, indicating that rich people like Weber's father could give their son's balls to have signed, but most of the kids Stan encountered could offer only notepads or scorecards. Accepting the revision, Weber plucked the clay ball from the image and shaped a small notebook in its place. Musial stressed the importance of this change. Florence Shinkle, the author of the article, summarized Stan's feelings on the issue: "The substitution of the notebook for the ball had changed the child into an ordinary fan—one of the thousands upon thousands that Musial had made it a point to sign autographs for, staying late after every game. . . . " Musial remarked on the importance he placed on autographing for fans explaining that "old-time players took care of fans."[49]

On January 21, 1969, Musial was elected to the Hall of Fame on the first ballot. He received 93.2 percent of the votes cast. Many had suggested that he should have received unanimous support, but, when asked, Stan expressed no disappointment with the vote. Pointing out that he had way more than the 75 percent minimum, he indicated that he "was just happy [he] was elected." As was the custom, the ceremony was held outdoors on the steps of the Hall of Fame in Cooperstown in July. It was an overcast day and a light drizzle fell on the participants. Also included in this induction class were catcher Roy Campanella, and two old-timer-committee selections, pitchers Stan Coveleski and Waite Hoyt. When the moment came for Musial to deliver his acceptance speech, the sun suddenly broke through the clouds as if on cue. Pat Dean, wife of Dizzy, remarked that "the sun always shines on Stan the Man." While thanking his elderly mother, who was in the audience, he had to choke back tears as he explained how she had constructed baseballs out scraps of various sorts of material. In paying tribute to his late father he recounted the oft-told story of his father's desire that his eldest son take up college studies rather than professional baseball. As the main theme of his address Stan expanded on his frequently stated conviction that young people should endeavor to pursue a college education and concluded with praise for baseball as a great game that will always remain a great game.[50] Clearly Stan enjoyed his association with the Hall of Fame, as is evidenced by his frequent attendance at the annual induction ceremonies and other festivities and meetings there.[51]

In his quiet way, Stan continued through the 1970s to have the right touch in a variety of businesses ventures, which included an increasing number of restaurants, hotels, sporting goods, and bowling alley operations. Musial's business pursuits mostly thrived into the 1980s, but, as he delegated more of the responsibilities to others some of his businesses did not live up to expectations. Realizing in the late 1980s that his fame made sports memorabilia the best and most appropriate endeavor for him to carry into his later years, he sold or dissolved all of his businesses with the exception of his memorabilia company—Stan the Man, Inc. Though Stan would still often give autographs without charge when approached in person, he realized that things he autographed were being sold by others for hefty amounts and—in view of the fact that he could readily control the production of his personally autographed merchandise—he decided to market the substantial commodity his good name had become. With his understanding of business practices Stan never encountered the underpayment-of-income-tax problems that afflicted Hall of Famers Duke Snider and Willie McCovey, who faced legal difficulties for being less cautious about their autograph-for-pay activities.[52] Visiting the Web site of Stan the Man, Inc. as I was finishing this book in 2007, I found that Musial's prices were modest in view of the price gouging practices of memorabilia venders one encounters in other precincts of the Internet, as well as in the shops along the Mainstreet of Cooperstown. Most small items—autographed photos, prints, caps, and so forth—were in the $75 to $100 range, and there was also a service where Stan would sign and return items sent to him by fans for $100. Within the context of the twenty-first century's culture of celebrity, Stan had found a way to support himself by signing things. The iconic *Saturday Evening Post* cover painting by John Falter showing Musial in autographing mode was, perhaps, receiving a new sort of fulfillment.[53] Jack Buck pointed out an interesting irony of the prospering of Musial's memorabilia business. By the mid-1990s Stan had probably already made far more money from his autograph enterprises than he had earned in total income from his long career as a professional baseball player.[54] Stan had bowed to the realization that his fame had become its own industry. Though he was too often neglected in the baseball books, he was still a household word to baseball fans at large. He could bank, literally, on being famous for being famous. After the turn of the century in the year 2000, his popularity—always far-reaching in the older generation of fans—was increasingly catching the attention of younger collectors who had done their homework in baseball history. Having outlived many of his former rivals he was increasingly becoming, more emphatically than ever before, one of a kind—*the* man, indeed.

Health concerns slowed Musial down for a time in the 1980s. Hospitalized first with a gastric ulcer and then with prostrate cancer, Stan, who was also at the time facing concerns over some of his businesses, fell into a period of depression from which he was rescued by a letter from his daughter Gerry, who reminded him that he should smile to make "the world smile with you." It was the right message at the right time. After recovering from his early-detected cancer, Musial became a public advocate for periodic prostrate cancer examinations.[55]

Stan's harmonica was a constant companion whenever he needed to appear in public. The whipping out of the harmonica and launching into an impromptu performance became a familiar part of his public persona. He would perform such ditties as "Red River Valley" and "Wabash Cannon Ball" on all sorts of occasions, including Hall of Fame banquets and Roy Clark's *Hee Haw* television show. Bandleader and trumpeter Al Hirt performed "backup" to Musial the musical on more than one occasion.[56] In addition to his tuneful exploits, Stan had kept up a bag of tricks as a magician ever since he began getting a rise out of teammates with such antics in the 1940s. On his trip to Japan, in his continuing role as a Cardinals vice president in 1968, Stan received considerable press attention for one of his favorite tricks, which involved having the victim use an invisible knife to make cutting motions toward an unpeeled banana, after which the victim was induced to peel the fruit and find that it had, indeed, been sliced in several places. Both Japanese and American newspapers took note of this delightfully silly achievement in stories on the Redbird excursion. Stan was, of course, delighted that the trip was another successful competitive venture to Japan for the Cardinals. Their winning of thirteen games, while losing five, was the most wins by an American major league team touring in Japan since the Cardinals won fourteen, while losing only two, in 1958. That trip was discussed in chapter 8 of this book. Treated royally once again in Japan, Stan greatly enjoyed the trip.[57]

To say that Stan's ventures as "the life of the party" were ploys to overcome the limitations of shyness[58] is a valid observation, but such explanations do not do full justice to the meanings of Stan's efforts to be an entertaining companion. Bob Broeg wrote an article for *The Saturday Evening Post* in 1954 in which he tried to get at the essential matter of who Stan was. Frustrated that most sports writers found nothing "colorful" about Stan, Broeg set out to dispel the myth that "the only interesting thing about him is his ball playing." Musial was resisting Broeg's proposal of the idea of an authorized biography to be written by Broeg with the close involvement of Musial, an idea which was to bear fruit ten years later in the form of the autobiography—*Stan Musial, The Man's Own Story*, a tale told in Broeg's adjective-heavy writing style but meant to convey Musial's personal account of his life. Unable, in the mid 1950s, to persuade Musial to go along with the writing of a full-length biographical study, Broeg hoped that his article on "The Mystery of Stan Musial" would enable him to make clear to his fellow sports writers, and the world in general, just how interesting a fellow his beloved friend really was.[59] In commenting on Broeg's earnest article Jerry Lansche, a recent Musial biographer, jokingly asserted that Broeg's quietly affectionate essay could hardly have persuaded anyone that Musial was a colorful guy: "That Stan laughed at his own jokes and watered his lawn wasn't exactly headline news; Broeg had unwittingly added to the idea that the Cardinal legend was, indeed, colorless."[60] In reality, though, Broeg's article did touch upon the central elements that made Stan an attractive figure, and it's basic points have been echoed in the accounts of Lansche, Giglio, Robinson, and many others. If we read between the lines of everything that has been written about The Man, we can discover that there are several important things that need to be remembered about Stan Musial: He was capable of a disciplined concentratrion, he was determined to be as good as he could be, he was fiercely proud and loyal, he liked to be liked, and he loved to laugh.

Some of Stan's virtues seem almost of a Victorian nature, and are, therefore, difficult to discuss in the booze-and-broads context of the typical behind-the-scenes sports story. It is clear that he was devoted to his parents and deeply sensitive about the telling of any tales that would make clear the full extent of the poverty of his family as he was growing up. Broeg and other sports writers were sternly admonished by Stan not to comment at any length on the home that Stan grew up in, although Stan did eventually take Broeg to see it. Stan, by all accounts, adored his wife Lil and pointedly refused any and all offered opportunities to be disloyal to her. Many have noted his dedication to church attendance. He was a Catholic who did not think it acceptable to miss Mass.[61] One of Stan's children reported to Giglio that among the few things their father could be stern about were instances when family members wanted to allow sleepiness to get in the way of getting up in time for church.[62] Musial's disciplined concentration was, no doubt, undergirded by his faith. Not overtly religious outside of church, Stan was, nonetheless, spiritually disciplined at the bat and in his life. Concentration was always key. He finally had to retire from playing, not so much because of a decline in physical ability, but because of the fall-off he noticed in 1963 in his ability to concentrate at bat.[63]

It seems likely that Stan's knack for bringing his physical talents to bear upon specific tasks in the field of play was enabled by the training in gymnastics his father insisted his son have. The turnverein style of training he experienced when tiny gave him the ability to make his body perform as a fine-tuned instrument. That training and a continuing reliance on calisthenics help explain Musial's surprising strength and durability. People who met him casually were sometimes surprised that this great athlete was not more obviously muscular, but it was the nature of the musculature Stan developed from his youngest years that made him great. His strength was allied with the ability to whip his torso to bend, to stretch, to rotate, and to tumble. Where conventional ballplayers would dive for balls in the outfield, Stan would follow through his dive with a somersault, furthering fielding performance through exercises in tumbling.

In the early pages of his book Giglio makes much of Stan's reliance, throughout his life, on mentors. This is an important point. From the days of his childhood Musial's drive to transcend the limitations of his circumstances was helped by advisors that he sought out and relied upon. Ambitious to make himself great in his chosen field and determined to overcome every limitation or lack of knowledge,

Stan understood, from the days of his childhood, that help could be found and lessons could be learned[64] Stan's famed humility seems fundamentally aligned with his openness to advice. Proud of his accomplishments, yet always attributing the greatness of his successes to how "lucky" he had always been, Stan relentlessly ran forward, always determined to take one more base, in life as well as on the field.

Stan's fierce pride is obvious and does not need demonstration, but it is, perhaps, easy to underacknowledge as one reviews accounts of what a nice guy he was. More than one discussion of Stan's performance betrays the fanatical level of his dedication to doing well. If he had one hit, he felt he had to have at least one more. If he had two hits, he was grimly determined to not let the next one get away. If he had three hits or four, he was positively consumed with desire to go out and get one more to make it a perfect day. He was not easily satisfied, in part, it appears, because of his dedication to being what he felt he had to be for his fans, but, most of all, for himself.

Stan was also a man who loved to be loved. He was exquisitely sensitive to those around him. Far from the stereotype of the boorish, self-involved athlete, Stan was always aware of the perimeter of watchers beyond the action on the field. He could block them out when he was playing, which was key to his concentration, but before and after games or when he was eating in a restaurant or walking down the street he was uniquely in tune with his fans' desire for a piece of him. It seems quite right that the image of Stan signing autographs for kids has become a kind of primary image with regard to his legend. There was idealism to his outgoing behavior in this regard and there was the desire he seems to have had to be loved by fans. To say that he understood the value of having a nice-guy reputation in no way diminishes the value of his openness to fans. His elderly turn toward selling his signature does not seem a betrayal of his tendency to make himself available. Fans can still find the door to Stan easy to open.

Related to Musial's desire to be liked is his remarkably odd penchant for goofy magic tricks and practical jokes. Yes, his antics were a cover for shyness, but they went further than that. He became a performer at parties and banquets, as he had been on the ball field. By dedicating himself to the improvement of his musical feats, jokes, and tricks Stan converted a weakness, his shyness about public appearances, into an unusual sort of strength. He loved to laugh and could see what laughter could do for a social situation. Public performance became one more challenging field for him to perform well in, and he worked hard to rise to such occasions.

Of course, all these aspects of The Man operated as one whole. As he rhythmically beat on lockers during a musical frivolity before the start of a game, he was also getting into the rhythm that he would need to hit the ball. His musical bent was one of his forms for heightening concentration during his days as a great hitter, rhythmical tappings in the dugout before his at bats were among the ways he used music to tune himself into the focus he needed to hit the baseball. After his retirement from the ball field, his harmonica became an extension of the rhythm he had relied on in the batter's box, as he continued to try to be as good as he could be as a public performer on the lecture circuit. He did not make any claims about the quality of his musical noodlings, but he strove, nonetheless, to perform as well as he could, endeavoring to hit a screaming line drive with every one of his public performances.

The awed respect, almost religious in nature, which Musial's talents and character had earned him by the end of his career as a player, can perhaps best be observed in James Michener's description of the crowd reaction to the great ball player as he and Stan and a number of other famous people toured the country campaigning for John Kennedy in the fall of 1960. As one after the other of the celebrities were announced to the large crowd at a typical campaign stop the scenario was always repeated. The introduction of each big name—actor Jeff Chandler, actress Angie Dickinson, Pulitzer Prize winning authors Michener and Arthur Schlesinger, millionaire Ethel Kennedy, and so forth—the crowd reacted with mild recognition and scattered handclaps; but when Musial stepped forward the atmosphere turned electric. "Then Stan Musial appeared, and before the announcer could name him, a low rumble rose from the crowd, and men pressed forward, dragging their boys with them, and one man shouted, 'It's Stan the Man!' And a great cry rose from the night, and Musial walked into the glare, a tall, straight man in his late thirties, an authentic American folk here, and the men fell back to let him pass. . . . As we disappeared into a waiting car I heard one rancher say to his son, 'For the rest of your life, Claude, you can tell people about this night. You saw Stan Musial.'"[65]

Toward the end of his career, Stan's teammates had a plaque made to express their feelings of admiration for him. Broeg's article on the "Mystery of Stan Musial" ends with the quotation of the inscription on that plaque. In the center of that salute is a mention that Stan is an "outstanding artist in his profession."[66] That statement is a good note on which to end this chapter. Stan was always a performer devoted to his fans and their hopes for what they might see him do; he was an artist always dedicated to a "standard of excellence"[67]; a perfectionist never willing to allow himself to fall short of the high expectations of his audience.

NOTES

1. James Giglio, *Musial: From Stash to Stan the Man* (Columbia: University of Missouri Press, 2001), 275–276.

2. Stan Musial and Bob Broeg, *The Man Stan ... Musial, Then and Now* (St. Louis, MO: Bethany Press, 1977), 230; Giglio, *Musial*, 275–279.

3. Cleon Walfort, "Musial Sought More Time at Home, but Hasn't Found It Amid Four Jobs." *Milwaukee Journal*, May 24, 1964.

4. "Cardinals Give Musial Free Hand to Encourage Physical Fitness." *Syracuse Herald American*, March 22, 1964; Giglio, *Musial*, 275–279.

5. Musial and Broeg, *The Man Stan*, 229–230.

6. Ibid., 230–232.

7. Giglio, *Musial*, 275.

8. Ogden Nash, "The Tycoon." *Life*, September 5, 1955, 87.

9. Walfort, "Musial Sought More Time at Home, but Hasn't Found It Amid Four Jobs." *Milwaukee Journal* (May 24, 1967).

10. Giglio, *Musial*, 277–278.

11. "Musial Leaves Hospital." *St. Louis Post-Dispatch*, September 4, 1964; Giglio, *Musial*, 277.

12. Musial and Broeg, *The Man Stan,* 231.

13. John Snyder, *Cardinals Journal* (Cincinnati, OH: Emmis Books, 2006), 480.

14. Ibid., 486.

15. Red Schoendienst and Rob Rains, *Red: A Baseball Life* (Champaign, IL: Sports Publishing, 1998), 144.

16. Musial and Broeg, *The Man Stan*, 232–233.

17. Peter Golenbock, *The Spirit of St. Louis: A History of the St. Louis Cardinals and Browns* (New York: HarperCollins, 2000), 478.

18. Bob Gibson and Lonnie Wheeler, *Stranger to the Game* (New York: Viking Penguin, 1994), 127.

19. Shirley Povich, "Stan the Man Enters New League." *Washington Post*, January 29, 1967.

20. Uncredited newspaper clipping in National Baseball Hall of Fame and Museum Archive, Cooperstown, dated February 18, 1967.

21. Jimmy Cannon, "The (Lonesome) Man." *New York Journal American*, January 25, 1967.

22. Dick Young, "Young Ideas." *Daily News*, March 4, 1967.

23. Bob Broeg, "Musial and Schoendienst Are an Odds-On Entry." *St. Louis Post-Dispatch*, January 24, 1967.

24. Uncredited newspaper clipping in National Baseball Hall of Fame and Museum Archive, Cooperstown, dated May 6, 1967.

25. Nancy Osgood, "Lil Musial Marvels at Husband's Success." *St. Petersburg Times*, April 29, 1967.

26. Young, "Young Ideas."

27. Musial and Broeg, *The Man Stan*, 234–236.

28. Mel Freese, *The Glory Years of the St. Louis Cardinals, Volume 1, The World Championship Seasons* (St. Louis, MO: Palmerston & Reed, 1999), 226.

29. Bob Broeg, "Red and Stan Click as Players, Executives." *St. Louis Post-Dispatch*, September 5, 1967.

30. Golenbock, *The Spirit of St. Louis*, 481–482.

31. Ibid., 484.

32. Freese, *The Glory Years of the St. Louis Cardinals*, 249; Neal Russo, "Redbirds Saved by Swaps They Failed to Make." *St. Louis Post-Dispatch*, September 9, 1967.

33. Freese, *The Glory Years of the St. Louis Cardinals*, 256–257.

34. Bill McSweeney, The Impossible Dream: The Story of the Miracle Boston Red Sox (New York: Coward-McGann, 1968), 220–225, 240–242; Gibson and Wheeler, *Stranger to the Game*, 146–150; Joseph Stanton, *Cardinal Points: Poems on St. Louis Cardinals Baseball* (Jefferson, NC: McFarland, 2002), 67.

35. Al Hirshberg, "Trouble in Musial's Paradise." *Baseball Digest*, February 1968, 17.

36. Neal Russo, "Complacent Cards? Not Under Bing." *St. Louis Post-Dispatch*, December 23, 1967.

37. Giglio, *Musial*, 286–287.

38. Bob Broeg and Jerry Vickery, *The St. Louis Cardinals Encyclopedia* (Chicago, IL: Contemporary Books), 98.

39. Walfort, "Musial Sought More Time at Home, but Hasn't Found It Amid Four Jobs."

40. Musial and Broeg, *The Man Stan*, 236.

41. Neal Russo, "Smiles, Kisses and Tears at Musial Stature Unveiling." *Sporting News*, August 17, 1968, 23.

42. Benjamin Rader, *Baseball: A History of America's Game*, second edition (Urbana: Illinois University Press, 2002), 1–135.

43. Giglio, *Musial*, 291–295; 304–310.

44. Ibid., 280–283.

45. Steve Guback, "Musial's Sculptor Worrying–How to Put the Wiggle in Stance." *Washington Evening Star*, May 29, 1965.

46. Giglio, *Musial*, 280–283.

47. David Bonetti, "Going Public." *St. Louis Post-Dispatch*, May 29, 2005; Stanton, *Cardinal Points*, 41.

48. Giglio, *Musial*, 281.

49. Florence Shinkle, "Revived Statue Suits Stan the Man Just Fine." *St. Louis Post-Dispatch*, September 24, 2004.

50. Giglio, *Musial*, 287–289; Snyder, 511; Furman Bisher, "The Accidental Immortal." *Atlanta Journal*, January 23, 1969.

51. Jonathan Mayo, "Masterful Ceremonies: Induction Weekends at the Hall Have Provided Plenty of Memorable Moments." MLB.com, 2001.

52. Giglio, *Musial*, 290–298.

53. Michael Ruscoe, ed. *Baseball: A Treasury of Art and Literature* (New York: Hugh Lauter Levin Associates, 1993), 167.

54. Giglio, *Musial*, 297.

55. Ibid., 296

56. Gibson and Wheeler, *Stranger to the Game*, 150; Giglio, *Musial*, 298–299.

57. "Japan Land of Fun for Gift-Laden Cards." *Sporting News*, December 14, 1968, 29.

58. Giglio, *Musial*, 298–299.

59. Bob Broeg, "The Mystery of Stan Musial." *Saturday Evening Post*, August 28, 1954, 17–19, 50–52.

60. Jerry Lansche, *Stan "The Man" Musial: Born to Be a Ballplayer* (Dallas, TX: Taylor, 1994), 133.

61. Broeg, "The Mystery of Stan Musial." 17–19, 50–52.

62. Giglio, *Musial*, 215.

63. Musial and Broeg, *The Man's Own Story*, 236.

64. Giglio, *Musial*, 11.

65. James Michener, *Sports in America* (New York: Random House, 1976), 300.

66. Broeg, "The Mystery of Stan Musial," 52.

67. Glen Singer, "Stanley Frank Musial (A Paean)." *Elysian Fields Quarterly*, 23 (4) 2006, 75.

Stan the Man at the 2005 Hall of Fame Induction festivities warmly addressing the crowd, his infamous harmonica ready for action in his right hand. *National Baseball Hall of Fame Library, Cooperstown, NY.*

THE MAKING OF A LEGEND:
AN ENDURING REPUTATION

How good was Stan Musial? Perhaps Vin Scully's 1959 remark handled the question best: "How good was Stan Musial? He was good enough to take your breath away."[1] I will begin this chapter with an examination of the nature of Musial's performance. After that I will turn to the question of Stan's stature. How should we regard him as against the many other great players of the game? While questions of ranking are impossible to settle definitively, as such determinations are subject to the criteria chosen and the weight given to each factor, my vote will be to place Musial closer to the top of the scale than he has sometimes been placed by the many writers on baseball who exhibit a preoccupation with players identified with New York and Boston.

The central topic in any discussion of Stan Musial is obviously his extraordinary success as a hitter. Most of the myriad articles in magazines and newspapers from the early 1940s to the present address the relentless consistency of his performance at the plate. Excellence is always admirable and fascinating. We long to understand what enabled Shakespeare to be Shakespeare, Rembrandt to be Rembrandt. Such inquiries are as primary to the biographer's effort as they are to the historian's and the aesthetician's because the question of who the excellent performer was is inseparable from the excellent performance. Though his life and psychology do not "explain" Musial's achievement, the mystery of Stan's personality cannot be cleanly separated from the mystery of his Hall-of-Fame-quality hitting.

Musial's batting stance has provoked endless discussion. When he was first coming into baseball, many, including teammate Marty Marion, doubted that

Stan could have much success coming out of a stance like that.[2] In 1949, a *Time* cover story on "That Man" attempted to provide a full description of Stan's stance. "Before squaring off on the left side of the plate, he limbers up with a hula-like motion, bat held high above his head, hips and shoulders waggling. It looks a little ridiculous, but it helps loosen him up and opposing pitchers do not laugh. Before the pitch, he goes into a crouch in the far outside corner of the batter's box, stands motionless as a statue, his feet close together, knees bent, body slanted forward. . . . Musial's striding swing brings him diagonally forward in what is almost a flank attack on the ball. He can reach an outside pitch and send it lining into left field, or rifle it through the pitcher's box; he can meet a close-in pitch and thump it to right. . . . [He] can spray his hits around the full 90 degree arc of the playing field."[3] Pitcher Ted Lyons' remark that Musial, in his stance, "Looks like a kid peeking around the corner to see if the cops are coming,"[4] is a much quoted statement about the way Stan looked from the vantage point of the pitcher's mound. How fearful that vantage could be for the moundsman is betrayed by Warren Spahn's comment that, "Once Musial timed your fastball, your infielders were in jeopardy."[5] Branch Rickey described Stan's initial stance at the plate as "a fraud" that he emerged from as he swiveled toward the ball.[6] This explanation, though it sounds shrewd, is actually not a very useful observation. That Stan would have to emerge out of his corkscrew crouch to stride into his swing is obvious; just as it is obvious that Sadaharu Oh did not stay back on one leg once he had committed to his swing.

In 1951, when Ty Cobb was asked his views on Musial's infamous stance, he commented that, if Musial had played in the old days and had to face "the spitballers, emery ballers and others who roamed the diamonds in the early 1900s," he would have had to adapt a more open and variable stance. Declared Cobb, "Musial wouldn't take his present stance against the pitchers we saw— Rube Waddell, Addie Joss, Walter Johnson, Eddie Plank, Cy Young, and others. They gave you too many different kinds of pitches to let you stay in one place." As an after thought Cobb added that he could, however, remember one hitter of the older era who had some success with Musial's immobile-stance strategy: "There was one fellow who hit everybody from the same position, though. Hornsby. I think he was pretty close to being a right-handed version of Musial."[7]

Musial's success with his distinctive stance led many novice hitters to imitate it. So prevalent was the imitation that Stan felt compelled to declare on a number of occasions that imitating the Musial stance was a bad idea for young batsmen. "It's good for me," Stan explained to Jimmy Cannon, "because its natural with me." Hitters who imitated the famous corkscrew stance were, Musial warned, "hurting themselves more than they're helping themselves," by arranging their bodies in a way not suited to their skills and tendencies.[8]

One of the purposes of Stan's crouch was to reduce his strike zone and give the pitcher less opportunity to throw strikes that would be difficult to hit. Everything Stan did at the plate contributed to enhancing his chances of hitting the ball well. Curt Flood's quotation of the advice Musial gave him about hitting captures the matter in a nutshell: "Well, you wait for a strike. Then you knock the shit out of it."[9] In 1949 Stan explained in a more detailed way to a reporter how he viewed the opportunity provided by various positions of pitched balls: "I have a mental image of the strike zone—a vertical square just in front of the plate. When the pitch hits that square, I decide how to swing. If it's an outside pitch, I'll slice toward left. If it's inside, I'll come around and pull toward right."[10] He felt that his coming out of the crouch from deep in the batter's box was helpful against both the outside pitch, which he could easily poke into left field, and the inside pitch, which he could turn on quickly and drive with power to right. Musial commented more than once on his conviction that a hitter should avoid hitting fly balls to center field, where the best-fielding outfielder lurked and had the support of comrades to the left and right of him. A ball hit down either line, Musial reasoned, could only be fielded by one man who was often not as fleet as the centerfielder.[11] Because Musial was a spray hitter—who hit pitches to every field, and even, at times, to center, especially to right center and left center—fielders could not risk overplaying him in any one direction. Outfielders faced a dilemma similar to that faced by pitchers. Musial was versatile, variable, and opportunistic. No one strategy could be used against him with any assurance of success. Tim McCarver and Jack Buck both observed that Musial's knack for almost always hitting the ball on the sweet spot of the bat was crucial to his phenomenal hitting. The dents on his older bats would almost all be on the most potent part of the barrel. The screaming line drive was his characteristic hit. McCarver has also pointed out what a remarkable low-ball hitter he was.[12] This talent proved particularly valuable at Sportsman Park/Busch Stadium where Stan could lift low pitches up on to the pavilion roof or—even more impressively, when he really caught hold of one—out onto Grand Avenue. In later years Stan sometimes made the joke that he was a "low-ball hitter and a high-ball drinker."[13]

In the chapter of his autobiography in which he offered "Ten Tips on Hitting," Stan prefaced his listing of practical tips with some general principles that are perhaps more crucial than the tips that follow. Above all else, Musial urged hitters to combine relaxation with concentration. To explain how relaxation and concentration should not be seen as in contradiction Stan used the analogy of a cat stalking its prey. That the cat is relaxed and loose is evident, Stan argued, in the way the cat's tail swishes just before he pounces. The revolving tail prevents the cat from getting tense, leading up to the moment when the swishing stops and the cat jumps forward for the capture and the kill. This scenario, Stan felt, was equivalent to his wriggle in the box as he set up for the pitch. Like a cat, Musial relaxed himself in order to be ready for the total concentration necessary for a successful pounce. The relaxation factor, and his position deep in the batter's box, helped Musial to hold back his bat longer than most hitters. He could get away with this because of his ability to accelerate his bat rapidly as he engaged his swing just before meeting the bat.[14] One observer likened Stan's accelerating swing to the cracking of a whip. Another commentator suggested that Stan's pounce was like "a hungry man going at a thick juicy steak."[15]

Because keeping motivation and focus were essential to Stan's consistent high achievement at the plate, the possibility of achieving batting records sometimes served Musial as a means to keeping the concentration of his "pounce" at a high level of intensity even at times when fatigue or the dismal showing his team was making might have taken the edge off Stan's concentration. Though he downplayed records when interviewed by reporters, Musial's awareness that every successful blow would enhance his stature helped him maintain the intensity necessary to keep hitting well. Stan explained that the "added incentive of statistical proof of an achievement—that lasting evidence—enabled me to bear down longer, to concentrate better."[16]

Sculptor Carl Mose's description of Musial's body, quoted in the previous chapter, is also instructive here: "From chest to waist, he's like a wedge. That's where he got the power." Mose's conception of Musial was partly related to his surprise at the broadness of Stan's shoulders, which Mose measured at twenty-two inches across.[17] The well-defined musculature of Stan's torso was likely the result of Musial's physical conditioning in gymnastics from the days of his earliest childhood and his continuing development of his body through early career, off-season basketball play. Musial's remarkable hook shot was probably not unrelated to his vicious swings at the plate. Though slender in appearance, especially in the early part of his career, Musial's muscles were well-developed where they needed to be to enable the whiplike acceleration of his swing and the tumbling strategies he employed in his fielding. Marty Marion, Tim McCarver, and many others have commented on the surprising strength of Musial's musculature. "If you ever saw Stan undressed," Marion remarked, "he had a lot of muscles in his shoulders."[18] "Another thing about Musial," McCarver explained, "was his strength. The muscular shape of his back—the clumps of his muscles—they were centered. Man he was strong. Mays was like that, too."[19]

To accentuate the whipping action of his swing Musial employed a bat with a thick barrel and a thin handle. He would further thin his handles by sanding them down, which also had the advantage of making them easier to grip. His bat was relatively small for the major leagues, a Louisville Slugger M159. At the beginning of the season he used a thirty-four and a half inch bat that weighed thirty-four ounces, but then changed to a thirty-three-ounce bat toward the middle of the summer when he felt his strength sapped by the heat of summer. In the later years of his career he resorted to even lighter bats, going with thirty-one or thirty-ounce clubs.[20] He understood that bat speed was the key thing and the size of the lumber was of secondary importance.

The batting stance and style of Stan the Man were undoubtedly expressive of his personality as well as a means to hitting baseballs, but, just as it is difficult to discover exactly who an artist is by an examination of his brush strokes, so it is hard to find Stan revealed in his style at the plate. Crouching deep in the batter's box turned away from the pitcher, Musial was keeping himself held back in a powerful way. The notion that he was like a kid peeking around the corner is an appropriate analogy in several respects. The stance allowed Stan to hold what he had in reserve for as long as possible. He was hoarding his power as well as the available time, giving himself as much opportunity as possible to see the ball and to decide what to do. He was controlling his set up in a most careful way. In response to the arrival of the ball, another side of Stan's personality came into play. His swings were passionate and yet precise. The control of the situation was maintained in the exacting execution of the swing, and yet he could not have been a great hitter without the passion. This strategy of coiling back and then unleashing forward could probably not have worked as well had Stan not had a body trained in gymnastics.

Stan and others have commented on the importance of his excellent eyesight to his performance. Marty Marion once compared notes with Musial about eyesight: "Stan, how does the ball look to you? It looks like an aspirin tablet to me." Stan answered, "It looks like a grapefruit!" Marion confirmed that this was fact not brag, saying, "[Stan] wasn't lying. He had good eyes."[21]

Stan always claimed that he did not need to guess what the pitcher was going to throw. He determined which sort of pitch was headed his way by noting its speed. Familiarity with each pitcher's arsenal of pitches was essential to Stan's approach. Deceptive pitchers, who could throw several sorts of pitches at the same speed, sometimes gave Stan more trouble than the more famous pitchers of the time. Warren Spahn was an example of a great pitcher that Musial often hit hard. If he was concentrating properly, Stan felt he could usually determine what sort of pitch was headed his way and, no matter how good the pitcher was, he felt he could find a pitch to hit. As he explained in his autobiography in 1964: "If I free my mind of all distracting thoughts, I could tell what a pitch was going to be when it got about half way to the plate, whether the pitch was fast ball or a breaking pitch, which necessarily is at least a bit slower. Since hitting is timing, I could set myself for the fast ball, then adjust if concentration enabled me to see the pitch was something else."[22] In a 1997 interview Stan commented on this matter further, suggesting that when the count was in his favor, his ability to tell what was coming was infallible. "If you have a pitcher in a hole, you're not guessing. I never guessed. *I never guessed* . . . I was set and something told me . . . I had a sixth sense. I don't know what else you call it, but it never deceived me. It never deceived me."[23]

Stan has expressed surprise on several occasions at Ted Williams' claim to having been a guess hitter. It is possible that the actual practice of Musial and Williams was more similar than their disagreement on this point suggests, but Musial was never able to accept that any strategy involving regular guessing could work for most hitters. Stan firmly believed that a hitter with a good eye and a determined attitude should be able to figure out what was coming. "How can a great hitter like Williams be guessing?" Stan complained in 1997, going on to remark, "I couldn't imagine that he would do that because you come to the plate so many times every day, every game. You see so many pitches each time you're up. Now, how can you be guessing? That was a shocker."[24] In his autobiography, Musial indicated that he felt a key problem with guessing is that a batter's investment in a guess-determined expectation left him set him up to fail even if he guessed correctly. Guessing a slow pitch of any sort would leave a batter totally unable to deal with a fastball, and, Stan reasoned, if the expected slower pitch arrived, the batter might be too anxious to pounce on it, causing him to make less than his best swing. Musial believed a hitter should endeavor to look as well as he could and that looking should be unhindered by the preconceptions of guessing. Stan felt that an attitude that favored a notion of guessing left the player at the mercy of his emotions, whereas to have relaxed confidence that one can recognize what pitch was coming kept the hitter focused on his job at the plate. To explain the danger of anxiousness Stan used the example of the 3-0 count. When Eddie Stanky was his manager, Stan had frequent differences of opinion with him about what he should do when he was in the enviable hitting position of having three balls and no strikes. Stanky insisted that Stan should be ready to attack the fastball strike that was probably on its way when the count was 3-0, but Musial explained that he preferred to be taking all the way on a 3-0 count because he tended to get "overeager" when everyone in the ballpark knew a fastball strike was likely on the way and that overeagerness tended to throw off Stan's timing and judgment. Musial claimed he could hit better when the count was 3-1, and he could confidently adopt his usual relaxed strategy of carefully looking without excessive prejudgment.[25]

A trait that Musial shared with other great hitters of his era such as Williams and DiMaggio was a strong sense of self-confidence at the plate. As Stan declared to a reporter after his return from the Navy, "I know I can hit." He had made a similar declaration when he saw his first major-league game. He told the friend who had taken him to the game that he was sure he could hit the sort of pitching he was witnessing.[26] Early in his career he sometimes had doubts about his prospects as a pitcher, but he claimed always to have been confident with a bat in his hands. DiMaggio talked about the necessity of such self-assurance for anyone with hopes of having success at the plate, explaining that "The first requisite of the good hitter is confidence. No player can be a hitter without it." He went on to say that any player approaching the plate "with fear in [his] heart" should give up playing baseball.[27] Musial remarked that confidence could be particularly important when a batter has two strikes on him. Whereas some batters would choke up on the bat and anxiously aim to avoid a strikeout once they had two strikes on them, Musial felt that even though a batter "can't be choosy" when he has two strikes on him, a readiness to take a vigorous and confident swing was essential. Ted Williams once expressed surprise that a free swinger like Stan could manage to strike out so seldom. In a typical 600-at-bats season Musial would typically only strike out around twenty-five times.[28] Stan's low strike-out totals testify to the combination of refined skill and fearless demeanor that made him such a challenge for pitchers.

Musial felt that left-handed hitters have a considerable advantage in certain situations. With runners at first and second, for instance, Stan relished the big hole available to him on the right side of the infield as the first and second basemen inclined toward their respective bases to hold the runners on. In such cases Stan would lay off all outside pitches as long as he could, in hopes of getting an inside pitch he could drive to the right side to advance the runners and perhaps get a hit through the infield hole. Stan loved the extra step or two he had toward first base because of his left-handed position at the plate. At any time this was an advantage, but it was especially helpful in bunting situations. A fleet left-hander with good bunting skills could, Stan pointed out, boost his average by bunting from time to time. The extra steps toward first gave Musial a good shot at beating out the bunt, and the very fact of the bunt potential prevented the corner infielders from laying back as deeply as they would have liked.[29] Such canny left-handed strategies have been more recently evidenced in the opportunistic batting of Ichiro Suzuki, though, as Stan became more of a power hitter in the second half of his career and his foot speed decreased, he largely dropped the bunt-for-a-hit strategy from his arsenal.

The ten rules of hitting that Stan included in his autobiography as advice to young hitters reflected his belief that a pragmatic approach and a relaxed attentiveness are essential. Here is his list:

> 1. Get a bat that's light enough to handle easily.... 2. Hold the bat properly. Don't make a fist around a club.... 3. Don't imitate

anyone, unnaturally. Use a comfortable batting stance.... 4. Keep
your bat up, away from your body, and ready.... 5. Keep your eye on
the ball. Swing only at strikes.... 6. Take a level swing. Hit the ball
where it is pitched, pulling only the inside pitches, and send outside
pitches to the opposite field.... 7. Don't swing too hard or overstride.... 8. Practice holding back your swing on a pitch that fools
you. Hit confidently with two strikes.... 9. Don't try to guess what
the pitcher will throw.... 10. Learn to bunt. Play the team game.[30]

The complexities involved in judging who is better and who is best in a
sport like baseball are legion. Players who have played in different times amidst
different sorts of circumstances cannot easily be definitively judged one against
the other. I will here not try to nail Stan Musial in a particular place on the
scale from better to best. No historian of baseball would dispute that Musial
deserves a high ranking. Just how high is a matter for endless and largely futile
debate. To approach the problematic topic of rankings I would like to confine
myself largely to a consideration of what William Marshall and others have called
"The Great Triumvirate" of Musial, Ted Williams, and Joe DiMaggio. In my
examination of how these three superstars, who played in roughly the same era,
have been positioned in rivalry with each other in various baseball conversations
and rankings, I will be noting the ways in which they have been ranked and/or
discussed in relation to each other and, to a lesser extent, I will consider how
they stand in relation to everyone else. Having the Triumvirate as my main focus,
will enable my remarks to be more focused than they would have been had I
attempted to survey thoroughly and systematically the entire array of historically
significant players.

In recent books on sports in general and baseball in particular, there has
been an obsession with rankings. Some mathematically minded analysts employ
elaborate statistical schemes for adjudicating their lists. A variety of other criteria
are employed by other analysts. Some lists are the result of votes by groups of
interested parties or simply reflect the preferences of a small group of writers.
Many such books partake of the sports columnist's mentality, a state of mind
evident in most sports pages on a daily basis as well as on various sports talk
shows on television and radio; it is a state of mind that favors rapid-fire rhetoric
over careful consideration.

Let us start, however, with a writer who carefully considers his judgments.
William Marshall endeavors to be even-handed in his comments on The Great
Triumvirate in what his book's title calls *Baseball's Pivotal Era: 1945–1951*. His
take on the Williams-Musial-DiMaggio comparison seems the best sort of way to
approach such questions. He discusses the three stars in the context of the history

of their time and does not attempt to construct the impossible Olympus of baseball gods suggested by most other discussions of rank. The three are different sorts of talented men with abilities and achievements arising out of their individual strengths and circumstances. With regard to all three men, Marshall reminds us that in the prime years of Musial, Williams, and DiMaggio there were many challenges to hitters that were not the case for more recent stars. "Unlike in the decades that followed, during the Pivotal Era, the sacrifice fly rule was not in effect, strike zones were large, mounds were high, and the pitching, when every team had at least one ace, had not yet been watered down by expansion."[31] Marshall's account finds Williams to be the greatest hitter of the three, projecting, as many have, what Williams' records would have been had he not lost prime seasons to World War II and the Korean conflict. With regard to DiMaggio's less impressive numbers Marshall reminds us that Joe lost crucial years to military service and then was faced with continuing injury-related challenges in the postmilitary phase of his career. In Marshall's discussion as a whole, Musial comes off as the undisputed great man of the National League in his prime years, and, while it is implied that he more fully realized his potential than DiMaggio did his, the point is not emphasized. The focus is on telling the story of how amazing all three of these fellows were.[32]

In his 1999 book, *Baseball's All-Time Best Hitters: How Statistics Can Level the Playing Field,* Michael Schell contrasts his "The Adjusted List of Top Hitters" with what he calls "The Traditional List of Top 100 Hitters." There is an appearance of definitive objectivity to his second list, set up by the fact that his traditional list is simply a listing of hitters from highest career batting average to lowest career batting average. The obviously inflexible nature of his "Traditional List" puts it in the position of being something of a "straw man," making his adjusted list seem obviously more intelligent. Dr. Schell, whose day job is as a Professor of Biostatistics at the University of North Carolina, argues well for the legitimacy of his various criteria, and we can assume his math skills are on the mark, but the therefore-my-list-has-to-be-correct implication of his book is never as entirely convincing as the author suggests. Throughout his study he makes various decisions about what factors should be weighed and what weight they should be given; however, it is evident that arguments could be advanced against him on many of his small and large points and undermining any of his initial assumptions would obviously change how one regards his numerical outcomes. Ultimately his list is very interesting and admirable in its ambition, but does not, by any means, settle the question. As it turns out, the cause of Musial is advanced by the machinery of Schell's adjustment. Musial who had been ranked twenty-fourth in the list based on career batting average alone moves up to eighth place after the calculations. Williams remains ahead of Musial on both lists, but Ted actually goes down one slot going from fifth in the traditional list to sixth in the adjusted list. DiMaggio stays fairly low in both lists but comes up from thirty-third in the traditional list to the nineteenth position after Schell's calculations.[33] The gutsy demeanor of Schell's nerd-on-the-warpath demeanor makes his book fun to consider. Schell's writing procedure and rhetorical tack seem based on that of the infamous Bill James; however, Schell projects an air of mathematical confidence that goes beyond the more careful claims that James makes for his number crunchings.

A saving grace of the always stimulating writings of Bill James has, in fact, been his cautious detachment with regard to the math that lies behind his opinions. James is always a thoughtful writer whose arguments turn more on the logic of his reasoning than on a stipulation of statistical definitiveness, though he is, clearly, proud of his interpretations of which numbers are most important. As is the case with Schell, James' references to his calculations justifies and energizes his arguments, but, ultimately he argues his points more than he calculates them. His Win-Shares system is a platform for argumentation rather than an end in itself. In *The New Bill James Historical Baseball Abstract*, which he published in 2001, he considers players by position and ranks Ted Williams as the all-time number one at that position and Stan Musial following right after at number two. In remarks in several places in the book James makes it clear that Williams gets the nod for being the best hitter in baseball during his time, rather than for being the best all-around player, yet clearly such was the greatness of Williams hitting (and his potential for further hitting during his war years) that James puts him on top even though Musial was a much better fielder and base runner. The use of Win Shares to evaluate player greatness clearly treats Musial well. James points out that "Musial was the best player in the National League seven years—1943, 1944, 1946, 1948, 1949, 1951 (tied with Jackie Robinson), and 1952. Musial was the most successful player ever in MVP voting, but really, the vote still understates his value."[34] Of course, one interesting problem with considering Musial entirely as a left fielder is the considerable time he spent in right field and at first base. James places Joe DiMaggio in fifth place in center field—ranking him behind Willie Mays, Ty Cobb, Mickey Mantle, and Tris Speaker in positions one through four. The placing of Mantle higher than DiMaggio is well argued by James but has probably not been well-received by some Yankee fans. Certainly DiMaggio, who liked to be announced as the greatest living ball player, would not have liked how most of the recent rankings have regarded him. The legend of Joe's prowess as a fielder is given interesting treatment by James who discusses the oft-raised contention that Joe's two center-field-playing brothers, Vince and Dom, were better with the glove than Joe. In James' balanced treatment of this question, Joe

DiMaggio's hitting and fielding turn out, in James' view, to have been at a high enough level often enough to make him the top center fielder of his era.[35]

There is a cheerfully glib confidence about the rankings offered in *Who's Better, Who's Best in Baseball?* by journalist and broadcast writer Elliot Kalb. Although he refers to himself as "Mr. Stats," he does not appear to allow statistics much play in his determinations. Instead, he portrays his personal decisions as to where to rank players as the result of chats he has had with players, broadcasters, other journalists, and anyone else with an opinion to offer. One interesting assumption he makes is that modern ball players have to be given the edge because they are bigger and more athletic than their predecessors from long ago. He flatly pronounces at one point that, "If Alex Rodriguez has a career batting average that is exactly the same as a player who played in the 1920s, A-Rod has a big head start in these rankings over the other player."[36] This kind of thinking appears to be particularly strong in the sports broadcasting world centered in ESPN, whose little ten-best-of-all-time countdowns used as fillers between other sports programming outrageously favor the recent over the somewhat older, and barely seem to have any real knowledge of the more ancient stars and contests. Few of these "best-of" sequences ever cite any athlete or contest from more than twenty years in the past. A provocative challenge to this sort of thinking has been offered by Bill Jenkinson in his 2007 book, *Recrowning Baseball's Greatest Slugger: The Year Babe Ruth Hit 104 Homeruns*. Making use of extensive research into dimensions of ballparks and other factors, Jenkinson argues that older ballplayers need to be accorded much more respect than they have been in recent years.[37] Kalb's casual research methods do not seem to have hurt Ted Williams overmuch; he is ranked seventh; but Musial is placed down in the twenty-second position, one place beneath DiMaggio. Babe Ruth is treated fairly well by Mr. Kalb who ranks him number two, but in a surprising and provocative move he places Barry Bonds in the number one position.[38]

David Gentile's book, *Baseball's Best 1000*, came out just one year before Kalb's book, so he had also been witness to most of Barry Bond's best late-career great seasons, but Gentile comes to very different decision, placing Bonds in the nineteenth position, restoring Ruth to his accustomed stature at the top of the list, and giving Willie Mays the number two slot. Gentile's decisions (like Kalb's) are personal, and often highly surprising. He places Mickey Mantle in sixth place, one ahead of Williams in seventh and well ahead of Musial in the ninth position. DiMaggio follows Musial in the tenth position in this ranking. Gentile's book has an attractive encyclopedic quality with a thumbnail-sized picture for each of the 1,000 players. Gentile's effort to consider and appropriately place Negro League stars within his rankings adds to the authority of his overall project.[39]

The most stimulating of all the ranking books is by the great Ted Williams himself. *Ted Williams' Hit List: The Best of the Best Ranks the Best of the Rest* gives the top slot to the usual suspect, Babe Ruth, but then follows him with great players that Williams highly respected for a variety of reasons—Lou Gehrig, Jimmie Fox, and Rogers Hornsby. Williams had personal connections to Fox and Hornsby. Williams had played alongside Fox on the Red Sox during Fox's concluding seasons, and Hornsby was a batting coach in the Red Sox minor league system, who was generous with advice and help to a nineteen-year-old Williams. Despite the personal nature of some of Williams' choices, he argues for them eloquently in the rough-hewn, yet highly intelligent rhetoric to which he was prone. One of the delights of this book is the restraint shown by Williams' collaborator Jim Prime, which allows Williams' own voice, as passionate and persuasive as it is colloquial and quirky, to sound off. This is an element we certainly do not have in the Musial–Broeg collaborations, where Musial's voice always sounds like a version of Broeg's voice. Among the useful features of Ted's commentary are his remarks on the nature of the ballparks in which the various hitters performed. Williams has strong opinions on all factors that seem to him to be advantageous or disadvantageous to the hitter. On the issue of the Triumverate, Williams ranks DiMaggio at five, followed by Ty Cobb at six, and Musial at seven. Stating emphatically that "DiMaggio was the greatest all-around player I saw," Williams offers an important vote in favor of regarding Joe as the top guy in the Triumverate. Certainly Williams had extensive opportunity to watch Joe in action. So, when Williams declares that "DiMaggio ... was my idol," we have to take him at his word. Williams is, however, also high in his praise for Musial whom he calls, "the best hitter in the National League for almost 20 years."[40]

Williams feels that Musial's speed gave him a big advantage but notes too, that Musial "really roped" the ball, hitting line drives to all fields. Ted feels that he had a little more power than Stan but expresses the view that Stan's foot speed made up for that advantage and implies that Musial and Williams were counterparts of more or less equal ability. Williams appears to be conscious of the frequent comparisons that were drawn between him and Stan in the press over their many years of rivalry in the opposing leagues. In the care he takes in his comments on Stan, Ted seems desirous of avoiding any appearance that he regards himself as better than the popular Cardinals star. Williams' analyses of the hitting styles of the players on his "hit list" are always interesting and revealing glimpses into the craft and science of hitting. Williams describes Musial as, "a sweeper and an inside-outer and a ripper to right field," remarking on Musial's ability to hit to left field and the knack Stan also had for driving inside pitches to right. Williams rounds out the top ten places in his list by following Musial with Joe Jackson, Hank Aaron, and Willie Mays.[41] Williams also provides a "Gallery of Great

Hitters" in his book on *The Science of Hitting* in which he does not present the great hitters in a top-to-bottom hierarchy but clumps them in little categories. In the 1986 edition of that book Musial and DiMaggio are presented on the same page, Stan as one of "the top five left-handed hitters of all time" and DiMaggio as one of "the top five right-handed hitters of all time."[42]

Because my subject is Stan Musial, I would like to conclude my consideration of rankings by looking at a book that places Musial very close to the top of the list based on a statistical formula that favored balanced achievement in all phases of hitting. *Big Stix: The Greatest Hitters in the History of the Major Leagues* by Rob Rains places Stan Musial as the third best hitter in the history of the Major Leagues—Hank Aaron is named number one and Ty Cobb is number two. The less balanced performer, Ted Williams is deposited in twenty-fourth place. The book only considers the top twenty-five so Williams barely makes the cut this time. Joe DiMaggio does not even make that list. Babe Ruth is given eighth place in a tie with Pete Rose. Although Rains' study may seem eccentric because of the atypical nature of its rankings, it is, in fact, quite methodical in the nature of its calculations. Though all rankings are problematical and arbitrary in a variety of respects it is interesting to see that a case to place Musial higher than most of the usual suspects can certainly be made. Rains specifically points out that a case can be made for Musial as the best of The Great Triumverate. "Because Ted Williams played in Boston and Joe DiMaggio played in New York, the universal opinion in the late 1940s amd 1950s was that they were the two best players in the game. The player many observers were forgetting, however, was a member of the St. Louis Cardinals, at least according to the Rawlings rankings, he was the best of the three."[43]

Any survey of books that rank the great ball players leads ultimately to the conclusion that such books are written not because there is any real hope of deciding these matters but because people are anxious to buy books that provide such rankings, anxious to have someone tell them how heroic their heroes can be seen to be. In my little review of such rankings I have seen Musial ranked as low as twenty-two and as high as three. Though the matter cannot be settled here, it is valuable to keep in mind that much can be said in favor of ranking Musial higher than he often is.

Much can be said, too, about the nature of Musial's widespread fame and popularity in the middle part of the country. Whether or not Musial has received the respect he deserves in baseball history, it is clear that he will always be a sainted figure in the Redbird bastion on the Mississippi River and in the southern and western regions of the "Cardinal Nation" where people grew up listening to the chronicles of his exploits over the airwaves. It seems more than fitting that Stan Musial was asked to throw out the ceremonial first pitch as part of the pregame festivities for the fifth and deciding game of the 2006 World Series. Winning that game gave the Cardinals a world championship for the first time since 1982. Musial, who turned eighty-six the following November and was making this appearance as Mr. Cardinal sixty years after his last World Series, was seen as "a symbolic link to championships past."[44]

But perhaps the image of the frail, elderly Musial, garbed from head to toe in Cardinal red, throwing out that ceremonial first pitch in October of 2006 is not where I should conclude my effort to answer to the question I started this chapter with. The answer to the question, "How good was Stan Musial?" has to be sought ultimately in the hearts and minds of his fans, as is the case for all the great stars—DiMaggio, Williams, and all the rest. In Musial's case one might picture a young fan passionately listening to the exploits of Stan the Man coming to him over the radio waves, the announcer's voice crackling with static. The young fan could be Mickey Mantle or the Boyer brothers, country boys dreaming baseball dreams. In John Grisham's novel, *A Painted House* we have perhaps the most poignant account of such a fan, a small boy listening in 1952 in a country place far from the "perfect outfield grass" of an imagined Sportsman's Park while Stan Musial, "the greatest Cardinal of all time," stepped up to the plate, causing all the men in the country household to crowd closer to the radio, with the excitement mounting around the radio as the pitcher fell behind in the count with everybody on that front porch, and—in the boy's mind, everyone in the stadium—getting out of their seats. With two balls and no strikes on The Man, everyone knew that "a baseball was about to get ripped to some remote section of Sportsman's Park," because no pitcher could ever escape unscathed after falling behind Musial on a count. And then there was the crack of the bat and Harry Caray's breathless account of a run coming home to score and Stan dashing around to third for a triple.[45] Grisham, who grew up in Arkansas listening to the great Musial on just such a radio on just such a porch, knew, even as a child, the answer to the question; he knew the answer more intimately than Vin Scully ever could. How good was Stan Musial? He could take your breath away.

NOTES

1. Widely quoted. See, for instance, *Baseball Almanac*, http://www.baseball-almanac.com

2. Peter Golenbock, *The Spirit of St. Louis: A History of the St. Louis Cardinals and Browns* (New York: HarperCollins), 253.

3. "That Man." *Time*, September 9, 1940, 40.

4. Bob Broeg, "The Mystery of Stan Musial." *Saturday Evening Post*, August 28, 1954, 52.

5. *Baseball Almanac*, http://www.baseball-almanac.com.

6. James Giglio, *Musial: From Stash to Stan the Man* (Columbia: University of Missouri Press, 2001), 237.

7. Paul Chandler, "That Stan-ce No Go in Long Ago." *Baseball Digest*, September 1951, 11–12.

8. Jimmy Cannon, "'Don't Mimic Me'—Musial." *Baseball Digest*, November 1952, 33.

9. Curt Flood with Richard Carter, *The Way It Is* (New York: Simon & Schuster, 1971), 64.

10. Bill Fay, "Inside Sports." *Collier's*, May 14, 1949, 70

11. Stan Musial and Bob Broeg, *Stan Musial: "The Man's" Own Story as Told to Bob Broeg* (New York: Doubleday, 1964), 244; Mark Newman and John Rawlings, "Man to Man," *Sporting News*, July 28, 1997, 13.

12. Elliott Kalb, *Who's Better, Who's Best in Baseball?* (New York: McGraw-Hill, 2005), 145.

13. Mark Newman and John Rawlings, "Man to Man." *Sporting News* (July 28, 1997), 13.

14. Musial and Broeg, *Stan Musial*, 144–146.

15. Bob Broeg, "How Does Musial Do It?" *Sport Life*, January 1949, 28.

16. Musial and Broeg, *Stan Musial*, 245.

17. Steve Guback, "Musial's Sculptor Worrying–How to Put the Wiggle in Stance." *Washington Evening Star*, May 29,1965.

18. Golenbock, *The Spirit of St. Louis*, 253.

19. Kalb, *Who's Better*, 145.

20. Giglio, *Musial*, 237.

21. Golenbock, *The Spirit of St. Louis*, 253.

22. Musial and Broeg, *Stan Musial*, 245.

23. Newman and Rawlings, "Man to Man," 11.

24. Ibid., 12.

25. Musial and Broeg, *Stan Musial*, 253.

26. William Marshall, *Baseball's Pivotal Era: 1945–1951*. Lexington: UP of Kentucky, 1999, 326.

27. Joe DiMaggio, *Lucky to Be a Yankee* (New York: Grosset and Dunlap, 1951), 196.

28. Musial and Broeg, *Stan Musial*, 252–253.

29. Cannon, "'Don't Mimic Me'—Musial," 33–34.

30. Musial and Broeg, *Stan Musial*, 246–253.

31. Marshall, *Baseball's Pivotal Era*, 327.

32. Ibid., 324–339.

33. Michael Schell, *Baseball's All-Time Best Hitters: How Statistics Can Level the Playing Field* (Princeton, NJ: Princeton University Press, 1999), 3–151.

34. Bill James. *The New Bill James Historical Baseball Abstract* (New York: Simon & Schuster, 2001), 652–653, 720–721.

35. Ibid., 720–727.

36. Kalb, *Who's Better*, 1–7.

37. Bill Jenkinson, *Recrowning Baseball's Greatest Slugger: The Year Babe Ruth Hit 104 Home Runs* (New York: Carrol & Graf, 2007), 218–287.

38. Kalb, *Who's Better*, 9–28, 57–63, 135–145.

39. Derek Gentile, *Baseball's Best 1000* (New York: Black Dog & Leventhal, 2004), 7–22.

40. Ted Williams and Jim Prime, *Ted Williams' Hit List: The Best of the Best Ranks the Best of the Rest* (New York: McGraw-Hill, 1996), 29–89.

41. Ibid., 87–103.

42. Ted Williams and John Underwood, *The Science of Hitting* (New York: Simon & Schuster, 1986), 86. The first edition of this book appeared in 1970.

43. Rob Rains, *Big Stix: The Greatest Hitters in the History of the Major Leagues* (St. Louis, MO: Rawlings, 2004), 10–96.

44. "Game Five." *St. Louis Cardinals Gameday, 2006 Postseason Commemorative Edition*, 2006, 184.

45. John Grisham, *A Painted House* (New York: Doubleday, 2001), 59–61.

APPENDIX: CAREER AND POSTSEASON STATISTICS

APPENDIX: STAN MUSIAL'S MAJOR LEAGUE BATTING STATISTICS

REGULAR SEASON STATISTICS

Year	Club	League	G	AB	R	H	2B	3B	HR	RBI	BA
1941	St. Louis	National	12	47	8	20	4	0	1	7	.426
1942	St. Louis	National	140	467	87	147	32	10	10	72	.315
1943	St. Louis	National	157*	617	108	220*	48*	20*	13	81	.357*
1944	St. Louis	National	146	568	112	197*	51*	14	12	94	.347
1945	In Military										
1946	St. Louis	National	156*	624*	124*	228*	50*	20*	16	103	.365*
1947	St. Louis	National	149	587	113	183	30	13	19	95	.312
1948	St. Louis	National	155	611	135*	230*	46*	18*	39	131*	.376*
1949	St. Louis	National	157*	612	128	207*	41*	13*	36	123	.338
1950	St. Louis	National	146	555	105	192	41	7	28	109	.346*
1951	St. Louis	National	152	578	124*	205	30	12*	32	108	.355*
1952	St. Louis	National	154*	578	105*	194*	42*	6	21	91	.336*
1953	St. Louis	National	157	593	127	200	53*	9	30	113	.337
1954	St. Louis	National	153	591	120*	195	41*	9	35	126	.330
1955	St. Louis	National	154*	562	97	179	30	5	33	108	.319
1956	St. Louis	National	156	594	87	184	33	6	27	109*	.310
1957	St. Louis	National	134	502	82	176	38	3	29	102	.351*
1958	St. Louis	National	135	472	64	159	35	2	17	62	.337
1959	St. Louis	National	115	341	37	87	13	2	14	44	.255
1960	St. Louis	National	116	331	49	91	17	1	17	63	.275
1961	St. Louis	National	123	372	46	107	22	4	15	70	.288
1962	St. Louis	National	135	433	57	143	18	1	19	82	.330
1963	St. Louis	National	124	337	34	86	10	2	12	58	.255
Major League Totals—22 years			3026	10972	1949	3630	725	177	475	1951	.331

*indicates league leader

G = games; AB = at bats; R = runs; H = hits; 2B = doubles; 3B = triples; HR = home runs; RBI = runs batted in; BA = batting average

WORLD SERIES STATISTICS

Year	Club	G	AB	R	H	2B	3B	HR	RBI	BA
1942	St. Louis	5	18	2	4	1	0	0	2	.222
1943	St. Louis	5	18	2	5	0	0	0	0	.278
1944	St. Louis	6	23	2	7	2	0	1	2	.304
1946	St. Louis	7	27	3	7	4	1	0	4	.222

Source: http://baseball-reference.com.

BIBLIOGRAPHY

BIOGRAPHIES OF STAN MUSIAL

Giglio, James. *Musial: From Stash to Stan the Man*. Columbia: University of Missouri Press, 2001.

Grabowski, John. *Stan Musial*. New York: Chelsea House Publishers, 1993.

Lanshe, Jerry. *Stan "The Man" Musial: Born to Be a Ballplayer*. Dallas, TX: Taylor Publishing, 1994.

Musial, Stan, as told to Bob Broeg. *The Man, Stan: Musial, Then and Now*. St. Louis, MO: Bethany Press, 1977.

———. *Stan Musial: "The Man's" Own Story, as told to Bob Broeg*. Garden City, NY: Doubleday, 1964.

Robinson, Ray. *Stan Musial: Baseball's Durable "Man."* New York: G. P. Putnam's Sons, 1963.

BOOKS

Adomites, Paul, David Nemec, Matthew Greenberger, Dan Schlossberg, Dick Johnson, Mike Tully, Peter Palmer, Stuart Shea. *Cooperstown: Hall of Fame Players*. Lincolnwood, IL: Publications International, 2005.

Alexander, Charles. *Our Game: An American Baseball History*. New York: Henry Holt, 1991.

Allen, Lee. *The National League Story: The Official History*. New York: Hill & Wang, 1961.

Anderson, Dave. *Pennant Races: Baseball at Its Best*. New York: Doubleday, 1994.

Broeg, Bob. *The Greatest Moments in St. Louis Sports*. St. Louis: Missouri Historical Society Press, 2000.

Broeg, Bob and Jerry Vickery. *The St. Louis Cardinals Encyclopedia*. Chicago, IL: Contemporary Books, 1998.

Bullock, Steven. *Playing for Their Nation: Baseball and the American Military During World War II*. Lincoln: University of Nebraska Press, 2004.

Chadwick, Bruce and David Spindel. *The St. Louis Cardinals: Over 100 Years of Baseball Memories and Memorabilia*. New York: Abbeville Press, 1995.

Cohen, Richard and David Neft. *The World Series*. New York: Macmillan, 1986.

Connor, Anthony, ed. *Voices from Cooperstown: Baseball's Hall of Famers Tell It Like It Was*. New York: Macmillan, 1982.

Craft, David and Tom Owens. *Redbirds Revisited*. Chicago, IL: Bonus Books, 1990.

Creamer, Robert. *Baseball and Other Matters in 1941*. Lincoln: University of Nebraska Press, 1991.

DiMaggio, Joe. *Lucky to Be a Yankee*. New York: Grosset and Dunlap, 1951.

Durocher, Leo with Ed Linn. *Nice Guys Finish Last*. New York: Simon & Schuster, 1975.

Fleder, Rob, ed. *The Baseball Book*. New York: Sports Illustrated Books, 2006.

Flood, Curt. *The Way It Is*. New York: Simon & Schuster, 1971.

Freese, Mel. *The Glory Years of the St. Louis Cardinals, Vol.1: The World Championship Seasons*. St. Louis, MO: Palmerston & Reed, 1999.

Gentile, Derek. *Baseball's Best 1000*. New York: Black Dog & Levental, 2004.

Gibson, Bob with Phil Pepe. *From Ghetto to Glory: The Story of Bob Gibson*. Englewood Cliffs, NJ: Prentice Hall, 1968.

Gibson, Bob and Lonnie Wheeler. *Stranger to the Game*. New York: Viking, 1994.

Goldstein, Richard. *Spartan Seasons: How Baseball Survived the Second World War*. New York: Macmillan, 1980.

Golenbock, Peter. *The Spirit of St. Louis: A History of the St. Louis Cardinals and Browns*. New York: HarperCollins, 2000.

Grisham, John. *A Painted House*. New York: Random House, 2000.

Halberstam, David. *October 1964*. New York: Random House, 1994.

James, Bill. *The New Bill James Historical Baseball Abstract*. New York: Simon & Schuster, 2001.

Kahn, Roger. *The Era: 1947–1957*. New York: Houghton Mifflin, 1993.

Kalb, Elliott. *Who's Better, Who's Best in Baseball?* New York: McGraw-Hill, 2005.

Jenkinson, Bill. *Recrowning Baseball's Greatest Slugger: The Year Babe Ruth Hit 104 Home Runs*. New York: Carrol & Graf, 2007.

Leventhal, Josh, ed. *Baseball: The Perfect Game*. Stillwater, MN: Voyageur Press, 2005.

———. *The World Series*. New York: Black Dog & Leventhal, 2006.

Lieb, Frederick. *The St. Louis Cardinals: The Story of a Great Baseball Club*. New York: G. B. Putnam's Sons, 1945.

Marshall, William. *Baseball's Pivotal Era: 1945–1951*. Lexington: University Press of Kentucky, 1999.

McCarver, Tim with Phil Pepe. *Few and Chosen: Defining Cardinal Greatness Across the Eras*. Chicago, IL: Triumph Books, 2003.

McSweney, Bill. *The Impossible Dream: The Story of the Miracle Boston Red Sox*. New York: Coward-McCann, 1968.

Michener, James. *Sports in America*. New York: Random House, 1976.

Neyer, Rob and Eddie Epstein. *Baseball Dynasties: The Greatest Teams of All Time*. New York: W. W. Norton, 2000.

Rader, Benjamin. *Baseball: A History of America's Game*, 2nd ed. Urbana: Illinois University Press, 2002.

Rains, Rob. *Big Stix: The Greatest Hitters in the History of the Major Leagues*. St. Louis, MO: Rawlings, 2004.

———. *Cardinal Nation*. St. Louis, MO: Sporting News, 2002.

———. *The St. Louis Cardinals: The 100th Anniversary History*. New York: St. Martins Press, 1992.

Robinson, Ray and Christopher Jennison. *Greats of the Game*. New York: Abrams, 2005.

Schell, Michael. *Baseball's All-Time Best Hitters: How Statistics Can Level the Playing Field*. Princeton, NJ: Princeton University Press, 1999.

Schoendienst, Red and Rob Rains. *Red: A Baseball Life*. Champaign, IL: Sports Publishing, 1998.

Snyder, John. *Cardinals Journal*. Cincinnati, OH: Emmis Books, 2006.

Stang, Mark. *Cardinals Collection: 100 Years of St. Louis Cardinals Images*. Wilmington, OH: Orange Frazer Press, 2002.

Stanton, Joseph. *Cardinal Points: Poems on St. Louis Cardinals Baseball*. Jefferson, NC: McFarland, 2002.

Stark, Jayson. *The Stark Truth: The Most Overrated and Underrated Players in Baseball History*. Chicago, IL: Triumph, 2007.

Veeck, Bill with Ed Linn. *Veeck—As in Wreck*. New York: G. B. Putnam's Sons, 1962.

Williams, Ted and Jim Prime. *Ted Williams' Hit List: The Best of the Best Ranks the Best of the Rest*. New York: McGraw-Hill, 1996.

Williams, Ted and John Underwood. *My Turn at Bat: The Story of My Life*. New York: Simon & Schuster, 1969.

———. *The Science of Hitting*. New York: Simon & Schuster, 1986.

ARTICLES AND CHAPTERS

Anderson, Dave. "The Stuff of Legends: Stan, Ted." *New York Times* (June 9, 1990).

Appel, Marty. "The Last Immortals: Stan Musial and Bob Feller." In *Baseball: The Perfect Game*, edited by Josh Leventhal. Stillwater, MN: Voyageur Press, 2005.

Bonetti, David. "Going Public." *St. Louis Post-Dispatch* (May 29, 2005).

Biederman, Lester. "Musial . . . A Legend in Our Time." *Pittsburgh Press* (September 8, 1963).

Broeg, Bob. "How Does Musial Do It." *Sport Life* (January 1949).

———. "The Man Reveals Near Miss as '48 Bucco." *St. Louis Post-Dispatch* (April 6, 1963).

———. "The Mystery of Stan Musial." *Saturday Evening Post* (August 28, 1954).

———. "Red and Stan Click as Players, Executives." *St. Louis Post-Dispatch* (September 5, 1967).

———. "Remembrance of Summers Past." In *The National Pastime*, edited by John Thorn. New York: Warner Books, 1982.

———. "Stan Musial's Fight to Keep Playing." *Sport* (April 1963).

"Cardinals Give Musial Free Hand to Encourage Physical Fitness." *Syracuse Herald American* (March 22, 1964).

Carlin, Margaret. "Musial's Mother Cried … When He Quit Baseball." *The Pittsburgh Press* (September 15, 1963).

Cannon, Jimmy. "'Don't Mimic Me'—Musial." *Baseball Digest* (November 1952).

———. "The (Lonesome) Man." *New York Journal American* (January 25, 1967).

Carmichael, John. "Musial's Streak Ends the Hard Way." *Baseball Digest* (October 1950).

Chandler, Paul. "That Stance No Go in Long Ago." *Baseball Digest* (September 1951).

Cobb, Ty. "The Greatest Player of All Time Says: 'They Don't Play Baseball Any More.'" *Life* (March 17, 1952).

Crichton, Kyle. "Ace in the Hole." *Collier's* (September 13, 1947).

Dexter, Charles. "Musial—As Usual." *Baseball Digest* (September 1951).

Drees, Donald. "Ice Man Musial." *Baseball Digest* (November 1946).

Fay, Bill. "Inside Sports." *Collier's* (May 14, 1949).

Kahn, Roger. "The Benching of a Legend." In *The Baseball Book*, edited by Rob Fleder. New York: Sports Illustrated Books, 2006.

Key, Philip. "Good Time to Re-Do Musial Statue." www.STLtoday.com, 2005.

"Game Five." *St. Louis Cardinals Gameday, 2006 Postseason Commemorative Edition*, 2006.

Guback, Steve. "Musial's Sculptor Worrying—How to Put the Wiggle in Stance." *Washington Evening Star* (May 29, 1965).

Heinz, W. C. "Now There Are Eight." *Life* (May 1958).

———. "Stan Musial's Last Day." *Saturday Evening Post* (October 11, 1963).

"Japan Land of Fun for Gift-Laden Cards." *Sporting News* (December 14, 1968).

Knight, Ralph and Bob Broeg. "Country Keynotes the Cards." *Saturday Evening Post* (May 17, 1947).

Lawson, Earl. "Musial Wraps Up Game for Nationals." *Cincinnati Times-Star* (July 13, 1955).

Mayo, Jonathan. "Masterful Ceremonies: Induction Weekends at the Hall Have Provided Plenty of Memorable Moments." www.MLB.com, 2001.

McQueen, Red. "Cards Are a Hustling Team." *Honolulu Advertiser* (November 6, 1958).

———. "Cards in for Rough Time." *Honolulu Advertiser* (October 24, 1958).

———. "Musial Disappoints Japanese." *Honolulu Advertiser* (November 14, 1958).

"Musial Leaves Hospital." *St. Louis Post-Dispatch* (September 4, 1964).

Nash, Ogden. "The Tycoon." *Life* (September 5, 1955).

Newman, Mark and John Rawlings. "Man to Man." *Sporting News* (July 28, 1997).

Norris, Stephen. "Cardinals Care Dedicates Musial Field." www.stlcardinals.com (June 28, 2005).

O'Leary, Theordore. "A Rare Bird." *Sports Illustrated: St. Louis Cardinals World Series Commemorative Edition* (2006).

Osgood, Nancy. "Lil Musial Marvels at Husband's Success." *St. Petersburg Times* (April 29, 1967).

Paxton, Harry. "A Visit with Stan Musial." *Saturday Evening Post* (April 19, 1958).

Povich, Shirley. "Stan the Man Enters New League." *Washington Post* (January 29, 1967).

Russo, Neal. "Complacent Cards? Not Under Bing." *St. Louis Post-Dispatch* (December 23, 1967).

———. "Redbirds Saved by Swaps They Failed to Make." *St. Louis Post-Dispatch* (September 9, 1967).

———. "Smiles, Kisses and Tears at Musial Statue Unveiling." *Sporting News* (August 17, 1968).

———. "Vanek's Decision 25 Years Ago Made Stan Musial a Cardinal." *St. Louis Post-Dispatch* (January 1, 1962).

Saigh, Fred. "What Stan Musial Means to the Cards." *Sport* (July 1952).

Shinkle, Florence. "Revived Statue Suits Stan the Man Just Fine." *St. Louis Post-Dispatch* (September 24, 2004).

Singer, Glen. "Stanley Frank Musial (A Paean)." *Elysian Fields Quarterly* (Fall 2006).

Stang, Mark. *Cardinals Collection: 100 Years of St. Louis Cardinals Images.* Wilmington, OH, 2002.

Stanton, Joseph. "Eight Ways of Looking at a Musial." In *Horsehide, Pigskin, Oval Tracks and Apple Pie: Essays on Sports and American Culture*, edited by James Vlasich. Jefferson, NC: McFarland, 2005.

Stockton, J. Roy. "Rookie of the Year." *Saturday Evening Post* (September 12, 1942).

"That Man." *Time* (September 9, 1940).

Walfort, Cleon. "Musial Sought More Time at Home, but Hasn't Found It Amid Four Jobs." *Milwaukee Journal* (May 24, 1964).

Williams, Joe. "Frank Lane's Plan to Trade Musial Really Irked Man." *Pittsburg Press* (April 11, 1964).

VISUAL MATERIALS

Baker, Ernest Hamlin. *Cardinals' Stan Musial: Thirty Days Hath September* (magazine cover). *Time* (September 5, 1949).

Falter, John. *Stanley Musial* (painting). National Baseball Hall of Fame, Cooperstown, New York, 1954.

———. *Stanley Musial* (reproduction of painting). In *Baseball: A Treasury of Art and Literature*, edited by Michael Ruscoe. New York: Hugh Lauter Levin, 1995.

———. *Stanley Musial* (magazine cover). *Saturday Evening Post* (May 1, 1954).

Mose, Carl. *Musial* (bronze statue). Busch Stadium, St. Louis, MO, 1968.

Musial Memorabilia. St. Louis Cardinals Hall of Fame. Musial donated his personal collection of more than 1,000 items in 1992.

Musial Memorabilia for sale. www.stan-the-man.com.

St. Louis Cardinals Vintage World Series Films: 1943, 1944, and 1946. DVD. Major League Baseball, 2005.

Weber, Harry. *The Boy and the Man* (bronze statue). Missouri Sports Hall of Fame, Springfield, 2005.

———. *Stanley Frank Musial* (bronze statue). Busch Stadium, St. Louis, MO, 1998.

Wohlschlaeger, Amadee. *The Boy and the Man—Baseball's Bond* (sketch after painting). *St. Louis Post-Dispatch*, 1964.

Williams, Bill. *Stan Musial* (bronze bust). Hall of Famous Missourians, Jefferson City, 2000.

INDEX

About the Author

JOSEPH STANTON is an interdisciplinary scholar and poet who has published extensively on American art, literature, and culture. His *Cardinal Points: Poems on St. Louis Cardinals Baseball* (McFarland, 2002) chronicles and celebrates over one hundred years of St. Louis Cardinals baseball. His other books include *A Field Guide to the Wild Life of Suburban O'ahu, Imaginary Museum: Poems on Art, What the Kite Thinks, A Hawai'i Anthology,* and *The Important Books.* He has published in such sports journals as *Elysian Fields Quarterly, Aethlon: Journal of Sport Literature, Fan,* and *Spit Ball.* His work has also appeared in such journals as *Poetry, Harvard Review, Journal of American Culture, American Art,* and *Art Criticism.* An associate professor at the University of Hawai'i at Mānoa, he teaches courses in art history and American studies. His courses in sports culture include "Sports in America," "Baseball in American Culture," and "Art History of the Sports Film." His Ph.D. is from New York University.